Kenneth Cain Kinghorn

The Heritage of American Methodism

Foreword by Charles Yrigoyen, Jr.

The Heritage of American Methodism

Author: Kenneth Cain Kinghorn
Picture selection: Kenneth Cain Kinghorn
Publisher: Éditions du Signe - B.P. 94 - 67038 Strasbourg - France
Design and Layout: Carré Blanc
Director of publication: Claude Bernard Costecalde

© Éditions du Signe 1999 - ISBN 2-87718-870-1
© Abingdon Press 1999 - ISBN 0687-05500-8

Printed in Italy by G. Canale & C. S.p.A.- Borgaro Tse (To)

Foreword

There are more than 8,000,000 members of The United Methodist Church in the United States, making it one of the largest and most important religious bodies in the nation. Many of its members have grown up in United Methodism. Others have come to it later in life. Whether related to the church all their lives, or recently associated with it, too few know its history or appreciate its heritage. Each generation needs to discover or rediscover this important legacy.

What is United Methodism? Where did it come from? How did it develop? What is its mission? What has it accomplished? What are its beliefs? These are questions which this book seeks to answer, both in compelling words and superb illustrations. The advanced color printing technology used in this volume enables us not only to read history, but also to see it.

The story of United Methodism in America is complex. It involves the twists and turns we would expect of a denomination which began as a small movement in colonial America and steadily grew into the largest Protestant church in the land in the 19th century. The generous use of life stories and historical accounts found here illustrates how and why our church grew as it did.

The United Methodist Church, which is heir to three separate religious traditions—Methodism, the Church of the United Brethren in Christ, and the Evangelical Association—has experienced the exhilaration of substantial growth and influence, the challenge of theological and social controversy, the despair of painful divisions, and the jubilance of unions. On the pages that follow we trace the ideas and actions of men and women who were leading and representative figures in the unfolding epic of United Methodism from its birth to the present.

For those who are United Methodists this book is a sound reminder of our historic identity. Those who are not as familiar with United Methodism will find here in word and picture a succinct account of some of the most important chapters in the church's life and heritage.

Charles Yrigoyen, Jr.,
General Secretary of
the General Commission
on Archives and History of the
United Methodist Church

Preface

American Methodism began in the 1760s as a tiny seed that sprouted in the fertile soil of an emerging nation. When America's War of Independence ended in 1783, the Methodists were among the smallest and least impressive of the American religious movements. Other denominations in this country had enjoyed religious prominence for almost one and one half centuries. It is no exaggeration to say that during the last part of the eighteenth century most of the clergy of America's established churches regarded Methodism as an upstart company of religious zealots showing no promise of becoming a significant spiritual force in the new nation.

Nonetheless, to the surprise of many, within a few decades the Methodist Episcopal Church listed more members than the Congregational, Episcopal, and Presbyterian Churches combined. By 1850, American Methodism claimed one-third of all church members in the United States. Furthermore, Methodism's religious and social impact on nineteenth-century America was greater than that of any other religious movement. This remarkable achievement stands out as one of the most noteworthy developments in the nation's religious history. This book tells that astonishing story.

One way to write about the past is to report dates, genealogies, and facts. This approach is useful for scholars, and libraries should stock a good number of these kinds of books. Facts are to history what the skeleton is to the body, and the framework is essential. However, an exclusive concern with dates and facts fails to capture the incentives, dreams, and passions of history's participants. As a rule, we want to know the reasons that events unfolded and results occurred. We instinctively recognize that people's attitudes determine their actions and that their motives shape their methods. The *what* needs to include the *why*. This book, therefore, uses narratives and photographs to help the reader grasp the spirit and essential qualities of those who helped shape history's events. Through descriptions and pictures these pages seek to capture the unique genius and inspiring drama of American Methodism.

United Methodism enjoys a rich abundance of archival treasures, probably the most extensive of any Protestant denomination. In preparing these pages, I have used a number of primary sources, often quoting the very words of earlier generations. It has been necessary, of course, to use selective judgment in order to keep within reasonable space limitations. A single volume cannot contain all the personalities, issues, and events that comprise almost two dozen decades of United Methodist history. Therefore, I have included representative accounts that capture the essence of American Methodism.

To be sure, each person and event is specific and local. Specifics are, nevertheless, parts of the total. Particulars help make up the whole. The journal of an Ohio circuit rider who itinerated on horseback may well express the spirit of a missionary to the Northwest Territory who covered his circuit in a canoe. In the end, we understand the nature of Methodism by looking at its parts. *The Heritage of American Methodism* is about people, places, and concerns that shaped a great denomination. This legacy is worth knowing.

Kenneth Kinghorn

Contents

1 The British Legacy to American Methodism

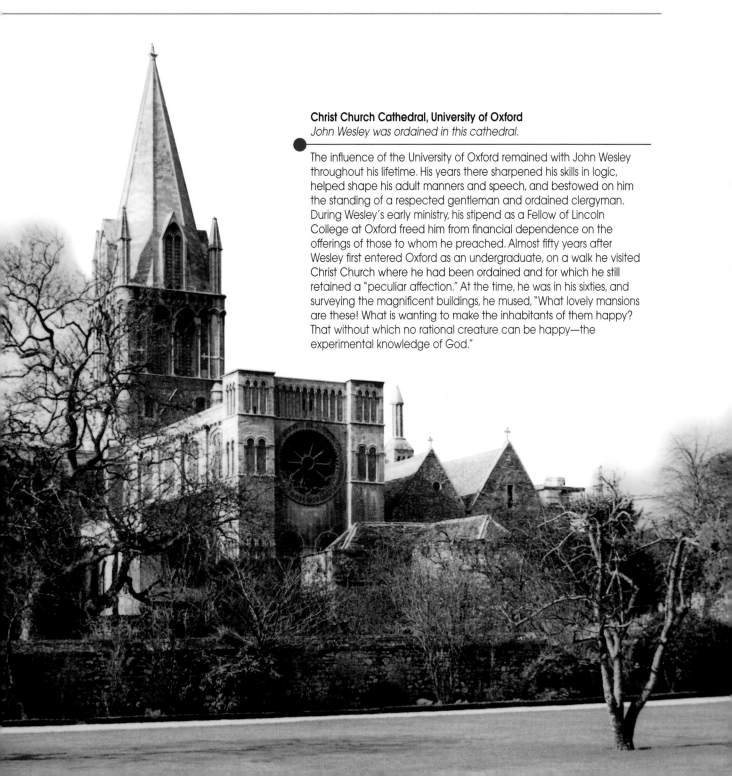

Christ Church Cathedral, University of Oxford
John Wesley was ordained in this cathedral.

The influence of the University of Oxford remained with John Wesley throughout his lifetime. His years there sharpened his skills in logic, helped shape his adult manners and speech, and bestowed on him the standing of a respected gentleman and ordained clergyman. During Wesley's early ministry, his stipend as a Fellow of Lincoln College at Oxford freed him from financial dependence on the offerings of those to whom he preached. Almost fifty years after Wesley first entered Oxford as an undergraduate, on a walk he visited Christ Church where he had been ordained and for which he still retained a "peculiar affection." At the time, he was in his sixties, and surveying the magnificent buildings, he mused, "What lovely mansions are these! What is wanting to make the inhabitants of them happy? That without which no rational creature can be happy—the experimental knowledge of God."

The story of American Methodism reaches back to the eighteenth-century Anglican rectory of Samuel and Susanna Wesley. These parents of John and Charles Wesley gave their children a superb home education. Susanna nurtured their minds and spirits, taming their wills without crushing their spirits. Patiently, she helped each child learn at a pace best suited to his or her ability. For the benefit of her children she wrote little books of instruction on religious themes. Later, in her children's adult years, she continued to enrich them through her counsel and encouragement. Although we credit John and Charles Wesley with founding Methodism, we can justifiably call Susanna Wesley the spiritual mother of Methodism.

Susanna Wesley (1669-1742)
Picture reproduced by permission of the Trustees for Methodist Church Purposes, Great Britain.

Mrs. Wesley's most important contribution to Methodism was the education and spiritual nurture she provided for her children. Education in the home consisted of two sessions per day—9:00 A.M. until noon, and 2:00 to 5:00 PM. The Wesley children's religious training included reading scripture, learning the catechism, memorizing collects, and saying prayers. Susanna also taught her children manners, ethics, and self-discipline. Through her sons John and Charles Wesley the influence of her parenting skills and Christian character reached out to all of England and into America.

Samuel Wesley (1666-1735)
This photograph was supplied by Peter Forsaith, Westminster College, Oxford, England and reproduced here by permission of the Trustees for Methodist Church Purposes, Great Britain.

Samuel Wesley, the father of John and Charles Wesley, influenced his children in a literary direction. He wrote persistently all his life, as did a number of his children. John Wesley wrote more than two hundred original works and edited at least a hundred others. Charles Wesley's production of hymns is legendary, and his brother Samuel Wesley, Jr., also wrote hymns. Some of the daughters of the Wesley home also wrote pieces of literary merit.

This portrait of the father of John and Charles Wesley passed through a London auction room in the 1960's, and a photographer captured a black and white photograph of this likeness. The portrait's present location and previous history are not known.

John Wesley (1703-1791), founder of Methodism

John Michael Williams painted this portrait of Wesley in 1742, and it is located at Wesley College, Bristol, England. Historians regard Williams' portrait as the best early adult likeness of John Wesley. Later, in 1754, John Downes made an engraving from this portrait. The Downes engraving appeared as the frontispiece to the first edition of John Wesley's *Notes Upon the New Testament,* now one of the doctrinal standards of American Methodism. The great number of portraits and engravings made of John Wesley during his life and after his death highlight the esteem in which Methodism's founder was, and is, held.

John and Charles Wesley's father also left a lasting impression on his famous sons. Despite his constant financial struggles, Samuel Wesley served faithfully as a pastor, and he labored diligently at scholarly projects. Although he left most of the children's education to his wife, he passed on to John and Charles a loyalty to the church and an appreciation for the enduring values of the Christian tradition. Also, he taught his children classical languages and the art of poetry. In sum, John and Charles Wesley inherited a superior religious and intellectual legacy from their childhood home at Epworth, England. This heritage left a significant imprint on the development of early Methodism.

The tomb of Samuel Wesley at Epworth Parish Church, the childhood church of John and Charles Wesley.
The tomb of Samuel Wesley, the father of John and Charles Wesley, is in the foreground. Photograph by H. O. Thomas.

Samuel and Susanna Wesley, the parents of John and Charles Wesley, served the Epworth parish from about 1696 to 1735. From infancy, the Wesley children learned knowledge and vital piety from their mother and father. Susanna supervised the education of each of the Wesley children, and each child excelled in academic work. John Wesley's sister, Mehetabel, was so advanced in learning that at the age of eight she read the New Testament in Greek.

Each morning when the household "school" opened, the children sang Psalms, as they did each evening. The older children read the Bible to the younger children, after which each child had private devotions. Samuel and Susanna Wesley bequeathed to their children a heritage of Biblical instruction, academic excellence, and godly example.

John Wesley, when seventy-five, walked alone in this Epworth churchyard and stopped by his father's grave. He said, "I felt the truth of 'one generation goeth, and another cometh,'" and he quoted the verse,

> The natal soil to all how strangely sweet!
> The place where first he breathed who can forget?

He wrote, "Epworth ... I still love beyond most places in the world."

The Oxford Methodists

Despite the advantages of their pious home, when John and Charles Wesley enrolled at the University of Oxford, they lacked an experiential knowledge of God. In later years John Wesley confessed that as a university student, he possessed "the faith of a servant, but not the faith of a son." On reaching the age of twenty-two, he, with his brother Charles, began an earnest religious search that continued as his chief lifetime concern. On learning of her son John's serious religious quest, Susanna Wesley wrote him, "In good earnest, resolve to make religion the business of your life."

In 1729 John and Charles Wesley joined with other like-minded students at Oxford to form a small religious society called the Holy Club. Under John Wesley's leadership, the group met regularly to read

Christ Church College, University of Oxford.
Photograph by John Walters.

In 1720 John Wesley entered Christ Church College at the University of Oxford. Later, he wrote that at the time he "had not so much as a notion of inward holiness." In 1725 he became intensely interested in religion and prepared for ordination in the Church of England. In 1726 John Wesley's superior ability as a scholar gained him an appointment at Oxford as a Fellow of Lincoln College. During his time at Oxford he helped organize the first Methodists.

Interior of Christ Church Cathedral at Oxford, site of John and Charles Wesley's ordinations.
Photograph by John Walters.

The legacy of the Church of England, in which John and Charles Wesley were reared, contributed to the development of Methodism in America. Anglican Bishop John Potter, who ordained John Wesley in Christ Church Cathedral, remained on good terms with Methodism's founder. Bishop Potter advised Wesley, "If you desire to be extensively useful, do not spend your time and strength in contending for or against ...things (that) are of a disputable nature; but in testifying against open notorious vice, and in promoting real, essential holiness."

from the Greek New Testament, study classic literature, pray, and hold theological discussions. These serious students carefully obeyed the standards of the Church of England, dutifully followed the rules of Oxford University, and regularly attended the sacrament of Holy Communion. They adopted strict disciplines for themselves, in the belief that an exacting way of life would help them gain "inward and outward right-eousness."

In addition to their spiritual and intellectual disciplines, the members of the Holy Club engaged in social ministries. They provided Christian literature, clothing, food, and fuel for people of meager means. To save money to share with the needy, these young men walked instead of rode, ate sparingly, and studied in chilly rooms to conserve fuel. Furthermore, they visited the Bocardo Prison in the City of Oxford where they ministered to those jailed for serious as well as trivial offenses. The Holy Club helped pay prisoners' debts and established a school for the children of the poor.

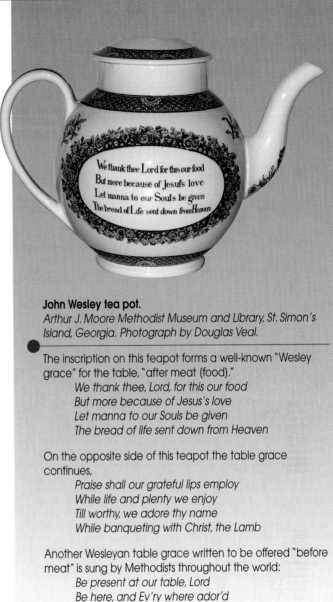

John Wesley tea pot.
Arthur J. Moore Methodist Museum and Library, St. Simon's Island, Georgia. Photograph by Douglas Veal.

The inscription on this teapot forms a well-known "Wesley grace" for the table, "after meat (food)."
> We thank thee, Lord, for this our food
> But more because of Jesus's love
> Let manna to our Souls be given
> The bread of life sent down from Heaven

On the opposite side of this teapot the table grace continues,
> Praise shall our grateful lips employ
> While life and plenty we enjoy
> Till worthy, we adore thy name
> While banqueting with Christ, the Lamb

Another Wesleyan table grace written to be offered "before meat" is sung by Methodists throughout the world:
> Be present at our table, Lord
> Be here, and Ev'ry where ador'd
> Thy creatures bless, and grant that we
> May feast in paradise with thee

George Whitefield (1714-1770). *This painting by an unknown artist was painted close to 1770. The original is located at the World Methodist Museum and printed here by permission of the museum. Note the "all-seeing eye of God" above the pulpit.*

George Whitefield was perhaps the most skilled orator among the early Oxford Methodists. Because his eyes did not properly focus, Whitefield's detractors referred to him as "Dr. Squintum." Whitefield pioneered the Methodist practice of field preaching without sermon notes. He visited America seven times, traveling from Georgia to Maine as "a flame of fire." His sermons deeply moved his hearers and brought many to faith in Jesus Christ. Whitefield inspired the founding of some fifty American colleges and universities, including the University of Pennsylvania, where his statue occupies a prominent position. Because of his belief in predestination and a "limited atonement" for the elect only, he parted company with John Wesley who held that Christ died for everyone and that all who trusted in Christ could be saved. Despite this theological disagreement, John Wesley and George Whitefield remained life-long friends.

The zealous young John Wesley believed that lukewarm Christianity was worse than open sin. Accordingly, he labored to bring every area of his life into submission to Jesus Christ. His zeal and that of his colleagues provoked ridicule. Other university students mocked the enthusiasm and self-denial of these fervent young men. Faultfinders heaped upon them such names as "Sacramentarians," "Bible Moths," and "Enthusiasts." The methodical disciplines of the members of the Holy Club caused critics to brand them "Methodists."

Despite their semi-monastic existence and devotion to good works, the Oxford Methodists fell short of gaining the certainty of God's love. They toiled at strict self-examinations, rigorous spiritual disciplines, and sacrificial good works. Still, the assurance of salvation eluded them. Their devotion consisted mostly of religious duties and good works, but these efforts failed to give them peace or joy. John Wesley was mired in what he later called a "spiritual wilderness."

The Strangely Warmed Heart

In 1735 John and Charles Wesley accepted an invitation from the Society for the Propagation of the Gospel to minister in the recently formed English colony in Savannah, Georgia. Charles Wesley served as a secretary to James Oglethorpe, founder and first governor of the Georgia Colony. John Wesley assumed responsibility as chaplain for the English colonists and as a missionary to the American Indians. Concerning his decision to go to Georgia, John Wesley wrote, "My chief motive is the hope of saving my own soul."

Despite their good intentions, John's and Charles's ministries in Georgia were not successful. While John Wesley was diligent and self-denying, he was also dogmatic and intolerant. The Native American Indians were not eager to embrace Christianity, as John and Charles had fantasized. Disappointingly, the British colonists did not respond with favor to their ministries. These failures intensified the spiritual despair of the Wesley brothers. The members of the Georgia Colony turned against John and forced him to return to England in late December, 1737. Charles had already sailed home, broken in spirit and in health.

Bocardo Prison, Oxford, England. *Photograph by H. O. Thomas.*

Here, the members of John Wesley's Holy Club visited prisoners. The Oxford Methodists examined new prisoners as to whether they bore malice towards those responsible for their imprisonment, whethe they repented of their sins, and whether they wished to receive Holy Communion. From their own limited means and by contributions from others, these young men assisted prisoners by supplying them with books, medicines, and other necessities. When possible they paid the debts of those that owed money, and arranged for their release.

On the return voyage to England, John Wesley contemplated his ineffective ministry and his lack of certainty of God's love. He wrote, "In vain have I fled from myself to America: I still groan under the intolerable weight of inherent misery... Go where I will, I carry my hell about me; nor have I the least ease in anything." His humiliating experience was inescapably leading him away from a focus on what he could do for God to a focus on what God could do for him.

John Wesley's celebrated heart-warming assurance of salvation finally occurred May 24, 1738, at a prayer meeting on Aldersgate Street in London. Afterward, John and some of his friends visited Charles to announce John's exhilarating religious experience. John declared simply to his brother, "I believe." Charles responded by relating his own conversion that had transpired a few days earlier. The happy band of believers sang a hymn that Charles had written to celebrate his own conversion—"Where Shall My Wandering Soul Begin?" At last, John and Charles Wesley had the inner witness of the Holy Spirit that they were in a right relationship with God.

Interior of Wesley Monumental Methodist Church, Savannah, Georgia. *Photograph by Douglas Veal.*

In 1875 Methodism's South Georgia Annual Conference adopted a plan to erect this church to recognize the contributions of John and Charles Wesley, the first Methodists to come to America. The church was erected on Calhoun Square, one of the twenty-four squares in the original plan for the city of Savannah, laid out in 1733 by James Oglethorpe, founder of the Colony of Georgia. Contributions for constructing the church flowed into the building project from throughout the United States, and from countries in Europe. Thus, this church belongs to all Methodists.

The first service in Wesley Monumental Methodist Church was held March 31, 1890. Each of the stained glass windows is dedicated to a historic Methodist personality. The Wesley window above the rear of the sanctuary features life-sized busts of John and Charles Wesley. At the top of the window is a globe, across which is written "The World is my Parish."

Their spiritual transformations had brought them from law to grace and changed them from legalists to evangelicals. Their experience of God's love gave them spiritual peace, an impulse for evangelism, and a sustaining motivation for addressing the evils of society. Having experienced spiritual liberty for themselves, these Oxford Methodists spent the rest of their lives spreading the good news of God's love.

The eighteenth-century Church of England had fallen into decline because it had neglected the essential doctrines on which it was founded. Methodism did not advocate any new doctrines; Methodism's purpose was simply to help the church recover its avowed message and mission. Many in the church, however, accused Methodism of introducing "new doctrines." John Wesley preached a sermon at St. Mary's Church, Oxford, in which he said, "It is the melancholy remark of an excellent man, that he who now preaches the most essential duties of Christianity, runs the hazard of being esteemed, by a great part of his hearers, 'a setter forth of new doctrines.' Most men have so lived away the substance of that religion, the profession whereof they still retain, that no sooner are any of those truths proposed...than they cry out, 'Thou bringest strange things to our ears.'"

We may condense early Methodism's doctrinal emphases under three headings: (1) *All can be saved*, (2) *All can know they are saved*, and (3) *Persons and*

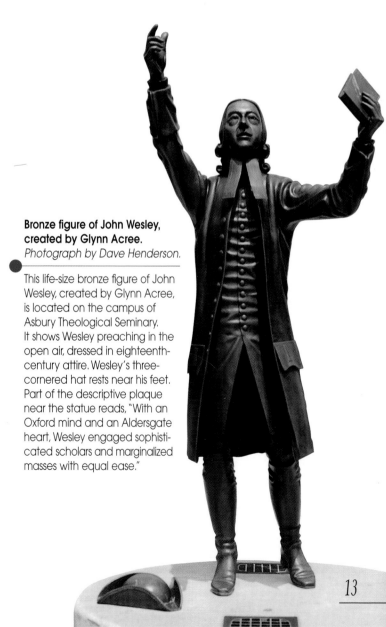

Bronze figure of John Wesley, created by Glynn Acree.
Photograph by Dave Henderson.

This life-size bronze figure of John Wesley, created by Glynn Acree, is located on the campus of Asbury Theological Seminary. It shows Wesley preaching in the open air, dressed in eighteenth-century attire. Wesley's three-cornered hat rests near his feet. Part of the descriptive plaque near the statue reads, "With an Oxford mind and an Aldersgate heart, Wesley engaged sophisticated scholars and marginalized masses with equal ease."

nations can be saved from the power of sin. The belief that all can be saved helped create faith in those who were trapped in the lowest levels of society and mired in the most desperate of spiritual conditions. The teaching that all can know they are saved gave hope to those whose personal experience of conversion made them aware of Christ living within them. The doctrine that all can be saved from the power of sin engendered love for God and neighbor that led to the spiritual transformation of individuals and society.

In 1738, the year of the evangelical conversions of John and Charles Wesley, religion in England had reached a low point. After visiting England, the French rationalist Charles Montesquieu wrote, "In France I am thought to have too little religion, but in England to have too much." Anglican Bishop George Berkeley declared, "Our prospect is very terrible and the symptoms grow worse from day to day." The soon-to-be Archbishop of Canterbury, Thomas Secker, stated, "The public rails at Christianity with little reserve, and the teachers of Christianity ridicule it without any reserve at all."

John Wesley. *This portrait was painted by Henry Edridge in Wesley's eighty-eighth year. Some think this picture was the last to be painted before Wesley's death.*

John Wesley wrote, "I have again and again, with all the plainness I could, declared what our constant doctrines are; whereby we are distinguished only from Heathens, or nominal Christians; not from any that worship God in spirit and in truth. Our main doctrines, which include all the rest, are three,—that of repentance, of faith, and of holiness. The first of these we account, as it were, the porch of religion; the next, the door; the third, religion itself."

Despite these dire assessments, within Wesley's generation Methodism's positive impact was enormous. The influence of John and Charles Wesley earned them the love and respect of the common folk, and eventually Westminster Abbey installed a memorial tablet commemorating them and their work. *The Cambridge Modern History* states that the most important positive influence in eighteenth-century England was "John Wesley and the religious revival to which he gave his name and life." Furthermore, the positive influence of British Methodism was to become an important influence in the new country named The United States of America.

An American Ministry

By the 1760s Methodism had found its way into North America through the ministries of two lay preachers who had been converted to Christ under Methodist preaching in their native Ireland. In 1768 John Taylor, a lay person, wrote John Wesley informing him of the existence of a Methodist Society recently begun in New York City. The letter urged Wesley to send a qualified preacher to assist this new Methodist congregation. Taylor concluded his letter by saying, "With respect to the money for payment of a preacher's passage over...we would sell our coats and shirts and pay it."

Responding to Taylor's compelling plea, John Wesley sent preachers to the American Methodists, whom he described as "sheep without a shepherd." Between 1769 and 1774 twelve British Methodist preachers came to America, either by John Wesley's appointment or with his consent. Due to the outbreak of war between America and Great Britain, these preachers (Asbury excepted) remained in this country for only a few years. Nevertheless, their American ministries greatly impacted the infant Methodist movement they so briefly served.

Eventually, it became evident to John Wesley that Methodist converts in this country needed an ordained clergy of their own. His entreaties to the Anglican bishops to provide an ordained ministry for America went unheeded. So he took steps to provide clergy for the American Methodists. In 1784 he ordained Richard Whatcoat and Thomas Vasey for ministry in America. Also, he consecrated Thomas Coke as American Methodism's first "superintendent" (bishop). United Methodist clergy persons now trace their ordinations back to Wesley's decisive action in providing an ordained ministry for America.

Liturgy

A second legacy from Great Britain is American Methodism's liturgy. Coke, Whatcoat, and Vasey brought with them to America a Book of Worship (actually, loose sheets) that John Wesley had prepared for the American Methodists. Wesley titled this liturgy *The Sunday Service of the Methodists in North America, with Other Occasional Services*. He borrowed these rituals from the Anglican *Book of Common Prayer*, adapting them for American Methodism. In his introduction to this work, Wesley wrote, "I believe there is no liturgy in the World, either in ancient or modern language, which breathes more of a solid, scriptural, rational piety, than the [Book of] Common Prayer of the Church of England."

In 1784 the American Methodists officially organized themselves into a new denomination. The founding conference (known as the "Christmas Conference") officially adopted Wesley's *Sunday Service*. For a time, some of the early Methodist preachers read prayers from this prayer book. However, most did not. The majority of them preferred to pray extemporaneously. Furthermore, they believed that they could address God more reverently and effectively with closed eyes. Thus, American Methodists eventually laid aside parts of the *Sunday Service* and conducted religious services less formally. However, American Methodism continued to use portions of Wesley's liturgy. Today, United Methodists use the familiar rituals of Holy Communion, Baptism, Marriage, Burial of the Dead, and Ordination derived from the *Sunday Service*.

Doctrine and Theology

Another British legacy to American Methodism pertains to doctrine. John Wesley prepared Articles of Religion for the new church. Its founding conference required all ordained ministers to conform their preaching and teaching to the doctrines articulated in these Articles. Additionally, American Methodism benefits from John Wesley's *Sermons* and *Notes Upon the New Testament*. United Methodism's present Discipline designates these writings as "the traditional standard exposition of distinctive Methodist teaching."

In 1808 American Methodism adopted Restrictive Rules guaranteeing that the Articles of Religion remain the church's doctrinal standards. These Restrictive Rules continue in present-day United Methodism's Constitution. The First Restrictive Rule states, "General conference shall not revoke, alter, or change our Articles of Religion or establish any new standards or rules of doctrine contrary to our present existing and established standards of doctrine." At the merger of 1968, the United Methodist Church added as a parallel standard of doctrine the Confession of Faith of the former Evangelical United Brethren Church.

Today's United Methodist Discipline states, "Our forebears in the faith reaffirmed the ancient Christian message as found in the apostolic witness, even as they applied it anew in their own circumstances. Their preaching and teaching were grounded in Scripture, informed by Christian tradition, enlivened in experience, and tested by reason. Their labors inspire and inform our attempts to convey the saving gospel to our world with its needs and aspirations."

John Wesley was not concerned with doctrinal hairsplitting. He knew that a preoccupation with theological minutia divides Christians and diverts them from their central mission "to reform the nation, particularly the Church; and to spread scriptural holiness over the land." Wesley was famous for his "catholic spirit" and his willingness to maintain fellowship with all Christians. For him, doctrine was not an end in itself. Rather, he saw doctrine as a means to keep Christians grounded in truth and bonded in love.

Wesley explained, "A catholic spirit is not speculative latitudinarianism. It is not an indifference to all opinions: This is the spawn of hell, not the offspring of heaven. This unsettledness of thought, this being 'driven to and fro, and tossed about with every wind of doctrine,' is a great curse, not a blessing; an irreconcilable enemy, not a friend, to true catholicism [ecumenism]. A man of a truly catholic spirit...is fixed as the sun in his judgment concerning the main branches of Christian doctrine." Wesley preached, "Let us keep close to the grand scriptural doctrines... Let us hold fast the essentials of 'the faith which was once delivered unto the saints.'"

Wesley remained flexible regarding matters of "opinion," such as issues pertaining to modes of baptism, styles of worship, and church order. However, he regarded Christianity's "essential doctrines" as non-negotiable. He wrote, "No person shall be allowed to preach or exhort among our people, whose life is not holy...nor any who asserts anything contrary to the gospel." United Methodism's Articles of Religion and Confession of Faith articulate the essential doctrines concerning the Trinity, original sin, the deity of Christ, the atonement, justification by faith, and the work of the Holy Spirit. Additional doctrinal standards are John Wesley's *Sermons* and his *Notes Upon the New Testament*.

Church Polity

John Wesley possessed an exceptional ability to organize people and create effective methods. He established a system that connected individuals, small groups, circuits, conferences, and central oversight. United Methodism's itinerant ministry helps keep local congregations in touch with the larger church and the larger church in touch with the congregations. This form of church government calls for bishops to supervise Annual Conferences and guarantee sound Christian teaching and effective ministries throughout "the connection." This system of polity contrasts with a congregational church polity that allows for only a loose connection of autonomous congregations.

Methodist polity rests on certain beliefs about church organization. (1) Each member is a part of the whole and cannot be separated from the larger community of believers. (2) The individual has a responsibility to the denomination, and the denomination has a responsibility to the individual. (3) The proper functioning of the church requires faithful leaders and loyal followers.

United Methodist polity assumes that all members share a common commitment to the doctrine and mission of the church. Harmony in the church depends on a common confession that there is "one Lord, one faith, one baptism, one God and Father of all, who is over all and through all and in all." In addition to the worship of the Holy Trinity, Methodist church polity assumes the willingness of individuals and congregations to set aside complete autonomy and function in mutually accountable ways. Clergy members of the church go where they are "stationed;" congregations receive and support the clergy assigned to them. The United Methodist form of church government provides Christians the opportunity to support each other in mutual love and respect.

Charles Wesley and the Wesleyan Hymns

Christians of every denomination prize the Wesleyan hymns as one of the most treasured legacies of eighteenth-century British Methodism. Charles Wesley's heart-warming experience of God's grace resulted in a flow of poems and hymns that continued throughout his lifetime. He wrote more than 6,000 religious poems and hymns, and he continued composing hymn texts until the time of his death. Some of these hymns were written for particular or passing occasions, and they lack permanent distinction. Nevertheless,

many hymnologists agree that the best of Charles Wesley's hymns deserve a place among the finest hymns ever produced in any language or century.

Charles Wesley (1707-1788). *Picture reproduced by permission of the Trustees for Methodist Church Purposes, Great Britain.*

The date and artist of this "lily portrait" are unknown. The lilies and Bible suggest that the portrait was painted about the time of Charles Wesley's ordination. Charles Wesley's greatest contribution to Methodism lies in the thousands of hymns he wrote, many of which are of enduring quality. Among his best known hymns are "Love Divine, all Loves Excelling," "Hark! The Herald Angels Sing," "Jesus, Lover of my Soul," "Soldiers of Christ, Arise," "O For a Thousand Tongues to Sing," and "Rejoice, the Lord is King." Charles Wesley's hymns continue to be sung by Methodists and by Christians of all denominations.

An important feature of the Wesleyan hymns is their extensive use of the Bible. There is scarcely a verse in all Charles Wesley's hymns that does not, however subtly, refer to some passage in scripture. The Wesleyan hymns touch on every important biblical teaching—creation, divine sovereignty, providence, sin, repentance, grace, the atonement, conversion, assurance, the Holy Spirit, faith, and sanctification. Some students of these hymns aver that if the Bible were lost, we could reconstruct much of it from the Wesleyan hymns.

John and Charles Wesley insisted that the language and imagery of hymns be suited to the ordinary worshiper. Accordingly, the Wesleyan hymns employ the power of verbs to thrust forward the text with clarity and force. The Methodists sang their hymns in their homes, at work, at their family altars, and in their formal religious services. These verses gave hope and joy especially to the poor and socially disadvantaged people for whom Methodism had a powerful appeal.

The most impressive edition of Wesley's hymns was the 1780 *Collection of Hymns for the Use of the People Called Methodists*. This hymnal contained 525 hymns, many from the pen of Charles Wesley. The hymns were arranged to make this collection "a body of experimental and practical divinity." John Wesley wrote in the hymnal's preface, "I do not think it inconsistent with modesty to declare that I am persuaded that no such Hymn Book as this has yet been published in the English language. In whatever other publication of a kind have you so distinct and full an account of scriptural Christianity?"

Many rank the 1780 Methodist hymnal as the grandest hymn collection ever published. Hymnologist Bernard Manning declared, "This little book ranks in Christian literature with the Psalms, the Book of Common Prayer, and the Canon of the Mass... You cannot alter it except to mar it; it is a work of supreme devotional art by a religious genius." John Julian's

On the left is # 4 Charles Street, Bristol, England, where Charles Wesley lived for twenty-two years. *Photograph reproduced by permission of the Charles Wesley Heritage Centre, Bristol, United Kingdom.*

The front rooms of this house still have their original grates and paneling. Charles traveled for twenty years as a Methodist evangelist and field preacher. When his stamina declined, he settled down, first in Bristol and then in London. Charles Wesley, the "sweet singer of Methodism," is reputed to have composed many of his 6,500 hymns in the front attic of this house. A number of these hymns rank as incomparable masterpieces. Charles Wesley dictated his last verses while confined to his deathbed.

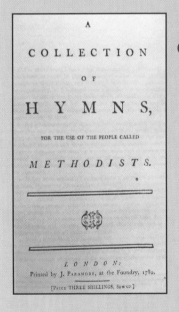

Title page of A Collection of Hymns for the Use of the People Called Methodists.

This 1780 *Collection of Hymns for the Use of the People Called Methodists* was the definitive collection of hymns to appear during the lifetime of John Wesley. As the culmination of a lengthy process of preparing a "general hymnbook," Wesley selected 525 hymns from more than fifty hymnbooks published during the preceding 43 years. The arrangement of the hymns was carefully designed to reflect the Wesleyan concept of the way of salvation and the pattern of Christian experience. In the introduction to this hymnal John Wesley wrote, "(1.) In these Hymns there is no doggerel, no botches, nothing put in to patch up the rhyme, no feeble expletives. (2.) Here is nothing turgid or bombast on the one hand, or low and creeping on the other. (3.) Here are no cant expressions, no words without meaning. Those who impute this to us know not what they say. We talk common sense, whether they understand it or not, both in verse and prose, and use no word but in a fixed and determinate sense. (4.) Here are, allow me to say, both the purity, the strength, and the elegance of the English language, and, at the same time, the utmost simplicity and plainness, suited to every capacity. Lastly, I desire men of taste to judge, (these are the only competent judges,) whether there be not in some the following Hymns the true spirit of poetry, such as cannot be acquired by art and labour, but must be the gift of nature. By labour a man may become a tolerable imitator of Spenser, Shakespeare, or Milton, and may heap together pretty compound epithets, as pale-eyed, meek-eyed, and the like; but unless he be born a poet, he will never attain the genuine spirit of poetry."

Dictionary of Hymnology concludes, "Charles Wesley is, perhaps, taking quality and quantity together, the greatest hymnwriter of all ages." The British legacy of Wesleyan hymns is an incomparable gift, greatly treasured by American Methodism.

The Legacy of Personal Influence

Eighteenth-century British Methodism bequeathed to American Methodism the influence of Christian heroes and heroines who were both inspired and inspiring. In addition to the legacy of John and Charles Wesley, these people and their works continue to enrich us today.

Significant among these individuals was John Fletcher (1729-1785), the most important English interpreter of the Wesleyan tradition. Following Fletcher's death, the British Methodist Conference Minutes recorded that he was "a pattern of holiness, scarce to be paralleled in a century." John Wesley said of him, "Within fourscore years, I have known many excellent men, holy in heart and life. But one equal to him, I have not known; one so uniformly and deeply devoted to God. So unblamable a man, in every respect, I have not found either in Europe or America."

If Fletcher was an inspiring saint, he was also a brilliant theologian. As is so often the case, he elaborated his theological ideas in the midst of controversy. In Fletcher's day, some stressed "special election" to the point of denying the need for God's chosen ones to obey the moral law. A few drew the extreme conclusion that because God's grace covers us, we can live as we please. This view is termed "Antinomianism," which means "against the law." In a series of essays called *Checks to Antinomianism*, Fletcher opposed Antinomianism as being both unbiblical and dangerous.

John Fletcher agreed with his theological critics on the solemn reality of original sin. He also agreed with them that our salvation rests entirely on the grace of God. However, he parted company with his detractors when he insisted that Christ died for all, not merely the elect. Fletcher also opposed the view that a personal response to God's grace has no place in human redemption.

John Fletcher (1729-1785). *Picture reproduced by permission of the Trustees for Methodist Church Purposes, Great Britain.*

John Fletcher's contribution to the Methodist heritage lies in his scholarship and the example of his personal piety. Early in life he learned to work in the French, German, Latin, Greek, and Hebrew languages. He served as a parish priest at Madely in England, and his preaching was instructive, eloquent and effective. Fletcher also produced a large body of useful writing that became standard reading for Methodists well into the nineteenth century. His writings focus on grace for all that believe (as opposed to grace only for the elect), the witness of the Holy Spirit to the human spirit, and Christian sanctification. Few writers have been able to match his ability to balance and reconcile seemingly opposite passages of scripture. John Wesley relied heavily on Fletcher as Methodism's most skillful polemicist. Some students today are rediscovering Fletcher's brilliant works.

It is generally acknowledged that Fletcher was one of the most saintly persons in Christian history. A non-Methodist contemporary said of him, "No age or country has ever produced a man of more enlivened piety or more perfect charity. No age has ever possessed a more apostolic minister. Fletcher in any communion would have been a saint." He was one of the few controversialists in the history of the church who wrote without bitterness; the qualities of love and fairness run through all his books and pamphlets. England's Lord Chancellor, wanting to honor Fletcher, offered to promote him to the office of a Canon, a Dean, or a Bishop. "Look, Mr. Fletcher," said the Lord Chancellor, "do you want anything?" Fletcher replied, "Thank you ... but I want nothing except more grace."

He defended the view that salvation comes entirely from the grace of God, and our resistance to the grace of God is the sole cause of damnation.

Fletcher wrote clearly, and he developed his theological arguments in a courteous and respectful manner. His knowledge and vital piety earned him the respect of almost everyone who knew his character or read his work. Thomas Coke, American Methodism's first bishop, borrowed extensively from Fletcher's writings. Similarly, Francis Asbury's journal often refers to Fletcher in highly favorable terms. The first Course of Study for American Methodist preachers required them to read John Fletcher's *Checks to Antinomianism*. Several generations of American Methodists were significantly influenced by his writings, and they printed many editions of his works.

Another British Methodist to enrich early American Methodism was the theologian Richard Watson (1781-1833). As did John Fletcher, Watson also wrote in the context of theological controversy. In both England and America certain leaders in the academy and the church were attracted to deism. The philosophy of deism holds that God is too transcendent to be concerned with individuals. Allegedly, we must rely entirely on our own resources. Deism also contends that we do not need divine revelation because human reason is adequate to gain the religious truth necessary for happiness and well-being.

Richard Watson refuted the philosophy of deism. Against deism's "natural religion," Watson championed "revealed religion," which means that God chose to reveal himself to us. He did so in the Bible and in Christ. Watson did not deny the insights of reason; he himself was a master logician. However, he effectively countered the deist notion that our understanding of God is restricted to the insights of reason.

Adam Clarke (c. 1760-1832). *Picture reproduced by permission of the Trustees for Methodist Church Purposes, Great Britain.*

Adam Clarke, an Irishman, was converted to Christ at the age of seventeen, under Methodist preaching, and he joined a Methodist class meeting. Digging in a garden at Wesley's Kingswood School, Clarke found a half-guinea, with which he bought a Hebrew Bible. From that point, he went on to become a brilliant scholar of the Bible in its original languages. Clarke had significant influence in British and American Methodism. He "combined evangelism with learning, simplicity with high society, and local pastoral care with wide connectional responsibility." Three times he served as president of British Methodism.

His scholarship won him a place in the Royal Irish Academy and numerous other learned societies. He knew at least sixteen languages and his reputation as a master of Latin, Greek, Hebrew, and Eastern languages was legendary. Clarke's most influential work was his multi-volume commentary on the Bible, "a help to a better understanding of the Sacred Writings."

Richard Watson (1781-1833), English Methodist preacher and theologian.

Richard Watson's intellectual brilliance surfaced early in his life. Before his sixth birthday he had read some eighteen volumes of a universal history. Watson became a Methodist preacher at the age of seventeen. His two-volume *Theological Institutes* took its place as the most influential theological work within British and American Methodism during the second and third quarters of the nineteenth century. He also wrote an important work on Methodist church government, a theological dictionary, and a standard biography of John Wesley. Watson's influence in American Methodism stems from his work as a careful theologian who presented Wesleyan theology in a clear and logical manner.

Watson also championed the view that Christ died for all people. In his day, some insisted that Christ died only for those elect whom God had chosen from before the creation of the world. They believed that non-elected people cannot be saved because Christ did not die for them—a view termed "limited atonement." A popular saying of the time was, "The elect will be saved, do what they will; the non-elect will be damned, do what they can." Watson defended the universal atonement of Christ and the doctrine that all can be saved (but not that all *will* be saved). He helped shape the Wesleyan position that our response to God's grace remains a necessary component of our salvation. Richard Watson's two-volume work, *Theological Institutes: Evidences, Doctrines, Morals, and Institutions of Christianity*, significantly influenced the preachers in early American Methodism.

Another important British Methodist scholar to influence American Methodism was Adam Clarke (c. 1760-1832), a leading Bible commentator of his day. Clarke combined an interest in serious

Elisabeth Ritchie Mortimer

Mary Bosanquet Fletcher

Sophia Cooke Bradeburn

Hester Ann Roe Rogers

scholarship with a concern for practical ministry. He served as an itinerant Methodist preacher, built schools, championed education for women, organized efforts to feed the hungry, published volumes of sermons, planned a retirement home for preachers, completed scholarly translations from the Coptic language, worked as an archivist for the British government, and translated the Bible into numerous languages.

Perhaps Adam Clarke's crowning achievement was his multi-volume commentary on the Bible, a project that took him forty years to complete. His goal was to help ordinary readers understand the meaning of scripture. His writing style was parallel to that of John Wesley, who wrote "plain truth for plain people." Clarke maintained that we should consider the Bible as "divinely inspired, and as containing infallible truth." To this day, many United Methodist preachers and lay Bible students in America have Clarke's commentaries on their bookshelves.

In a manner not typical in eighteenth-century England, British Methodism recognized women's rightful place in Christian ministry. British Methodism helped women confront inhibiting social customs, contest repressive structures, and challenge conventions that restricted women's opportunities to minister. The legacy of these Methodist women has vastly enriched the American church. This heritage includes godly character, intellectual power, public ministries, and effective leadership.

Examples of the influence of mature Christian character can be seen in people like Elisabeth Ritchie Mortimer, Mary Bosanquet Fletcher, Sophia Cooke Bradeburn, and Hester Ann Roe Rogers. These women lived humble lives of serene power and spiritual attainment. Often their ministries helped make possible the success of public leaders whose names received wider recognition.

Mary Bosanquet Fletcher wrote John Wesley a letter that constituted the first serious defense of women preachers in Methodism. She pointed out that the Bible contains instances of God's calling women to minister. Wesley recognized that God blessed certain women preachers who were anointed by God. Building on this British legacy, United Methodism now gives women the full recognition they deserve.

In our time the eighteenth-century British legacy to American Methodism is often forgotten or neglected. Still, those that understand this legacy know that it comprises a rich benefaction for the church today. John and Charles Wesley, along with other British Methodists, cared about the "dear Americans," and they did much to assist them. These British benefactors did not dream of the extent to which their lives and ministries would continue to enrich those who follow in their train.

Some Elect Ladies of early British Methodism.

Early Methodism was ahead of most denominations of the time with regard to offering opportunities for women to minister. This collage of pictures shows four important women of early British Methodism. *Top to bottom* Elizabeth Ritchie Mortimer, Mary Bosanquet Fletcher, Sophia Cooke Bradeburn, Hester Ann Roe Rogers. Elizabeth Ritchie Mortimer often entertained John Wesley in her home. Wesley wrote many letters to her, and she wrote a detailed account of John Wesley's final days. Mary Bosanquet Fletcher was the wife of John Fletcher, John Wesley's most valued assistant. Mary became Methodism's first woman preacher and an important lay theologian. Sophia Cooke Bradeburn was a friend of John Wesley and often hosted him in her home. On one occasion he wrote her, "Surely, you never can have need to use any ceremony with me. You may think aloud, and tell me all that is in your heart.... Give yourself to prayer; and then act, in the name and in the fear of God, as you are fully persuaded in your own mind." Hester Ann Rogers was a prominent Methodist lay woman in Great Britain whose writings influenced Methodists in America. She was converted to Christ under the preaching of John Wesley. From the time Rogers became a Methodist, she kept a diary, which was later published. Her writings in the influential *Arminian Magazine* were widely read. She published verse and encouraged Methodist preachers through extensive correspondence about religious issues. Her extensively circulated *A short Account of the experience of Hester Ann Roe Rogers,* an autobiography, inspired many thousands of readers.

2 *Methodism Comes to America*

Methodism existed in Great Britain for nearly thirty years before it successfully took root in America. Although John and Charles Wesley served brief terms as Anglican missionaries in Georgia during the 1730s, their efforts failed to plant Methodism in this country. After returning to England, the Wesleys successfully established Methodism in Great Britain, but they made no immediate plans to expand their work into America. Next, George Whitefield began a small Methodist society in Delaware in 1739, but that work also failed to survive. John and Charles Wesley and George Whitefield were the first Methodist ministers in America, but their efforts in this country produced no lasting organization. We trace Methodist beginnings in America to the work of others.

In the 1760s two Irish Methodist lay preachers—Robert Strawbridge and Philip Embury—immigrated to these shores. Without knowledge of each other, Strawbridge settled in Maryland and Embury located in New York. Both these pioneers established societies that mark the beginnings of American Methodism.

John Wesley monument in Savannah.

John and Charles Wesley served as missionaries to the Colony of Georgia, 1736-1737. They failed to establish Methodism in America as a continuing movement. Spiritually, they were not yet ready for this task, and they returned to England both humbled and disappointed. John Wesley wrote of his experience in America, "All the time I was at Savannah I was ... beating the air."

Compared to America's established denominations, these Methodist beginnings were small and, at the time, scarcely noticed. As the numbers of Methodists increased, however, they drew attention and then criticism. Some leaders in America's larger denominations regarded their established churches as superior to the humble Methodist societies. They objected to Methodism's enthusiastic preaching, loud singing, hand clapping, and shouting. The majority of Methodist preachers were neither culturally refined nor well educated—both marks against them. Some religious leaders even warned their congregations against attending Methodist meetings. Despite Methodism's unassuming start, however, it grew steadily and eventually became the most dynamic force in American religion.

Robert Strawbridge

The first permanent Methodist work in America, and the most influential, began with Robert Strawbridge, a self-reliant Methodist lay preacher. Around 1760 or 1761, Strawbridge and his wife, Elizabeth, left Ireland and settled in Frederick County, Maryland. Soon after his arrival, Strawbridge began a preaching ministry. He was an eloquent speaker, and he possessed a beautiful singing voice. Around 1773, in the house of John Evans, Strawbridge organized the first enduring Methodist society in America. Strawbridge's religious services attracted neighbors, and his ministry resulted in numerous Christian conversions. Some of these new converts became Methodist class leaders and preachers, making possible the starting of new societies. Later, Francis Asbury acknowledged in his journal, "Mr. Strawbridge formed the first society in Maryland—and America."

Robert Strawbridge (c. 1732-1781).

Around 1763, Strawbridge and his wife, Elizabeth, organized America's first permanent Methodist class meeting. While Elizabeth cared for family and farm, Robert preached throughout eastern Maryland, as well as in parts of Virginia, New Jersey, and Pennsylvania.

A contemporary of Strawbridge described him as being "of strong, muscular frame, about medium size, lean of flesh, black hair, dark, thin visage, the bones of his face projecting prominently, a pleasant voice, a melodious singer, and a great favorite among the children.... He appears to have been a general favorite in the community where he resided, for before any Methodist society was formed there, the neighbors were in the habit of cultivating his farm gratuitously and supplying the wants of his family, while he was dispensing the Word of Life abroad."

The John Evans House, site of American Methodism's first preaching station.

Under the ministry of Robert and Elizabeth Strawbridge, John Evans became the first convert in American Methodism. When Robert Strawbridge engaged in itinerant preaching ministries, Evans assumed leadership of the class meeting. This class soon moved to the John Evans home, built in 1764. The class continued to meet for 41 years. From 1768 to 1809, sixty-eight Methodist itinerants preached here, including Bishop Francis Asbury. In 1868 Strawbridge's pulpit was recovered from the attic of the Evans house, and the pulpit is presently displayed at the Lovely Lane Museum in Baltimore, along with some timbers from Strawbridge's first log meetinghouse.

Strawbridge deserves credit for a number of other "firsts" in American Methodism. He also helped win John Evans, American Methodism's first convert, although it seems likely that Strawbridge's wife Elizabeth was the more important influence leading to Evans's conversion. Robert Strawbridge's congregation built American Methodism's first meetinghouse, probably in 1764; it was a log structure erected about a mile south of the present town of New Windsor, Maryland. By 1800, Strawbridge's growing Methodist society had replaced its log meeting house with a stone chapel.

Although Strawbridge was not ordained, he believed that those under his spiritual care needed the sacraments. And so, in 1762 or 1763 he performed his first baptism, that of a child, making Strawbridge the first Methodist preacher in America to administer a sacrament. His doing so, however, went counter to Methodist principles. At that time, John Wesley insisted that Methodism was a religious society associated with the Church of England, and he instructed the Methodists to receive sacraments only from ordained Anglican priests. From Strawbridge's point of view, however, Wesley's policy failed to take into account that the Anglican sacraments were seldom or never available in many sections of America. So, he took matters into his own hands and offered the sacraments.

The Robert Strawbridge log meetinghouse, 1764.

This sketch is of the first Methodist chapel in America. It was 24 feet square, with a dirt floor. The logs were sawed for a doorway on one side; smaller openings were cut for windows, although it is uncertain whether windows were installed. Numerous Methodist preachers held services here, including Francis Asbury. Two of Robert and Elizabeth Strawbridge's children, Jane and Betsy, were buried under the place where the pulpit stood.

The Old Stone Chapel, 1783.

In 1783 American Methodism's first congregation built a stone chapel, called the "Old Hive," on land donated by Andrew Poulson. The two-story structure had galleries on three sides. After seventeen years, its walls began to crumble, and the congregation disassembled the structure. In 1800 the people rebuilt on the same foundation, and the floor and galleries were rebuilt in their original positions. Again in 1883, the church was rebuilt, removing the galleries and lowering the ceiling.

Rebecca Dorsey Ridgely (1739-1812). *This copy of a painting by John Hesselius appears here by permission of the Frick Art Reference Library.*

Mrs. Ridgely and her husband, Captain Charles Ridgely, generously befriended Robert Strawbridge by providing him a farm rent-free. The hospitality and generosity of people like the Ridgelys greatly assisted the early Methodist circuit riders in their itinerant ministries.

In 1789 Richard Whatcoat wrote in his journal an account of visiting the Ridgley residence (*original spellings and punctuation follow*): "Rode To Captin Ridgleys Held A watch Night the Revd John Coleman was Closeing his Discours as I arived I preach^d Bro^r Forster Exhorted &C The Fier Brok out then there was Crying praying and ... through the asembley which Continued till Twelv Then I Dismised the Congregation But Some Remained in Distress and Som Continued in prayer &C Till three I supose 10 or 12 found peace if Not More."

Old Rehboth Chapel.

This Methodist chapel near Union, West Virginia, was constructed in 1786 and is the oldest surviving Protestant church building west of the Allegheny Mountains. The building, measuring 21 by 29 feet, was constructed with a narrow gallery that seated almost as many people as the main floor. At the time it was built, forts in the area protected against Indian attacks. The first circuit rider assigned to this church was John Smith, whose journal reveals that the first Methodist ordination ceremony west of the Allegheny Mountains took place here in 1788. The service was in charge of Bishop Francis Asbury, who revisited this church several times.

This log building is typical of the hundreds of first-generation Methodist preaching houses erected across America from the 1760s through the next few decades. The protective roof system was added later to preserve the old log structure. Edward Keenan, who donated the site and erected the building, specified that the chapel must remain with the Methodists "as long as grass grows and water flows."

Strawbridge's ministry became an epicenter from which flowed powerful evangelistic currents that resulted in significant expansion. He received invitations to preach in other places, and his ministry reached out in wider and wider circles. His neighbors supported his itineracy by caring for his farm and providing for the temporal needs of his wife and children. From 1776 to 1781 Captain and Mrs. Charles Ridgely provided the Strawbridge family with a rent-free farm. Due to the assistance of the Ridgleys and other lay persons, Strawbridge was able to itinerate and thereby extend his ministry into eastern Maryland, Delaware, Pennsylvania, and Virginia. In all, he established thirty preaching stations, including at least six chapels. Francis Asbury tells in his journal that Maryland was a "veritable beehive" of religious activity.

A distinguishing mark of Strawbridge's ministry was the raising up of a number of "spiritual sons in the Gospel." These preachers became Methodist class leaders, exhorters, and itinerant preachers. Among them was Jacob Toogood, a slave and probably the first black preacher in American Methodism.

Strawbridge divided these Christian workers into bands of three or four for mutual support, accountability, and encouragement. They fanned out across the frontier to spread the Methodist message. These lay ministers visited in homes, prayed, sang hymns, and "exhorted" (encouraged) others to receive the grace of God. Some of Strawbridge's converts migrated across the Alleghenies, carrying the spiritual awakening into territories not yet charted. By the 1770s, almost half of Methodism's members and virtually all the American-born preachers lived in Maryland or Virginia—areas where Strawbridge's influence was particularly strong.

The records of early Methodism do not give adequate credit to Strawbridge for his accomplishments. As noted, he went against John Wesley's rule forbidding Methodist preachers to offer the sacraments. As a consequence of Strawbridge's sacramental ministry, Francis Asbury turned cool toward him and withheld his full approval. After 1775, Strawbridge's name does not appear in the official roster of Methodist preachers, likely because he ignored Methodist policy. Undaunted, Strawbridge, the "Methodist maverick," continued to evangelize and establish new Methodist congregations.

Robert Strawbridge continued his fruitful ministry until his death in 1781. Neighbors and converts carried his coffin to its burial site, singing the hymns of Charles Wesley that speak of the Christian's victory over death. This faithful minister of Christ was the first to plant continuing Methodist societies in America, and his ministry touched the lives of thousands. Robert Strawbridge deserves the designation "First Apostle of American Methodism."

The house where Strawbridge died (1781) and where his funeral was held (as was his wife's).

Strawbridge was buried in Wheeler's orchard near Baltimore. Richard Owen, one of Strawbridge's converts, preached his funeral sermon from the text, "Blessed are the dead that die in the Lord henceforth; Yea, saith the Spirit, that they may rest from their labors: and their works do follow them." In 1866, George C. Roberts, founder of the American Methodist Historical Society, had the couple's remains moved to Mount Olivet Cemetery, Baltimore, and placed in the "Bishop's Lot" alongside other Methodist worthies.

Philip Embury

Another Irish lay preacher, Philip Embury, also played a pioneer role in transplanting Methodism to America. Prior to coming to America, Embury was converted on Christmas Day, 1752. Later, in 1756, he heard John Wesley preach, and this experience inspired him to become a Methodist class leader and lay preacher. Poverty eventually caused Embury and some of his friends to immigrate to America in the hope of achieving a better standard of living. The group settled in New York but found no Methodist societies there. They became affiliated with a local church of another denomination, but they soon began to neglect their faith, not being as serious about it as when they had lived in Ireland. Although Philip Embury did not fall into flagrant sin, he no longer preached or conducted class meetings. He fretted over the religiously undisciplined lives of his friends but made no attempt to call them to serious Christian discipleship.

At this point, a Methodist heroine stepped forward and sparked a revival of religion among these Irish Methodist immigrants. She was a cousin of Philip Embury, named Barbara Heck. Mrs. Heck had become alarmed over the irreligious drift of her friends and relatives. In October 1766 she confronted her cousin, Philip Embury. Prostrating herself, she begged him with tears to begin preaching services. She declared, "You must preach to us, or we shall all go to hell together, and God will require our blood at your hands!" Embury responded, "How can I preach, for I have neither a [preaching] house nor a congregation?" Mrs. Heck rejoined, "Preach in your own house and to your own company first." He responded to her challenge, and they arranged to begin Methodist preaching in Embury's home.

Heck rounded up the first congregation, consisting of Embury, herself, her servant, and three others. After singing and prayer, Embury preached and then formed the small congregation into a Methodist class. Week by week, the attendance increased, and new worshipers were converted to Christ. The growing numbers required the congregation to move to a larger meeting place. They located in an "upper room" a few doors from an army barracks of the British occupying forces. Here, Embury preached

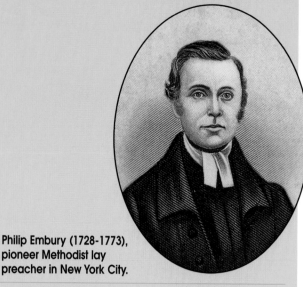

Philip Embury (1728-1773), pioneer Methodist lay preacher in New York City.

In 1766 Embury organized the first Methodist society in New York City. Those who knew him reported that he was modest and that he "gave evidence of feeling what he said to others." He often wept as he preached. A small book of family records was passed down to Embury's son. A leaf in this slender volume contains an entry penned by Philip Embury on Christmas Day, the first anniversary of his spiritual birth. He wrote, "On Christmas day;—being Monday ye 25th of December, in the year 1752; the love shone in to my Soul by a glimpse of his Redeeming love: being an Earnest of my redemption in Christ Jesus, to whom be glory for Ever & Ever. Amen. Phil. Embury." After coming to America, Embury earned the appellation "Apostle of Methodism in New York."

Barbara Ruckle Heck (1734-1804), "The Mother of American Methodism."

Due to Barbara Heck's persistence, Philip Embury opened his home for the first preaching service in New York City. Six people, including a black maid, attended this service. Barbara Heck combined the qualities of perseverance, self-control and patience. As the society grew, Mrs. Heck conceived a plan for the edifice of old John Street Church in New York City, a design that she believed God had given her. The New York Methodist Society approved her plan and constructed the building. Mrs. Heck's zeal for evangelism won her a hallowed place among the founders of American Methodism.

without compensation, and he organized two more classes. Additional helpers joined this work, including some British soldiers. Embury preached elsewhere in the city, including the almshouse, where the poor eagerly heard his sermons.

From the start, both in Maryland and in New York, black and white Methodists worshiped together. One of the members of Embury's original class meeting was Betty, a servant of Barbara Heck. Betty gained permission to invite other blacks to come to the Methodist meetings.

These additional "Africans" soon formed themselves into a separate class. The letters and journals of those who ministered in New York reveal that more than half of the early Methodists in that area were persons of color. Yet when the New York Methodists constructed their first building it included a ladder stairway to the "slave gallery" for persons of color. Despite this practice, Methodism grew to include thousands of black members. Some served as class leaders and preachers.

Drawing of Philip Embury's house in New York City.

Here, in the autumn of 1766, Embury preached the first Methodist sermon in New York. The first tiny congregation grew steadily, and soon Methodism was firmly established in the area. Embury's work in New York and Strawbridge's work in Maryland and Virginia began a Methodist momentum that by 1800 saw almost 65,000 Methodists "in society" in American Methodism. Several times that number attended Methodist preaching services.

Captain Thomas Webb

Philip Embury's New York congregation was astonished when an imposing stranger appeared at one of the services. He was Captain Thomas Webb, an officer in the British army. He wore a regimental uniform and sword. Although Webb's initial appearance created apprehension, the fears of the people dissipated when he took part in the singing and worship. At the close of the service, this striking man introduced himself as "a soldier of the cross and a spiritual son of John Wesley." He informed the congregation that he was a Methodist lay preacher, and he offered to assist the congregation. Webb's service among these early New York Methodists proved immensely helpful. When he preached, he wore his uniform and placed his sword across the pulpit. His colorful presence drew crowds to hear his powerful sermons.

A contemporary Methodist preacher said of Thomas Webb, "He experienced much of the power of religion in his own soul; he wrestled day and night with God for that degree of grace which he stood in need of that he might stand firm as the beaten anvil to the stroke, and he was favored with those communications from above which made him bold to declare the whole counsel of God." Young John Adams (later the second U.S. President) heard Webb preach. Adams remarked, "He was one of the most fluent, eloquent men I ever heard. He reaches the imagination and touches the passions very well, and expresses himself with great propriety."

Again, growth required Philip Embury's New York congregation to move to a new place of worship. This time, the group selected a rigging loft where workmen repaired sails. The room measured 18 by 60 feet, and the congregation furnished it with benches and a preaching stand. Embury's congregation met on Sunday mornings at 6:00 and on Thursday evenings, times that did not conflict with the services of the established churches.

Captain Thomas Webb (1724-1796).

In 1768 this British army officer helped raise funds for the first Methodist church in New York City, personally pledging thirty pounds. It is doubtful that this church could have been built without his help. Thomas Webb also went to Philadelphia where he found a class formed earlier by James Emerson, who had been converted under the preaching of George Whitefield. Webb organized this group into Philadelphia's first Methodist society. In 1769 his financial assistance made it possible for Joseph Pilmore and the Philadelphia congregation to purchase St. George's Church. Webb also took Methodism to Delaware, where he preached in Newcastle, Wilmington, and other areas. When Webb returned to England, he entreated John Wesley to send preachers to America.

Assessing the worth of Thomas Webb, John Wesley said, "The captain is all life and fire; therefore, although he is not deep or regular, yet many, who would not hear a better preacher, flock to hear him, and many are convinced under his preaching." Thomas Webb's work as a preacher, encourager, and patron proved invaluable to the early Methodists in America.

The rigging loft quickly became overcrowded, as it "could not contain half the people who desired to hear the word of the Lord." In 1768 the congregation leased still another site in New York on John Street and erected a chapel 42 by 60 feet. At the time, New York had a tax-supported state church, and the law did not permit congregations of other denominations to build churches. The Methodists built their meeting place with a fireplace and a chimney so that it could be classified as a house. They called it Wesley Chapel. When John Wesley received news of the new chapel he sent the congregation money, books, and a clock.

The Rigging Loft.

During 1767-1768 the early New York Methodists worshiped at this meeting place located at 120 William Street in New York City. Philip Embury and Thomas Webb led this congregation, assisted by several converts who were members of a regimental band of the British occupying forces. The congregation grew and soon made plans to build Methodism's first church in the area. At the time, the population of New York City was about 15,000.

Original John Street Church and parsonage.
This drawing by J. B. Smith is in the Museum of the City of New York, and it appears here by permission of the museum.

In August 1768 Philip Embury's Methodist society purchased two lots on John Street in New York City. Assisted by 250 subscribers, the congregation promptly erected a meetinghouse on the property and named it Wesley Chapel. Embury oversaw the construction of the edifice, which cost between 600 and 800 pounds. Here, America's first Methodist General Superintendent, Thomas Coke, preached his initial sermons in this country. In 1789 the conference of Methodist preachers met here and authorized Thomas Coke and Francis Asbury to take formal congratulations to George Washington on his election as the first president of the United States. In 1817 the original John Street church was razed to make room for a larger edifice that was completed in 1818. In 1840 the city's widening of John Street required the demolition of the 1818 structure. In 1841 Bishop Elijah Hedding dedicated a new building.

John Wesley's Official Missionaries to America

George Whitefield was probably the first person to urge Wesley to send Christian workers to America. In September 1764, Whitefield wrote Wesley from Philadelphia, "Here is room for a hundred itinerants." Then, Thomas Webb wrote on behalf of the New York society, imploring Wesley to send preachers to America. At about the same time, Thomas Bell, a British immigrant and cabinetmaker, wrote from Charlestown that the Americans "are running wild after this world.... And are not these lost sheep? And will none of the [British] preachers come here?" In 1768 Methodists in Maryland and New York, independently of each other, sent "pressing calls" to John Wesley asking for assistance in the growing Methodist work in America.

John Wesley was convinced of the need in America for missionaries, and he became determined to send "helpers" as soon as practicable. He believed strongly that Christians, especially new converts, required adequate pastoral care. He wrote, "I am more and more convinced, that the devil himself desires nothing more than this, that the people of any place should be half-awakened, and then left to themselves to fall asleep again. Therefore I determine, by the grace of God, not to strike one stroke in any place where I cannot follow the blow." The aging Wesley was not able to go to America himself, and the growth of Methodism in England required the full measure of his time and energy. He would need to send others on this mission to America.

In 1769 John Wesley took specific action. That year, the British Methodist Conference of Preachers met at Leeds. Wesley stated to the conference, "We have a pressing call from our brethren of New York (who have built a meetinghouse) to come over and help them. Who are willing to go?" The following day, two young ministers volunteered, and within two weeks they sailed for America. Their names were Richard Boardman and Joseph Pilmore. Although the British Methodists were in debt, the ministers at the conference in Leeds contributed 70 pounds—20 pounds for the passage for the two volunteers and 50 pounds toward the debt of the New York chapel. After a stormy voyage of nine weeks, Boardman and Pilmore reached Philadelphia and immediately began their ministries.

Richard Boardman (1738-1782)

Joseph Pilmore (1739-1825)

John Wesley commissioned these two British Methodist preachers as the first official Methodist missionaries to America. They arrived together at Gloucester Point, New Jersey October 24, 1769 and began immediately to minister. The two men preached in America until the winter of 1774 when political tensions between the American Colonies and Great Britain forced them to return to England.

Richard Boardman is described as "a man of great piety, of an amiable disposition, and possessed of a strong understanding." John Wesley said that Boardman was "a pious, good-natured, sensible man, greatly beloved by all who knew him." He preached with compelling ability and positive results. Through his example of selfless service, Richard Boardman helped establish and shape an infant Methodism in America. His steady hand and faithful service gave both direction and inspiration to the early Methodists along the eastern seaboard.

Joseph Pilmore was also a preacher of deep piety and personal power. Prior to coming to America, Pilmore made the following covenant with God: "First. I do this day, give up and devote my soul to thee, O my God, to be altogether and forever thine. I submit myself to thy yoke, and wait for thy continual guidance in all things. Let all my thoughts be pure and holy: let all my desires centre in thee, and all my affections be placed entirely upon thee: And in order to that, do thou, O my God, wean me from all my fondness for created enjoyments, and let me be entirely crucified unto the world, and the world unto me. Secondly. I offer up my body to be for ever thine; therefore, I pray that thou wouldst keep me from all pollution and defilement, and keep me chaste and clean, as a temple for thee, that thou mayest dwell for ever in my heart, and be glorified by my soul and body, which are thine; and at last, raise me up from the dust of death, to dwell among thy saints in glory. Thirdly. I hereby promise to spend all my time in thy service, and all my talents to thy glory and honour. Jos. Pilmore."

Richard Boardman

Richard Boardman was a year older than Pilmore, and Wesley selected Boardman to serve as his "Assistant" in America. At the time, the term assistant designated those who, under John Wesley's oversight, supervised the work of a circuit. Boardman began his work in New York, and Pilmore ministered in Philadelphia. Three times yearly, the two preachers exchanged places of service. These two men also preached in other colonies, spreading Methodism in ever-widening circles.

Due to frequent meetings and the time-consuming demands of horseback travel, their schedules were rigorous. Boardman preached four sermons a week and met with the society on Wednesday evenings. He wrote in a letter, "The rides are long, the roads bad, and the living very poor. But what more than compensates for these difficulties is a prospect of advancing the Redeemer's kingdom in bringing sinners to the knowledge of the truth as it is in Jesus. In the greater part of this round [circuit] the people were wicked and ignorant to a most lamentable degree, destitute of the fear and regardless of the worship of God. But such a reformation is wrought among them as shows the amazing love and almighty power of God."

Boardman received a salary of $15 per quarter. Due to this arrangement, the early American Methodists often referred to the preacher's remuneration as "quarterage." At that time Methodist preachers had no parsonages. They itinerated most of the time and received food and lodging from volunteer hosts along their circuits. The Methodists did not formally discuss parsonages until the conference of 1800, and several more decades passed before they built homes for their preachers.

Despite continuous travel and numerous inconveniences, Boardman and Pilmore continued to improve their minds by persistent reading. The Methodist Societies economized by allowing Boardman and Pilmore only four quires of writing paper a year—a quire being a set of four sheets folded once. To overcome this limitation, these two preachers bought paper out of their meager salaries. Their need for writing paper underscores the importance they attached to their studies. Their reading and writing resulted in ever more effective sermons, which attracted growing crowds.

In November 1769 Boardman wrote John Wesley that the people were so eager to hear the word of God that only one-third of the crowds could cram into the preaching place. A layman, Edward Evans, penned a letter to Wesley: "Your dear young men, I mean Brother Boardman and Brother Pilmore, have been a welcome and an acceptable present to us.... I find them truly sincere, and heartily concerned for the good cause. Their fervency and labour therein greatly delights me. The Lord is with them, and owns and blesses [them] greatly to the people."

Boardman had a special empathy for the black community. In 1769 he wrote John Wesley, "The number of Blacks that attend the preaching affects me much. One of them came to tell me she could neither eat nor sleep, because her Master would not suffer her to come to hear the word. She wept exceedingly, saying, 'I told my Master I would do more work than ever I used to do, if he would let me come [to religious services]; nay, that I would do every thing in my power to be a good servant.'" Happily, this woman experienced a glorious conversion and continued in joy until her death. Boardman recounted the story of her passing in a letter written in 1771:

> I have lately been much comforted by the death of some poor negroes, who have gone off the stage of time rejoicing in the God of their salvation. I asked one, on the point of death, 'Are you afraid to die?' 'O no, said she; I have my blessed Saviour in my heart; I should be glad to die: I want to be gone, that I may be with him for ever. I know that he loves me; and I feel I love him with all my heart.' She continued to declare the great things God had done for her soul, to the astonishment of many, till the Lord took her to himself. Several more seem just ready to be gone, longing for the happy time when mortality shall be swallowed up of life.

As Wesley's first Assistant in America, Boardman exercised an important ministry of encouragement among the newly recruited Methodist preachers. Pilmore recorded in his journal that at a conference of preachers, Boardman "preached a most excellent sermon on the important work of the Gospel Ministry." Boardman impressed on the new preachers the seriousness of their work, the essentials of Christian doctrine, the need for disciplined living, and the importance of Methodist polity.

Joseph Pilmore

If Boardman had a fruitful ministry, Joseph Pilmore was equally useful. After he had preached only a month in Philadelphia, the Methodist chapel could not accommodate half the people who came to the services. He recorded in his journal, "There appears such a willingness in the Americans to hear the word, as I never saw before. The number of blacks that attends the preaching affects me much." On another occasion he wrote, "In the evening, preached to a large congregation with great freedom.... Afterwards I admitted a very hopeful young man into the Society, and concluded the day in praise to God for the great and effectual door he has opened in this City for the preaching of his precious Gospel. The sacred fire is spreading wider and wider and the prospect continually grows brighter and brighter!"

The crowds of people inspired the Philadelphia congregation to move to a larger building. In 1769 the congregation purchased St. George's Church, a half-finished structure that another denomination was forced to abandon. The new building quickly filled with eager worshipers.

St. George's Methodist Episcopal Church, Philadelphia.

This structure is the oldest standing building in American Methodism. The edifice was erected in 1763 and purchased by the Methodists in 1769. In the beginning, this building had a dirt floor, and Methodism's first three conferences were held here prior to the addition of flooring, plaster, and paint. Originally, candles resting in black tin sconces hanging on the walls lighted the church. Candle chandeliers dangled from the ceiling. (Candles cost about fifteen cents a pound, and when they burned low the remaining "stumps" sold for about eight cents a pound.) The leaky stovepipe was often patched with clay, and smoke sometimes permeated the air. Because the stove was not adequate for good heating, the women brought foot-warmers to church.

Interior of historic St. George's Church after its restoration.
Photograph reproduced by permission from Old St. George Church.

A German Reformed congregation began the construction of St. George's Church in 1763. The original builders named the church St. George's, in the futile hope that the Anglican Church would help with its completion. When the original congregation sold it to the Methodists, the church retained its name. Bishop Francis Asbury worked tirelessly to raise money for the building's completion. Because of its size (55 by 85 feet) and seating capacity (over one thousand), Asbury referred to this church as the "Cathedral of Methodism."

St. George's Church has a rich history. In October, 1779 the first hymn collection published by an American Methodist society was printed for St. George's Church. In this church Joseph Pilmore gave the first public statement of Methodism's doctrine and polity, and American Methodism's first prayer meeting was held on December

8, 1769. American Methodist Watch Night services began in this building, and here Francis Asbury preached his first sermon in America. Richard Allen, the first American black preacher to receive a license to preach, received his certificate here in 1784. In 1789 John Dickens organized the Methodist Book Concern in St. George's Church. This congregation assisted in the organization of over one hundred Methodist churches. Over the years, the church has been expanded and remodeled. The church now maintains a valuable archival collection of papers, books, and historical treasures. The balcony from which this photograph was taken seats 568 people.

St. George's Church remains today as one of American Methodism's historic landmarks and the oldest Methodist edifice in continuous use in America. In addition to his work in Philadelphia, Pilmore organized Methodist societies in Maryland, Virginia, and South Carolina.

Joseph Pilmore appointed probably the first female class leader in America—Mary Thorne. When the occupying British army temporarily commandeered St. George's Church, Mrs. Thorne hosted the Methodist Society in her home. She became a good friend to Joseph Pilmore and Richard Boardman, both of whom affectionately called her "Mollie." The archives collection at St. George's United Methodist Church, Philadelphia contains a letter that Boardman wrote to Mary Thorne: "My Dear Friend: I find it good [to] plow and sow in hope. The time for gathering in will come. O! my dear friend, did we but see the fullness of blessing laid up for us in Christ Jesus [to make] us strong in faith, earnest in prayer, satisfy our objections and supply all our wants, while out of this fullness we received grace for grace. Yet a little while and Jesus will call us home. May we get fully ready. Heaven will more than compensate for all the little difficulties and trials we have suffered in this world."

A Lasting Legacy

Wesley's missionaries to this country did incalculable good and helped nourish the growing vine of American Methodism. In total, John Wesley sent eight missionaries to America—Richard Boardman and Joseph Pilmore (1769), Francis Asbury and Richard Wright (1771), Thomas Rankin and George Shadford (1773), Martin Rodda and James Dempster (1774). The onset of America's War of Independence, however, prompted all these workers except Francis Asbury to return to England.

George Shadford typifies this first generation of Methodist preachers. John Wesley sent Shadford to America with the simple statement, "I let you loose, George, on the great continent of America. Publish your message in the open face of the sun, and do all the good you can." Although Shadford ministered only five years in America before

George Shadford (1739-1816).

Shadford was one of eight missionaries that John Wesley sent to America between 1769 and 1774. He ranked among the most effective preachers in first-generation American Methodism. His cheerful personality and winsome sense of humor endeared him to his hearers. Shadford labored mostly in Maryland and Virginia, where thousands were converted to Christ under his ministry. As the American Revolution approached, certain American patriots persecuted him because he was a British citizen. In the midst of this political turmoil, Francis Asbury felt called to stay in America, while Shadford felt impressed to return to England. He said to Asbury, "I may have a call to go, and you to stay."

Shadford returned to England, where he had a long and fruitful ministry. Toward the end of his life he wrote, "I see more than ever the preciousness of time, and the wisdom of improving it to the best purposes: the living every moment for God, the buying up every opportunity; the necessity of being more spiritual in my conversation, in order to grow in grace; the talking in company not about worldly things, but about our souls, God and Christ, heaven and eternal glory."

When a doctor informed Shadford that he was dying, Shadford exclaimed, "Glory to God!" During his final hours he was asked if all was clear before him. He replied, "I bless God it is.... Victory through the blood of the Lamb!" His final words were, "I'll praise, I'll praise, I'll praise." The early American Methodists regarded George Shadford as "a man of warm impulses, great energy, and remarkable usefulness." Few preachers had more winsome charm or preached with such guileless dignity.

returning to England, his time here was highly effective. Shadford's simplicity, prayerfulness, good humor, and powerful sermons helped kindle revivals in which thousands of people came to Christ. His preaching inspired many young men to become Methodist circuit riders.

Sometimes the Methodist services were accompanied by unexplainable physical manifestations among the people. Jesse Lee, American Methodism's first historian, and a participant in these events, reported, "It was quite common for sinners to be seized with a trembling and shaking, and from that to fall down on the floor as if they were dead; and many of them have been convulsed from head to foot, while others have retained the use of their tongues so as to pray for mercy, while they were lying helpless on the ground or floor.... It was truly affecting to see [Christians] collecting round the penitent sinners, and praying for them...until some of the mourners would get converted; and then to see the young converts leaping up with streaming eyes and calling upon all present to praise God for what he had done for their souls." Lee concluded, "In that revival there were some things which might be called imprudent; yet... it was thought to be dangerous to try to stop the irregularities, for fear of stopping that gracious work which the Lord was so strangely carrying on."

If American Methodism was to continue, it could not rely solely on British missionaries. The movement needed homegrown preachers. So, the story of American Methodism moved into a new chapter, with the raising up of native-born American itinerants. Their journals and diaries, along with accounts written about them, contain thousands of pages that detail the exciting adventures of these young men who helped bridge Methodism's transition into its second generation of ministry.

The first native-born American to enter the Methodist itineracy was William Watters. He was the only American-born preacher to attend American Methodism's first conference, held in 1773, and in 1778 he was the first to preside over a conference of his peers. These colleagues reported that Watters was the only preacher on the opposite side of a controversy that treated them with respect and affection.

William Watters (1751-1827). *Photograph supplied by the courtesy of the United Methodist Commission on Archives and History at Drew University.*

Watters, the first American-born itinerant preacher, wrote "a short account" of his "Christian experience and ministerial labors." In that work he stated, "I had no one to tell me of the evil of sin, or to teach me the way of life and salvation. The two (priests) in the two parishes, with whom I was acquainted, were both immoral men, and had no gifts for the ministry... The blind were evidently leading the blind, and it was by the mere mercy of God that we did not all fall into hell together."

Then, as a young man, Watters heard several Methodist preachers, including Robert Strawbridge. Conviction for sin seized his heart, and in a Methodist prayer meeting his "heart and eyes melted" because of the depth of his spiritual need. He returned to his home and fasted for three days. Then, Methodist friends came to pray with him. Watters wrote, "The Lord heard and appeared spiritually in the midst of us. A divine light beamed through my inmost soul, and in a few minutes encircled me around, surpassing the brightness of the noonday sun. Of this divine glory, with the holy glow that I felt within my soul, I have still as distinct an idea as that I ever saw the light of the natural sun, but know not how fully to express myself so as to be understood by those who are in a state of nature, unexperienced in the things of God." Watters was twenty years old, and he immediately joined a Methodist class.

Watters began preaching at the age of twenty-one. Robert Williams, a Methodist preacher from England, took him under his wing and helped him become an effective circuit rider. He was "a man fervent in spirit, prudent in counsel, indefatigable in labor, saintly in piety."

Although Watters was a successful itinerant, poor health eventually required him to "locate," that is, cease traveling as a circuit rider. He continued to minister as best he could until he died in 1827. Matthew Simpson regarded Watters as "diligent, deeply pious, and very useful." William Watters was the first of tens of thousands of American-born Methodist itinerants who followed in his train, preaching the Methodist gospel of full salvation for all that believe.

Francis Asbury

Of the missionaries that Wesley sent to America, only Francis Asbury chose to remain permanently. He based his decision to stay in this country on his sense of a divine call to do so. As the first rumbles of America's War of Independence were beginning, Asbury wrote, "I can by no means agree to leave such a field for gathering souls to Christ as we have in America. ... [N]either is it the part of a good shepherd to leave his flock in time of danger: therefore, I am determined by the grace of God not to leave them, let the consequence be what it may." Asbury articulated his vision for America in a letter to George Shadford: "O America! America! It certainly will be the glory of the world for religion! I have loved, and do love America.... O let us haste in peace and love, where we shall know, love, and enjoy God and each other, and [our] differences...will be done away." Asbury's legacy consists of the pattern of his holy life, the inspiration of his preaching, and the example of his leadership.

Hints of the devotional life of Francis Asbury appear on almost every page of his journal. He read such books as Richard Baxter's *The Saint's Everlasting Rest*, Thomas a Kempis's *Imitation of Christ*, and John Bunyon's *The Pilgrim's Progress*, but the Bible was his constant companion. His daily habit of arising before 5:00 AM to study scripture enabled him instantly to locate almost any passage in the Bible. He worked with Hebrew, Greek, and Latin to help him better understand the nuances of scripture.

In addition to Asbury's constant reading of the Bible, his prayer life stood out as one of the most

Francis Asbury (1745-1816). *Permission to reproduce this picture is given by the World Methodist Museum, Lake Junaluska, NC. Photograph by Dave Henderson.*

This photograph is of Frank O. Salisbury's original oil painting of Francis Asbury. Salisbury compared the extant prints of Asbury and painted this famous likeness. The painting represents Bishop Asbury at the age of 39, the time of his election in 1784 as a bishop of the newly formed Methodist Episcopal Church.

characteristic marks of his life. Even though his travels required him to spend much time in the saddle, he devoted three hours to prayer each day. Circumstances often required that he pray in the forest in the cold and rain. Bishop Asbury's journal contains more regrets about being deprived of time for prayer than about the physical discomforts he endured on the circuits. Speaking at Asbury's funeral, Ezekiel Cooper said that Asbury "appeared to have nothing to do with the things of the world, only as they promoted the cause of God."

Asbury also bequeathed to his preachers the example of sound preaching. He wrote in his journal, "Lord, keep me from...preaching empty stuff to please the ear, instead of changing the heart." Asbury made no attempt to appear intellectual or brilliant. Instead, he preached from plain texts and spoke from his heart to the people's hearts. He was an effective preacher, not especially because of his oratorical skills, theological dexterity, or strong voice. Rather, his preaching reached people because his sermons brought God to them and them to God. He was primarily concerned with helping his listeners hear the word of God and respond to its eternal implications. For him, knowledge was less important than wisdom, and he championed the biblical truth that the fear of God is the beginning of wisdom.

Asbury's leadership skill eminently fitted him for supervising preachers and governing the church. As a leader among the Methodists, he had no equal in his day. His intuitive understanding of people and situations was exceptional, and he had an extraordinary ability to assess the strengths and weaknesses of the preachers. One biographer states, "Many things, which proved to be pivotal decisions which were timed and executed with unerring precision, he seemed to do in a perfectly casual way."

Although gifted with uncommon instincts and excellent leadership abilities, he did not rely on whims or hunches. Before making decisions, he gathered information by interviewing others, carefully studying the preachers' reports, and continuously visiting throughout the conferences. He kept notes on the preachers, so he could assign them to circuits where they could most effectively serve. He sent the eccentric preachers Lorenzo Dow and Peter Cartwright to take Methodism into new settlements, where they would create interest and excitement. Afterwards, he sent to those places preachers who could bring discipline, order, and nurture to the new circuits. Bishop Asbury knew that some preachers were suited to establishing beachheads, and others were more effective at bringing congregations to maturity.

Asbury's travels throughout Methodism gave him comprehensive insights into the church's needs and opportunities. His quick discernment, humble leadership, fair-minded administration, moral courage, and selfless service earned him the esteem and affection of those he served. They acknowledged that he was first among the preachers in sacrificial service and ceaseless labors. His example helped transform his generation of Methodist preachers into heroes of the faith, and he inspired countless lay people to serve Christ and neighbor. After two hundred years, the influence of Francis Asbury continues in the church.

Because the American Methodist movement was thriving, thoughts of forming a new denomination entered into the minds of some. In the 1770s, however, the preachers were not ready to take that step. In 1773 Thomas Rankin, one of Wesley's missionaries, called the preachers to American Methodism's first conference, which met at St. George's Church in Philadelphia. The ten preachers who attended (most of them citizens of the United Kingdom) agreed to keep American Methodism under the authority of John Wesley. As a sign of their loyalty to Wesley and to the Church of England, they voted to refrain from giving sacraments. This first generation of preachers from Great Britain had planted Methodism in America and bequeathed to this country a legacy of inestimable value. Yet it remained for others to take American Methodism into its next phase—that of becoming a new denomination. This step was completed eleven years later, in 1784. By then, with the exception of Asbury, the British missionaries had returned to England and the time had come for the Americans to establish their own church.

Equestrian statue of Francis Asbury (1745-1816). *This statue, created by Everette Wyatt, is located adjacent to Asbury Theological Seminary. Photo by Dave Henderson.*

Asbury's personal example and pioneering work earned him the highest esteem among American Methodists. For forty-one years he traveled on horseback an average of 6,000 miles yearly; he crossed the Alleghenies sixty times. The early growth of American Methodism is due, in large part, to his heroic and sacrificial ministries. Asbury averaged at least one sermon a day during his American ministry. He was consecrated bishop at 39 and died in active service in his seventy-first year. When he became bishop in 1784, American Methodism consisted of less than 15,000 members and about 80 preachers. At his death in 1816, he was the senior bishop of a church of more than 211,000 members and more than 700 itinerant preachers, most of whom he personally ordained. More than any other person, Francis Asbury is responsible for shaping American Methodism into America's most dynamic nineteenth-century denomination.

3 *American Methodism Becomes a Church*

The formation of American Methodism as a new church constitutes one of the most dramatic stories in the nation's religious history. Methodism in this country began about 150 years after an Anglican colony settled in Virginia and the first Pilgrims established themselves in Massachusetts. From Methodism's humble beginnings, by the mid-nineteenth century it had grown into the largest and most significant Protestant church in America. Its success stemmed from its biblical fidelity, unique organization, and sacrificial service.

Most early Methodists served God without thought of personal gain or earthly advancement. Many of them passed into eternity without monuments or books to remind us of their labors. Happily, though, Methodism's historians kept bet-ter-than-average records and faithfully chronicled the lives of a number of the church's heroes and heroines. From these accounts we understand how American Methodism developed into such a large and influential church.

The United Methodist Archives and History Center.
Photograph by Darlene Shoop.

This center is located on the campus of Drew University. The center has four levels, about six miles of shelving, a spacious 180,000 cubic foot archival vault, and a vast collection of books, documents, records, photographs, and artifacts pertaining to the history of the United Methodist Church and its antecedent denominations. In its almost two and one-half centuries of existence, American Methodism has published a rich legacy of historical materials. The Archives and History Center at Drew is the official denominational repository for these materials.

The Persecution of Methodists

The early American Methodists faced opposition and even persecution. Often, the clergy of other denominations denounced the Methodist preachers for "preaching delusions," "working to deceive others," "spouting heretical doctrines," and "promoting wild singularities." These "wild singularities" included dramatic preaching, exuberant worship, and weekly class meetings where the members shared their innermost selves. In the seventeenth and eighteenth centuries, most of the states supported established churches, and these entrenched denominations did not welcome new religious groups. In some places it was against the law for non-established religious groups to hold services. For instance, Francis Asbury wrote in his journal, "I was fined near Baltimore five pounds for preaching the gospel."

Because they received the sacraments in Anglican Churches, the early Methodists struggled to overcome the perception that their political loyalties were with England instead of America. Furthermore, in 1776 the Methodists in Virginia opposed the idea of abrogating the privileged position of the Church of England as the established church in that colony. Methodist loyalty to the Anglican Church caused many American patriots to draw the unwarranted conclusion that the Methodists were not in sympathy with American dreams of political independence. Also, it was well known that the Anglican *Book of Common Prayer* contained prayers for England's royal family, a reality that cast additional suspicion upon the Methodists.

Furthermore, some of the Methodist preachers were pacifists. They declined to take up arms against *any* foe. In a time of growing tension between America and England, several of America's colonies required their citizens to take "loyalty oaths." These oaths obligated able-bodied men to take up arms against King George's army. Because some of the Methodists (who were pacifists) refused to bear arms, the civil authorities viewed them as disloyal Americans. This awkward situation sometimes led to the persecution of Methodists.

In 1775 John Wesley published a widely circulated booklet, titled *Calm Address to Our American Colonies*. That work opposed America's independence from Great Britain and urged the

An American Rifleman at the time of the War of Independence.

The Maryland Oath mandated that young men swear to hold no loyalty to the King of England, and required Maryland's male citizens to bear arms against the British army. Other states required similar loyalty oaths. Many of the early Methodist preachers were pacifists and would not sign an oath to bear arms. Consequently, local authorities persecuted them for their alleged sympathies with Great Britain.

colonies to remain loyal to the British crown. Understandably, John Wesley's *Calm Address* worked against the Methodists in America. Furthermore, most of Wesley's missionaries in America sympathized with the government of Great Britain. Thomas Rankin, Wesley's chief assistant in America from 1773 to 1778, openly advised the American Methodists not to side with the colonists in their struggle against England. Jesse Lee, American Methodism's first

Thomas Rankin (1738-1810).

Beginning in 1773, Rankin served in America as John Wesley's General Assistant and Superintendent. He was a strong disciplinarian who brought order and stability to the Methodist societies. However, his rigid personality and strict discipline kept him from winning the hearts of the Americans. As well, Rankin's lack of support for the Colonial cause generated resentment and led to a strained relationship with the Americans he came to serve. He remained in America even after the start of the War of Independence, but he returned to England in 1778. Rankin has the distinction of having presided over the first conference of American Methodist preachers in Philadelphia in 1773.

historian, wrote, "If a person was disposed to persecute a Methodist preacher, it was only necessary to call him a *Torry* [sic], and then they might treat him as cruelly as they pleased."

During the colonial period numerous Methodist preachers suffered beatings, fines, and jailings. Caleb Pedicord, a circuit rider, was whipped so severely that he bore scars for the rest of his life. A mob tarred his colleague Philip Gatch solely because the mob's leader raged over his wife's conversion under Gatch's preaching. Freeborn Garrettson was beaten into insensibility because his pacifism prevented him from joining the Maryland Militia. In 1780, town authorities in Cambridge, Maryland imprisoned Garrettson as a suspected British sympathizer. The jail had a dirty floor and two open windows that allowed a cold east wind to blow through the cell. He remained in jail for a month, without a trial. The jailer released Garrettson only because Francis Asbury appealed to the governor of Delaware to intervene. Later, Thomas Ware reflected on those difficult times: "Being denounced from the pulpit as illiterate, unsound in our principles, and enthusiastic in our spirit and practice...the multitude...were imboldened [sic] to attack us; and it was often a matter of diversion to witness how much they appeared to feel their own superiority." Persecution kept many of the circuit riders from making their rounds. Asbury lamented that during the American Revolution so many Methodist preachers were in jail that he could not supply all the societies with pastors.

Freeborn Garrettson (1752-1827).

Garrettson was a native-born American who learned about Methodism through the ministries of Robert Strawbridge, Joseph Pilmore, and Francis Asbury. Converted to Christ at the age of 23, he immediately became an itinerant Methodist preacher. On entering the itineracy, Garrettson freed his slaves and thereafter consistently opposed every form of human bondage.

During the Revolutionary War Garrettson suffered more persecution than any other American Methodist preacher. Because he objected to the shedding of blood, he refused to take the Maryland Oath that required young men to go to war against the British Colonial Government. He was imprisoned, beaten, frequently stoned, threatened with guns, shot at, and, after one severe beating, left for dead on the road.

In 1784 Francis Asbury selected Garrettson and Harry Hosier to notify Methodism's preachers of the upcoming conference that would form the Methodist Episcopal Church. In the new church Garrettson served under Bishop Francis Asbury as a traveling preacher and presiding elder. Garrettson itinerated extensively, and he helped establish Methodism throughout New York State and the newly settled territory to the west. Next to Francis Asbury, Garrettson was the most important leader in early American Methodism.

Eventually, Garrettson and his wife built a commodious home where they offered hospitality to itinerant Methodist preachers. During his ministry he became known as a wise counselor and pre-eminent peacemaker. He won thousands to Christ, and in 1819 he became one of the founders of Methodism's missionary society.

Dorchester County Jail, Cambridge, Maryland.

Here, Freeborn Garrettson was imprisoned for preaching the Gospel and, allegedly, for being "one of King George's men."

Thomas Ware (1758-1842).

As a young man, Ware was a member of the founding Christmas Conference of the Methodist Episcopal Church, and he kept a record of its decisions. Years later, he summarized his recollections of that conference in the January 1832 *Methodist Magazine and Quarterly Review*. He wrote, "Nearly fifty years have now elapsed since the Christmas Conference, and I have a thousand times looked back to that memorable era with pleasurable emotions; have often said it was the most solemn convocation I ever saw; I might have said sublime, for during the whole time of our being together in the transaction of business of the utmost magnitude, there was not, I verily believe, on the conference floor or in private, an unkind word spoken, or an unbrotherly emotion felt. Christian love predominated, and under its influence we kindly thought and sweetly spake the same."

However, other documents reveal that there were some "sharp words" spoken between Thomas Coke and Thomas Vasey. Moreover, Francis Asbury clashed with William Glendinning (a former Presbyterian) about the proposed episcopal form of government for the new church. Nevertheless, harmony prevailed in the end, and the new church gained unanimous support from those who attended the Christmas Conference.

It was with deep emotion that the despised and persecuted Methodist ministers gathered for their annual conferences and tearfully sang together:

> *And are we yet alive,*
> *And see each other's face?*
> *Glory and praise to Jesus give,*
> *For his redeeming grace.*
>
> *Preserved by power divine*
> *To full salvation here,*
> *Again in Jesus' praise we join,*
> *And in his sight appear.*
>
> *What troubles have we seen,*
> *What conflicts have we passed,*
> *Fightings without, and fears within,*
> *Since we assembled last!*
>
> *But out of all the Lord*
> *Hath brought us by his love;*
> *And still he doth his help afford,*
> *And hides our life above.*
>
> *Then let us make our boast*
> *Of his redeeming power,*
> *Which saves us to the uttermost,*
> *Till we can sin no more.*

In time, the Methodist preachers overcame the accusations that they were disloyal citizens. A number of pacifist Methodists demonstrated their willingness to serve in the military forces as non-combatants. Non-pacifist Methodists took up arms as regular members of George Washington's Continental Army. After the War of Independence, Methodism's circuit riders, now free from political liabilities, resumed their itinerant ministries. Methodist revivals broke out in numerous places, and the church began to grow. Jesse Lee recalled, "As soon as the national peace was settled.... The Lord prospered us much in the thinly settled parts of the country...the work greatly revived, and the heavenly flame of religion spread far and wide."

The Need for Sacraments

John Wesley opposed the notion that the Methodists would ever form an independent denomination. Originally, he planned that the Methodists in America and Great Britain would remain as religious societies within the Church of England. Wesley, therefore, instructed the American Methodists to attend Anglican services and to receive sacraments from ordained priests.

A large percentage of Anglican priests in America, however, were not friendly toward the Methodists. Some Anglican priests labeled the Methodist preachers "illiterate creatures void of all prudence and discretion." The Anglican clergy were quick to accuse the Methodist preachers of encroaching on Anglican parishes. Most significantly, Anglican priests did not welcome the Methodists at their communion altars.

In turn, Methodists considered many of the Anglican priests to be lacking religious passion and spiritual wisdom. Some priests abused alcohol and gave inadequate attention to their pastoral responsibilities. The American Methodists turned away from priests that were worldly in conduct and speech. Serious-minded Methodists regarded them as being as unfit as they were unwilling to provide them with the sacraments. The first Methodist *Discipline* declared, "We are thoroughly convinced, that the Church of England, to which we have been united, is deficient in several of the most important Parts of Christian Discipline; and that (a few Ministers and Members excepted) it has lost the Life and Power of Religion." As a consequence of these circumstances, thousands of Methodist children had not been baptized, and many Methodist families had seldom or never partaken of the Lord's Supper.

Only a few Anglican clergymen, as exceptions to the rule, supported the American Methodists. Three sympathetic priests especially demonstrated their cordiality toward the Methodists— Samuel Magaw, Charles Pettigrew, and Devereux Jarratt, all warm friends of Francis Asbury. These priests gladly administered sacraments to the Methodists and supported their revivals. Jarratt stated in his *Autobiography*, "In order to remedy the complaint of the want of ordinances ...I took long rides through several [Methodist] circuits, to baptize their children [and] administer the sacrament.... All which I did without fee or reward." The American Methodists received much encouragement from the kindness and sacrificial service that Magaw, Pettigrew, and Jarratt extended to them.

Eighteenth Century Anglican Chapel in Virginia.

This 18th century Anglican chapel was similar to the one pastored by Devereux Jarrat (1733-1801), an ordained Anglican priest who especially befriended the Methodists. Jarrat first came into contact with the Methodists through the preaching of Robert Williams whom he described as "a plain, simple-hearted, pious man."

In a time when most of the Anglican clergy in America had little to do with the Methodists, Jarratt attended their revivals, preached at their conferences, encouraged their preachers, and offered them sacraments. Jarratt was particulary supportive of the Methodist revivals. He wrote that through Methodism many profligates had been "effectually and lastingly changed into pious, uniform Christians".

Francis Asbury said of Jarratt, "He was first who received our despised preachers—when strangers and unfriended, he took them to his house, and had societies formed in his parish." Jarratt was disappointed when the American Methodists formed a separate church, but cordial relationships with the Methodists were restored several years prior to his death.

Given the unwillingness of most Anglican priests to serve the Methodists, American Methodism faced a crisis regarding the sacraments. Wesley's rule forbidding the Methodists to administer the sacraments worked well enough in England where Anglican priests were available to baptize and serve Holy Communion to the members of Methodist societies. In America, however, most of the Methodists were not baptized members of the Anglican Church. It was impracticable for the American Methodists to look to Anglican churches for the sacraments.

When the American preachers met for their first conference in 1773, out of respect for John Wesley they agreed to refrain from administering the sacraments. Yet, despite the decision of the 1773 conference, in the succeeding months a growing number of Methodist preachers in the southern states grew increasingly restless. They saw no good reason to abide by the conference decision. These preachers believed that God had called them to a full ministry that included the proclamation of God's word *and* the administration of the sacraments. After six more years of frustration, without consulting with the preachers in the northern states, these impatient southerners met for a conference in Fluvanna County, Virginia. They voted to ordain each other, as well as all other Methodist preachers who wanted to administer the sacraments.

News of the decision of this conference reached Francis Asbury and the northern preachers, causing them consternation. At the time, they still hoped that American Methodism could find a way to comply with John Wesley's instructions to keep Methodism tied to the Anglican Church. Led by Asbury, a committee of northern preachers visited the southern preachers and entreated them to cease administering the ordinances of the church. To avoid a schism, the southern preachers agreed temporarily to refrain from sacramental ministries until they could correspond further with John Wesley about the matter. Still, the lack of access to baptism and Holy Communion persisted as a dilemma for the Methodists. The growing movement needed an ordained clergy.

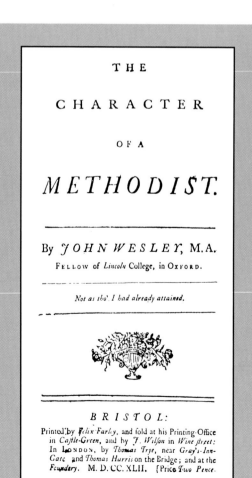

THE

CHARACTER

OF A

METHODIST.

By *JOHN WESLEY*, M.A.

FELLOW of *Lincoln* College, in OXFORD.

Not as tho' I had already attained.

BRISTOL:

Printed by *Felix Farley*, and fold at his Printing-Office in *Castle-Green*, and by *J. Wilson* in *Wine-street*: In LONDON, by *Thomas Trye*, near *Gray's-Inn-Gate* and *Thomas Harris* on the Bridge ; and at the *Foundery*. M.D.CC.XLII. [Price Two Pence.

The Character of a Methodist.

In 1742 John Wesley wrote a widely circulated tract that he named *The Character of a Methodist.* He wrote this piece to show that Methodism is not an off-beat sect. Rather, he showed that Methodism accords with the Bible and the historic church. This tract distinguishes between opinions and fundamental Christian doctrines that are essential to the faith. He contended that we should treat the opinions of others with respect, but opinions are not central to biblical faith, and they should not divide Christians.

In answering the question "Who is the Methodist?" Wesley stated, "A Methodist is one who has 'the love of God shed abroad in his heart by the Holy Ghost given unto him'; one who 'loves the Lord his God with all his strength'... For as he loves God, so 'he keeps his commandments'. Not only some, or most of them, but all, from the least to the greatest... Whatever God has fobidden he avoids; whatever God has enjoined he doth—and that whether it be little or great, hard or easy, joyous or grievous to the flesh... All the commandments of God he accordingly keeps, and that with all his might... All the talents he has received he constantly employs according to his Master's will ; every power and faculty of his soul, every member of his body... Nor do the customs of the world at all hinder his 'running the race which is set before him'... His soul is 'renewed after the image of God', 'in righteousness and in all true holiness'. And 'having the mind that was in Christ' he 'so walks as' Christ 'also walked'".

"Ordination Means Separation"

John Wesley understood the need for the American Methodists to have the sacraments. He appealed to the bishops of the Church of England to consecrate an Anglican bishop for America, but his appeals failed to generate a favorable response. In the meantime, America's war with England ended in October 1781 with the surrender of Lord Cornwallis to General George Washington at Yorktown, Virginia. America was no longer bound to England, and the slender thread linking American Methodism with the Anglican Church had finally broken. In 1784, Francis Asbury wrote John Wesley, "We are in great need of help. A minister [ordained], and such preachers as you can fully recommend, will be very acceptable."

The circumstances demanded an immediate resolution to the problem of the sacraments, and Wesley knew it. So he took the monumental step of ordaining ministers for America. He also consecrated American Methodism's first "superintendent"—or bishop. He was aware that this decision would result in the separation of American Methodism from the Anglican Church, but he saw no other solution. He justified his decision to ordain Methodist ministers for America on the following grounds:

• The American Revolution had separated the United States from England, and the Church of England had no authority in the new nation.

• There were few Anglican priests in America, and most of these were unfriendly toward the Methodists.

• The English bishops had failed to consecrate a bishop for America, thereby signaling no interest in providing for the spiritual needs of the colonies.

• Wesley believed that the episcopacy was an *office*, not an *order*. In principle, as an Anglican presbyter he had the authority to ordain.

• Wesley had a responsibility for overseeing the Methodists, whom the Anglican Church neglected or opposed.

Wesley declared, "By a very uncommon train of providences, many of the provinces of North America are totally disjoined from their mother-country, and erected into independent States. The English Government has no authority over them, either civil or ecclesiastical." He believed that it was more important for him to provide for the growing Methodist movement than to adhere to the requirements of the disinterested Anglican bishops. Wesley selected Thomas Coke as American Methodism's first General Superintendent.

Thomas Coke (1747-1814).
This copy of an original painting by Frank O. Salisbury appears here by permission of the World Methodist Museum, Lake Junaluska, North Carolina. Photograph by Dave Henderson.

Coke was educated at the University of Oxford, and received ordination as a priest in the Church of England. During his early ministry he became a Methodist and joined John Wesley's cadre of preachers. Wesley came to rely on Coke as a valuable assistant, and at Methodist conferences Coke sometimes presided in Wesley's stead.

In 1784 John Wesley consecrated Thomas Coke as the first superintendent of American Methodism. He sent Coke to America with instructions to ordain Francis Asbury and name him as a co-superintendent of the newly formed Methodist Episcopal Church.

Coke was a prolific writer, producing a six-volume commentary on the Bible, a history of the West Indies, as well as sermons and addresses on theological subjects; with Henry Moore he co-authored the authorized biography of John Wesley. Coke's ministry was not confined to England and the United States. He spent his last years as a traveling missionary to other countries. Coke had inherited a fair fortune from his father and gave generously to the work of the gospel. He was on a mission to begin a work in India and Ceylon when he died at sea. Although Thomas Coke's length of service in American Methodism was far less than that of Francis Asbury, Coke's good spirit, generosity, and wisdom enhanced his contributions as the first bishop of American Methodism.

Richard Whatcoat (1736-1806). *This eighteenth-century painting by an unknown artist appears here by permission of the World Methodist Museum, Lake Junaluska, North Carolina. Photograph by Dave Henderson.*

Richard Whatcoat served for fifteen years as an itinerant Methodist preacher in England prior to his coming to America. Unlike Coke and Vasey, Whatcoat stayed in this country for the remainder of his life.

In 1800, the American preachers chose Whatcoat as the third bishop of the church (after Francis Asbury). As a bishop, Whatcoat itinerated over the eastern seaboard and inland as far as Kentucky and Tennessee. He gained a reputation for being one of the most saintly men in early American Methodism. After his death the conference Minutes stated the he was "dead to envy, pride and praise." Asbury said of him: "A man so uniformly good I have not known in Europe or America."

Coke was a graduate of the University of Oxford, a Doctor of Civil Law, and a leader among the British Methodists. Wesley did not ordain Coke, because Coke was already an ordained clergyman in the Church of England. Wesley, however, did consecrate him for his work as a superintendent (although the Americans preferred the term bishop). Wesley also ordained two lay preachers for America—Richard Whatcoat and Thomas Vasey. Wesley instructed Coke to ordain Francis Asbury and appoint him a co-superintendent of American Methodism.

John Wesley's decision to ordain clergy for the American Methodists created an ecclesiastical uproar throughout England. His brother Charles bitterly protested these ordinations. He pointed out (correctly) that "ordination is separation." John Wesley responded to his critics: "Here [in Great Britain] there are bishops who have a legal jurisdiction: in American there are none, neither any parish ministers. So that for some hundred miles together there is none either to baptize or to administer the Lord's Supper. Here, therefore, my scruples are at an end; and I conceive myself at full liberty, as I violate no order, and invade no man's right, by appointing and sending labourers into the harvest."

Thomas Vasey (c. 1746-1826).

Thomas Vasey was orphaned at an early age, and his wealthy uncle made him heir of his estate. However, Vasey's conversion to Christ aroused his uncle's displeasure, and he disinherited Vasey for becoming a Methodist. When Wesley ordained him and sent him to America, Vasey had already itinerated as a Methodist preacher in England for nine years. He was a man of gifted intellect, and his message centered on the person of Jesus Christ.

Contemporaries said that he preached "the freeness and fullness of the salvation of the gospel." After spending a short time in America, he returned to England and continued to preach there until his death in 1826.

Thomas Coke, Richard Whatcoat, and Thomas Vasey sailed for America on September 18, 1784, and docked in New York on November 3. On disembarking, they received a warm welcome. In less than two weeks, Coke and his associates met with Asbury at Barratt's Chapel in Kent County, Delaware. They shared with him the plan to ordain an American Methodist ministry and organize "an Independent Episcopal Church." The men agreed to meet December 24 in Baltimore at Lovely Lane Chapel to organize the new church. At that time, American Methodism had 83 preachers, 64 stations and circuits, and 14,988 members.

Wesley's plan was that the new American church come under his supervision. Francis Asbury, however, contended that it should be an American church. He understood, to a degree much greater than did John Wesley, the democratic spirit of the American people and their passion for self-reliance. This knowledge helped him persuade Thomas Coke that British supervisors who lacked an intimate understanding of American ways could not effectively govern from afar. Asbury knew that if American Methodism was to succeed, it must enjoy the freedom of self-determination. As well, Francis Asbury deserves the credit for insisting that the structure of the new church have the consent of the preachers. Asbury informed Coke that he (Asbury) would serve as a superintendent only if the preachers elected him to serve. The church would not be an extension of an individual or a committee; rather, authority would reside in the conference of preachers. The American Methodist bishops were to preside over the conferences and appoint preachers to their stations, but decisions of policy would be made by the vote of the conference membership. Bishops were not to be free to appoint their successors; the conferences would elect bishops. Asbury's insight and persuasive powers proved determinative for the success of the new church.

Barratt's Chapel.

This Methodist meeting house, one of the first churches built in the state, is located ten miles south of Dover, Delaware. Freeborn Garrettson organized the original Methodist society here in 1778. Phillip Barratt, a member of this society, contributed the land for this chapel, built in 1780. During the building's construction a detractor contended that it was unnecessary for the Methodists to build the chapel "for by the time the war is over, a corn-crib will hold them all." Barratt's Chapel was the site of the first administration of the Lord's Supper by an ordained Methodist preacher.

Barratt's Chapel is a Methodist shrine, because Thomas Coke and Francis Asbury met here soon after Coke's arrival in America with authorization from John Wesley to ordain Asbury and consecrate him a bishop. At Barratt's Chapel, Coke and Asbury conferred with other Methodist preachers to lay plans for American Methodism's organizing Christmas Conference in 1884. Thus, the building is sometimes called the "Cradle of American Methodism." Note that the ground level windows flanking the main entrance have been changed into doorways. Prior to the Civil War, the congregation changed these windows to doors to create separate entrances to the balcony for the black worshippers.

American Methodism Becomes a Church

Coke and Asbury assigned Methodist preachers Freeborn Garrettson and Harry Hosier the mission of notifying the American Methodist preachers of the conference set to begin December 24, 1784. Accordingly, the two departed "like an arrow, from North to South," to spread the news of the forthcoming conference whose purpose was to organize the new church. On horseback, the two men covered about twelve hundred miles in six weeks. Sixty of the eighty-three Methodist preachers received sufficient notice to enable them to attend the conference.

The organizing conference of the Methodist Episcopal Church began at 10:00 AM on December 24, 1784, and it continued until January 2, 1785.

We refer to that gathering as the "Christmas Conference." The preachers met in Baltimore at Lovely Lane Methodist Chapel. The first order of business was the reading of John Wesley's letter appointing Thomas Coke and Francis Asbury joint superintendents over American Methodism. The conference members "cordially approved" the letter and turned their attention to naming the new church. The assembled preachers decided against a Congregational or a Presbyterian polity. American Methodism would have an episcopal government. That is, the bishops would appoint preachers to their places of service. Accordingly, the preachers approved the name suggested by John Dickins—the Methodist Episcopal Church.

Lovely Lane Chapel, Baltimore.

This Methodist meetinghouse was the site of the 1784 Christmas Conference, the organizing conference of the Methodist Episcopal Church. To ready the chapel for the Christmas Conference, the Baltimore Methodists brought in a stove and installed backs for the benches. Lovely Lane Chapel typifies the earliest style of Methodist architecture, which was simple and unadorned. Others of these early Methodist houses of worship were the original John Street Church in New York City (1768) and Barratt's Chapel in Delaware (1780). These plain meetinghouses had no steeples, cupolas, bells, belfries, or paint. Once, seeing a bell perched on a Methodist church, Bishop Francis Asbury wrote, "Here is a bell over the gallery ... may it break! It is the first I ever saw in a house of ours in America; I hope it will be the last." Asbury and first-generation Methodists believed that money spent on church decorations detracted from focused worship and Methodism's ministry to the needy. The Baltimore congregation erected this structure in 1774, and it was demolished in 1786. Due to crowding, the floor collapsed on two occasions. Today, a historic plaque marks the site where the building once stood.

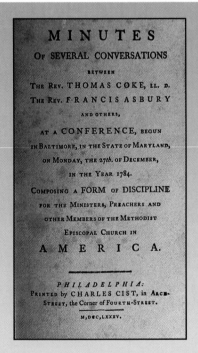

MINUTES OF SEVERAL CONVERSATIONS BETWEEN THE REV. THOMAS COKE, LL. D. THE REV. FRANCIS ASBURY AND OTHERS, AT A CONFERENCE, BEGUN IN BALTIMORE, IN THE STATE OF MARYLAND, ON MONDAY, THE 27th. OF DECEMBER, IN THE YEAR 1784. COMPOSING A FORM OF DISCIPLINE FOR THE MINISTERS, PREACHERS AND OTHER MEMBERS OF THE METHODIST EPISCOPAL CHURCH IN AMERICA.

PHILADELPHIA: PRINTED by CHARLES CIST, in ARCH-STREET, the Corner of FOURTH-STREET. M,DCC,LXXXV.

Discipline of the Methodist Episcopal Church.

In 1785 American Methodism's organizing conference published its first *Discipline*, along with John Wesley's Sunday Service and his "Collection of Psalms and Hymns." The church's *Discipline* serves as a book of polity, church law, doctrine, instruction, and procedure. A revised second *Discipline*, published in 1786, was the last to include Wesley's Sunday Service. The church printed yearly revisions of the *Discipline* until 1792, after which time revisions ordinarily were made each quadrennium. Since 1968, the church has placed liturgical materials in a separate volume, the Book of Worship.

"The Ordination of Francis Asbury, December 27, 1784."
This engraving, by A. Gilchrist Campbell, is patterned after a painting by Thomas Coke Ruckle.

Surrounding the kneeling Francis Asbury, from left to right, are Bishop Thomas Coke, Richard Whatcoat, Thomas Vasey, and William Philip Otterbein. Earlier in 1784 John Wesley had consecrated Coke, an Anglican priest, American Methodism's first "superintendent" (bishop). At that time Wesley also ordained Whatcoat and Vasey for ministry in America. Otterbein, a fraternal guest at the Christmas Conference, was to become one of the principal founders of the Church of the United Brethren.

On Christmas day Thomas Coke, assisted by Richard Whatcoat and Thomas Vasey, ordained Francis Asbury a deacon. On the two succeeding days Asbury was ordained an elder, then consecrated a superintendent. Philip William Otterbein, a close friend of Asbury (and later the founder of the Church of the United Brethren), assisted in Asbury's consecration. The conference also ordained more than a dozen men for the Methodist ministry.

The newly formed church adopted Twenty-Five Articles of Religion as its doctrinal standards. Earlier, John Wesley had abridged them from the Church of England's XXXIX Articles of Religion. The Methodist Episcopal Church also established additional doctrinal standards—John Wesley's *Standard Sermons* and his *Notes Upon the New Testament*. Methodism's first historian, Jesse Lee (1758-1816) observed, "The Methodists were pretty generally pleased at our becoming a church, and heartily united together in the plan which the conference had adopted. And from that time religion greatly revived." William Watters captured the general sentiment: "We became, instead of a religious society, a separate church. This gave great satisfaction through all our societies."

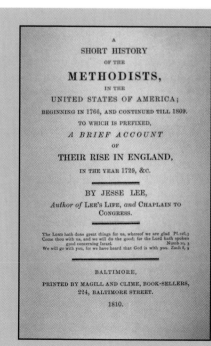

American Methodism's first history.

Jesse Lee (1758-1816) was American Methodism's first historian. His *Short History of the Methodists* (1810) chronicled the events in which Lee himself was sometimes a participant. Ironically, at the time when Lee wrote American Methodism's first history, the Methodist Conference did not support its publication. Lee's contemporaries averred that the facts recorded in his work were so well known that their publication was not necessary. Undaunted, however, Lee gathered a list of private subscribers to underwrite the book's publication. He wrote in the Preface, "I desire to shew to all our societies and friends, that the doctrines which we held and preached in the beginning, we have continued to support and maintain uniformly to the present day." Lee was at times critical of Francis Asbury, and Asbury opposed the publication of Lee's book. In ways not foreseen by Lee's contemporaries, his *Short History of the Methodists* has proven an invaluable source of information that otherwise would have been lost.

Lee was one of Francis Asbury's first traveling companions, and he sometimes held conferences for the bishop when Asbury was ill. The United States House of Representatives elected Lee its chaplain five times. In 1814 he became chaplain of the Senate. Perhaps Lee's crowning achievement was his planting of Methodism in New England. He is called Methodism's apostle to that region.

Francis Asbury as Bishop

Francis Asbury had come to America as a Methodist missionary just two weeks after his twenty-sixth birthday. On the voyage he wrote in his newly begun journal, "Whither am I going? To the New World. What to do? To gain honour? No, if I know my own heart. To get money? No. I am going to live to God, and to bring others so to do." Asbury arrived in Philadelphia in 1771 and quickly adopted America as his new home. He sympathized with America's resistance to British control and the colonists' displeasure over "taxation without representation." Asbury believed in Methodism's message and method as the best means for all Americans to "live to God, and to bring others so to do." He wrote in his journal, "The doctrines [the Methodists] preach, and the discipline they enforce, are, I believe, the purest of any people now in the world."

The young missionary took advantage of every opportunity to advance American Methodism, whether the circumstances were pleasant or disagreeable—and there were more of the latter than the former. He wrote, "I am willing to suffer, yea, to die, sooner than betray so good a cause by any means. It will be a hard matter to stand against all opposition...but through Christ strengthening me I can do all things."

On his arrival in America, one of Asbury's most important actions was to establish itinerant preaching. Richard Boardman and Joseph Pilmore, who had arrived in America two years earlier, were inclined to adopt a settled ministry in cities. Asbury was convinced that an itinerant ministry was crucial if Methodism was to reach the people on the advancing American frontier. Although Asbury was younger than Pilmore and Boardman, he exerted leadership by word and example. He recorded in his journal, "My brethren seem unwilling to leave the cities, but I think I shall show them the way." He began a ceaseless itinerant ministry that would characterize American Methodism for decades.

Asbury also took the lead in "raising up" American-born preachers. At the time of the War of Independence, the other British Methodist missionaries returned to Great Britain. It became imperative to replace them with American preachers. Asbury possessed an uncommon aptitude for judging character and

Bishop Francis Asbury on the circuit.

This painting by Kenneth Wyatt is located at Asbury Theological Seminary.
Photograph by seminary staff.

ability. Indeed, he gained great respect for his ability to "read men." When he found suitable candidates, he enlisted them as Methodist preachers. Throughout his long tenure as bishop, Asbury encouraged the preachers to read, improve their pastoral skills, and elevate the level of their preaching. He personally mentored a number of the young preachers, some of whom were barely old enough to need to shave. Many of those he recruited were people of ordinary ability, but possessed of extraordinary spiritual commitment, zeal, and determination. He recorded in his journal, "The Lord hath done great things for these people, notwithstanding the weakness of the instruments, and some little irregularities."

At the end of the War of Independence, John Wesley wrote a letter to the American preachers urging them, "Let all of you be determined to abide by the Methodist doctrine and discipline published in the four volumes of [John Wesley's] *Sermons* and the *Notes upon the New Testament*." Later, in 1798, Bishops Coke and Asbury published a special edition of the *Discipline* with "explanatory notes." In that work the bishops declared to the church, "Far from wishing you to be ignorant of any of our doctrines, or any part of our discipline, we desire you to read, mark, learn, and inwardly digest the whole." These bishops were not interested in splitting theological hairs or delving into philosophical speculations. Rather, they urged the preachers to keep to the grand doctrines of the church—repentance, faith, and holiness. Far from being sectarian, Methodism adopted a theology that articulated the important central doctrines of Christianity. In matters of "opinion only" (those things not pertaining to the essentials of the Christian faith), the Methodists were free to "think and let think." In matters of basic Christian teaching, however, they remained immovable. The bishops were convinced that only Christianity's biblical message would enable Methodism "to reform the continent and spread scriptural holiness over these lands."

The bishops based their belief on the admonition that John Wesley had written in *Thoughts Upon Methodism*. In that piece Wesley declared, "I am not afraid that the people called Methodists should ever cease to exist either in Europe or America. But I am afraid, lest they should only exist as a dead sect, having the form of religion without the power. And this undoubtedly will be the case, unless they hold fast both the doctrine, spirit, and discipline with which they first set out." Wesley proceeded to clarify the beliefs of the people called Methodists. He wrote:

What was their fundamental doctrine? That the Bible is the whole and sole rule both of Christian faith and practice. Hence they learned, (1) That religion is an inward principle; that it is no other than the mind that was in Christ; or, in other words, the renewal of the soul after the image of God, in righteousness and true holiness. (2) That this can never be wrought in us, but by the power of the Holy Ghost. (3) That we

receive this, and every other blessing, merely for the sake of Christ: And, (4) That whosoever hath the mind that was in Christ, the same is our brother, and sister, and mother.

Bishops Coke and Asbury were determined to retain both the "form of godliness and the power thereof."

As a bishop, Asbury provided administrative cohesion and direction for American Methodism. Three factors characterized his episcopal leadership: he maintained a fixed course based on scripture; he worked toward gaining consensus among the preachers; he personally modeled an inspiring example of sacrificial service. Under his leadership, Methodism established itself in almost all the settled areas east of the Allegheny Mountains. Before he died, the westward march of Asbury's itinerant preachers had reached as far as Missouri and Arkansas.

Francis Asbury had not come to America to seek fame; such a notion was far from his mind. Yet he became one of the best known people in America. A letter from England addressed simply to "The Revd. Bishop Asbury, North America" was delivered to this notable man. On October 15, 1924, Augustus Lukeman's equestrian statue of Francis Asbury was unveiled in our nation's capital. President Calvin Coolidge gave the dedication address (printed in the October 16, 1924, New York Times), in which Coolidge declared:

A great lesson has been taught us by this holy life. It was because of what Bishop Asbury and his associates preached...that our country has developed so much freedom and contributed so much to the civilization of the world.... How many temples of worship dot our landscape! How many institutions of learning, some of them rejoicing in the name of Wesleyan, all trace the inspiration of their existence to the sacrifice and service of this lone circuit rider! He is entitled to rank as one of the builders of our nation.

Throughout his forty-five years of American ministry, Asbury maintained close ties with the preachers and lay people throughout the connection. He understood and loved the American people, and his apostolic vision remained strong throughout his ministry in his adopted country. He rode 270,000 miles on horseback, preached

16,000 sermons, ordained 4,000 ministers, and presided over 224 Annual Conference sessions. The highest yearly salary he ever received was eighty dollars.

In Francis Asbury's address to the 1816 General Conference he said, "Only recollect as far as your observation will go, what God hath done by [Methodism] in...less than 50 years in America, and what wonderful things he may do for us and our successors in future years if we stand fast in the Gospel doctrine and pure Apostolic ordination, discipline and government into which we have been called and now stand." This conference was Asbury's last; he died later in the year.

From the beginnings of American Methodism in the 1760s to the death of Francis Asbury in 1816, the church saw astonishing growth. In less than a third of a century American Methodism moved beyond the status of a society attached to the Church of England and dependent on John Wesley. It became a self-directed American church with a form of government that enabled the preachers to make consensual decisions. In the several decades following Bishop Asbury's death, American Methodism grew into the largest and most influential denomination in America.

Francis Asbury. *This equestrian statue, sculpted by Augustus Lukeman, is located at Drew Theological Seminary in Madison, New Jersey. Photograph by Darlene Shoop.*

When Asbury arrived in America, he discovered that the Methodists were becoming lax in their discipline. He determined "to lay the ax at the root of the tree of irregularity." By that statement he meant that he was determined to establish discipline in the Methodist societies according to the Wesleyan rules. His fair and firm episcopal leadership molded the Methodists into a veritable army of righteousness that broke down strongholds of evil and significantly influenced American society.

4 From Small Beginnings to National Prominence

In 1776, the year of the signing of the Declaration of Independence, American Methodism ranked as one of the smallest religious groups in the nation. At that time, less than one out every 800 Americans was a Methodist. Methodism had no ordained clergy, and the movement was little known. No one referred to Methodist places of worship as churches; people called them meetinghouses, preaching stations, or chapels. In 1783 Ezra Stiles, Congregational minister and president of Yale College, forecast that there would be little room in America's future for the "westleians [Wesleyans] and Baptists."

President Stiles was clearly mistaken. Within a few decades of its beginnings, American Methodism's membership grew to be larger than the combined memberships of the Congregational, Episcopal, and Presbyterian Churches. By 1812 one out of every 36 U.S. citizens was a Methodist. The astonishing growth continued. By 1850, the Methodists claimed one-third of the entire church membership in America. The drama of early Methodism's advance from small beginnings to national prominence constitutes one of the most remarkable developments in American religious history. It is a grand legacy that continues to inspire and instruct.

The growth of the new church cannot be attributed to the decisions of a conference or to the sociological trends of the times. Rather, it was due to the labors of courageous and dedicated souls whose primary aim was to take the gospel to those whose lives had not yet come under the influence of God's saving love.

The Circuit System

Early in his ministry, Bishop Francis Asbury observed a steady stream of people rafting down the Ohio River and trekking across mountains to settle in Kentucky, Tennessee, Ohio, and Indiana. He expressed the burden of his heart when he wrote in his journal, "We must send preachers after these people." Methodism's itinerant preachers and system of circuits constituted an ideal means of "winning the west." Until 1819 Methodism did not have a designated missionary society, because the entire Methodist movement considered itself to *be* a missionary society. Leading the church's front-line attack against the devil and his works was an ever-expanding system of circuits supplied by traveling preachers, called circuit riders. These dedicated men played a decisive role in turning untold numbers of people from sin to righteousness.

When Francis Asbury arrived in America in 1771, he began his ministry by itinerating, and through his decades of service, he never abandoned that ministry. When he assigned preachers to their fields of service, he instructed them to establish chains of preaching places, called circuits. When the circuit riders arrived in an area, they frequently found that lay people had already planted Methodism prior to their arrival.

From 1773 to 1790 America's population grew by seventy-five percent. And during that same period the circuit system increased American Methodism more than 5,500 percent. In 1798 Bishops Coke and Asbury reminded the church, "*Our grand plan*, in all its parts, leads to an *itinerant ministry…* There is nothing *like this* for keeping the whole body alive from the centre to the circumference, and for the continual extension of that circumference on every hand." The circuit system guaranteed that every Methodist society would have preaching and pastoral leadership. As late as 1830 more than nine of ten Americans lived in communities smaller than 2,500. Often, the only religious services available to these people were those led by circuit-riding preachers.

The circuit riders were familiar with John Wesley's statement, "It is your business to bring as many sinners as you possibly can to Repentance, and…to build them up in the Holiness, without which they cannot see the Lord." American Methodism's first *Discipline* stated, "Our call is to save that which is lost. Now we cannot expect them to seek us. Therefore we should go and seek *them*… The greatest Hindrance to this you are to expect from rich, or cowardly, or lazy *Methodists*." The circuit system enabled the preachers to stay close to the people. The thousands of personal contacts helped bond the people to the Methodist societies.

The circuit system kept congregations from forming closed or ingrown congregations, as was the case with some denominations. The itinerant ministry linked each society to a circuit, each circuit to a district, each district to a conference, and each conference to the denomination. The circuit system also had the advantage of enabling the bishops to send preachers where they would have the best effect. Earlier, John Wesley had written, "This preacher has one talent, that another. No one whom I ever yet knew has all the talents which are needful for beginning, continuing, and perfecting the work of grace in a whole congregation." Bishop Asbury recorded in a private notebook his assessments of the preachers' abilities, and he used these observations in appointing the preachers. He sent the more refined preachers to town pulpits and the less refined preachers to rural and frontier areas. Preachers, of course, were expected to go where they were "sent." With but few exceptions, the preachers consented to the bishops' assignments.

The Circuit Riders

The early circuit riders were often responsible for large territories. Their circuits sometimes encompassed circumferences of from 200 to 500 miles, and some circuits were even larger. Elijah Woolsey's Methodist circuit near Albany, New York, required almost eight hundred miles of travel, taking between eight and nine weeks to cover. The preachers carried in saddlebags the necessary supplies of clothing, food, books, and paper. In 1798 Francis Asbury assigned John Kobler to cover "the North-Western Territory to form a new circuit and to plant the first principles of the Gospel." As late as 1835, a single Methodist district included Northern Illinois and Northern Iowa. When the preachers received their assignments at Annual Conference, they went forth into fields of service where there were inadequate chapels, few cities, and no parsonages. The circuit riders traveled continuously, preached morning and evening, and rested only a few days a month. These dedicated preachers needed fine horses, for which the *Discipline* required good care.

To start a new circuit, a frontier preacher would follow a trail until he came to a cabin. He would announce that he was a Methodist preacher sent by the bishop to begin Methodist work in the area. Often, the surprised homesteader would invite the preacher to a meal and overnight lodging. While at that house the circuit rider would teach, preach, and exhort. Then, if the householder agreed, the preacher would make arrangements to add the location to his circuit as

Circuit Rider's Saddlebags.

These saddlebags are located in the World Methodist Council Museum, Lake Junaluska, North Carolina. *Photograph by Dave Henderson.*

Gathering a crowd.

Methodist preachers entered into new areas to establish Methodist societies. Here, the preacher has mounted a makeshift platform where he is preaching. Bishop Asbury reported that preaching took place in homes, tobacco houses, paper-mills, poor houses, forts, and woodland clearings. Other places for preaching were log cabins, houses, barns, Masonic halls, warehouses, theaters, and riverboats. Taverns were on the frontier, and sometimes the circuit riders preached in tavern barrooms. On one occasion, a listener heard a Methodist circuit rider preach in a gambling house. The listener said that in the time of Jesus some made the house of God a den of thieves, but that now the locals had made a den of thieves into a house of God.

a new preaching station. Prior to the preacher's next visit, it was not uncommon for the hosts to have invited their neighbors to the service.

A Methodist itinerant preacher in Iowa wrote, "I preached where Quasqueton now is when there were but four families in the vicinity and no others within sixteen miles.... I always followed up the frontier to the last house." People in the remote districts had no theaters, little entertainment, and few amusements. Frontier folk looked forward to the next arrival of the circuit rider because he provided them news, excitement, and powerful sermons. Irreligious people also came to hear the preacher, if only out of curiosity.

Many of the circuit preachers became impressive orators, and some developed unique styles. James Axley, for example, employed ventriloquism in his sermons. He used his second voice to state the views of the devil, and he answered the devil with quotations from the Bible. The eccentric Lorenzo Dow sometimes began his sermon by thundering that he would announce the latest news from hell. Occasionally, a circuit preacher would point his finger at a sinner in the congregation and announce, "Thou art the man!" Sometimes the targeted person would fall to his knees and cry out to God for salvation from his sins.

In 1800 the average yearly salary of Congregational ministers was $400, while the Methodists preachers' average salary was $80. Often, the Methodist preachers did not receive the remuneration promised them. Some preachers had no coats, so on their long winter rides they covered themselves with blankets. In 1790 Bishop Asbury rode into Tennessee where he observed, "I found the poor preachers indifferently clad, with emaciated bodies, and subject to hard fare;

On one occasion Bishop Francis Asbury attended a camp meeting at Rushville, Ohio. On Saturday about 20 drunken rowdies invaded the camp, vowing that they would break up the meeting. One of the preachers asked the gang's leader to remove his followers from the camp. The gang leader became enraged and struck a violent blow to the preacher's face, knocking him down. Brother Birkhammer, an exceedingly stout man, seized the bully and crushed him down between two benches with one thrust of his arm. The gang's second-in-command rushed to aid his companion, and Mr. Birkhammer knocked him down as well. Birkhammer held down the two men until the sheriff arrived and took them to a judge, who gave them a heavy fine. One old brother stood safely on the sidelines, and when the fray had ended he declared, "We will have peace in God's house, if I have to fight for it!"

When peace was restored, Bishop Asbury went to the pulpit and stated that he had advice for any rowdies remaining in the camp: "You must remember that all our brothers in the church are not sanctified, and I advise you to let them alone; for if you get them angry, and the devil should get into them, they are the strongest and hardest men to fight and conquer in the world. I advise you, if you do not like them, to go home and let them alone." The camp meeting continued until Tuesday morning, and over one hundred were converted to God and joined the church.

yet I hope they are rich in faith." In one of the conferences, a number of preachers reported that they had not received their (meager) salaries. Bishop Asbury led the conference in prayer:

Lord, we are in thy hands and in thy work. Thou knowest what is best for us and for thy work, whether plenty or poverty. The hearts of all men are in thy hands. If it is best for us and for thy church that we should be cramped and straitened, let the people's hand and hearts be closed. If it is better for us; for the church, and more to thy glory that we should abound in the comforts of life; do thou dispose the hearts of those we serve to give accordingly. And may we learn to be content whether we abound, or suffer need.

The work of the circuit riders required fortitude and innovation. When Jesse Lee arrived in Norwalk, Connecticut, he began his ministry on the street, assembling his first congregation by singing a hymn. John King preached his first sermon in Baltimore from a blacksmith's block. In many cases, organized societies (congregations) grew out of meetings held in homes, taverns, barnyards, jails, schools, courthouses, on front porches, and beside rivers. In 1784 the Methodists had only sixty Methodist chapels, but more than eight hundred preaching places. Conference minutes listed some of the preaching places not by the name of a church, but by the home that accommodated Methodist services.

Sometimes the circuit riders faced malicious people who spitefully interrupted the services. The preachers learned to meet mischief-makers head on. James Harvey Wilbur, affectionately known as "Father Wilbur," was preaching at a camp meeting when two disturbers ignored his warnings to desist from their trouble making. During a hymn Wilbur marched down the aisle while singing in resonant tones. He reached the rascals, whose conversation prevented them from seeing his approach. While continuing to sing, he knocked their heads together with shocking force. Wilbur marched back to the pulpit without missing a note, and the rogues caused no more trouble.

Because the American frontier lacked law and order, the circuit riders often had no one but themselves to rely on for protection. It was not uncommon for cutthroats, hoodlums, drunkards, and thieves to attack the preachers on the trail. Peter Cartwright, a frontier preacher, tells in his *Autobiography* about a hoodlum who planned to push Cartwright's carriage into a creek:

There was but one way to pass to my carriage. At night I lay watching, with a good stick in my hand; and presently I saw William take hold of my carriage, and begin to turn it, in order to run it down the bank into the creek. I slipped out, and rushed upon him.... I was in the only pathway; and he, fearing a good knock-down, leaped over the bank right into the deep hole of water, and came out on the other side, and ran off. Cartwright tells that William came to the worship service on Sunday night with a string of frogs, strung on a piece of hickory bark, intending to slip them around Cartwright's head while he prayed. Cartwright concluded the story: "While he was seeking an opportunity to do this, the mighty power of God fell on him.... Many of the very worst rowdies that attended this meeting were struck down and converted to God; and thus ended the Frog Campaign. About seventy joined the Church."

Whether on the trail, in a small service, or at a camp meeting, the circuit riders needed to deal with troublemakers. Stephen George Roszel preached at a camp meeting where a group of "rowdies" regularly tried to break up the meetings. Roszel took the leader into the woods and bested him at fisticuffs. He then fixed the culprit's neck between two rails of a fence and left him trapped all night. The next day, the miscreant's

Peter Cartwright (1785-1872).

In 1801 in a camp meeting Peter Cartwright was converted from an irreligious life, and he immediately joined the Methodist Episcopal Church. He quickly became a preacher and came under the influence of William McKendree and Francis Asbury. Cartwright preached in Kentucky, Tennessee, Ohio, Indiana, and Illinois. He became widely known for his quick wit, sense of humor, and his readiness to use his tongue to preach for Christ or his fists to challenge the rowdies who sought to interrupt his meetings. He served twenty years as a circuit rider and fifty years as a presiding elder. Some called him the "Paul Bunyan of Methodist evangelism." Cartwright was active in planning the extension of Methodism beyond the Mississippi River. Although not well educated, he championed the founding of Methodist colleges.

In his Autobiography, Peter Cartwright wrote, "A Methodist preacher ... when he felt that God had called him to preach, instead of hunting up a college or Biblical institute, hunted up a hardy pony of a horse, and some traveling apparatus, and with his library always at hand, namely, Bible, Hymn Book, and Discipline, he started, and with a text that never wore out nor grew stale, he cried, 'Behold the Lamb of God, that taketh away the sin of the world.' In this way he went through storm of wind, hail, snow, and rain; climbed hills and mountains, traversed valleys, plunged through swamps, swam swollen streams, lay out all night, wet, weary, and hungry, held his horse by the bridle all night, or tied him to a limb, slept with his saddle blanket for a bed, his saddle or saddle-bags for his pillow, and his old big coat or blanket, if he had any, for a covering. Often he slept in dirty cabins, on earthen floors, before the fire; ate roasting ears for bread, drank butter-milk for coffee, or sage tea for imperial (tea and cream); too, with a hearty zest, deer or bear meat, or wild turkey, for breakfast, dinner, and supper, if he could get it. His text was always ready, 'Behold the Lamb of God.'"

Methodist camp meeting in the backwoods, c. 1849.

and loneliness. Their work required courage and physical fortitude because of the challenges presented by swamps, swollen rivers, hostile Indians, outlaws, and incessant insects. They encountered skunks and bears, and sometimes wolves followed them menacingly. Methodist circuit riders often spent nights sleeping under the stars, uncertain when or if they would find shelter. George Shadford once became lost in the woods when the weather was very cold and the snow was a foot deep. He knew that he could freeze if he remained all night in the woods. He knelt to pray for God's direction. Arising from prayer, Shadford heard the faint bark of a distant dog. The nearly frozen man followed the sound and came to a plantation, where he was saved from probable death. Some circuit riders, indeed, did die from the hardships on the trail. Of the 737 Methodist preachers who died before the middle of the nineteenth century, over 200 had not yet reached their thirty-fifth birthday.

partners in mischief released him, and the group never again disrupted the camp meeting. Looking back on the intrepid circuit riders, one-time president of the American Historical Society, Franklin Jameson, described them as "keen, hearty men, whose outdoor life kept them healthy in mind and body, and whose grasp on the real world had never been relaxed by education.... They appeared to be surrounded by a kind of holy 'knock'em down' power that was often irresistible."

These soldiers of the cross faced difficult circumstances, enduring hunger, dampness, cold,

In Ohio, James Finley's circuit consisted of thirty-two preaching stops, and the circuit took

Stephen George Roszel (1770-1841).

Roszel was an eminent member of the Baltimore Conference, serving for more than fifty years as a leading preacher in Virginia and Maryland. He was an able presiding elder, effective debater at conference, and a renowned preacher of power and excellence. One of his contemporaries said of him, "He had a ready command of thought and language, and as a debater had very few superiors... He possessed the most indomitable perseverance; whatever object he might have in view he pursued it with untiring zeal, and subordinated every agency within his reach to its accomplishment. His commanding qualities as a debater gave him great influence on the floor of the General Conference, and there were few men of his day who had an eye and a hand more constantly or more effectively on the great interests of the Church than he."

After his death, the 1841 Minutes of his conference commemorated him as "a man possessing singular courage, fortitude, constancy, and benevolence. As a preacher he was bold and uncompromising in declaring the whole counsel of God. Blessed with a strong mind, a ready elocution, and great physical powers, he was well qualified to do the work of a Methodist traveling preacher."

The Circuit Rider.
This drawing done by A. R. Waud appeared in black and white in several publications during the nineteenth century.

In 1810 Jesse Lee, Methodism's first historian, wrote, "The Revolutionary War being now closed, and a general peace established, we could go into all parts of the country without fear; and we soon began to enlarge our borders, and to preach in many places where we had not been before." Methodist preachers accompanied, or quickly followed, almost every wagon train of pioneers that headed into America's unsettled wilderness. Arguably, the Methodist preachers were the most well-known people on America's frontier. In Methodism's early period, Bishop Asbury appointed some preachers to circuits larger than states. "Allowances" (salaries) were meager, and often not paid. As they made their preaching rounds, circuit riders slept in the open air or in the cabins and barns of the people. These preachers forded rivers, snaked through swamps, risked attack by Indians, endured insects, suffered snakebites, often went hungry, and suffered sickness in solitude. These intrepid men gained respect throughout America. During stormy weather, people joked, "There is nothing out today but crows and Methodist preachers."

President Theodore Roosevelt, in a celebrated speech, paid the following tribute to Methodism's traveling preachers: "The whole country is under a debt of gratitude to the Methodist circuit riders, the Methodist pioneer preachers, whose movement westward kept pace with the movement of the frontier... ministering to (the) frontiersman's spiritual needs, and seeing that his pressing material cares, and the hard and grinding poverty of his life did not wholly extinguish the divine fire within his soul."

quarters at a miserable little hut. It was our only chance. It was getting dark; no other house for several miles, and the Bishop was sick and in great pain.... We carried him into the house, and laid him half dead upon a miserable bed, in a dirty room, which served as a parlor, bed-room, dining-room, and kitchen." Many circuit riders preferred to sleep in the forest or on the open grassland to avoid the crowded and grubby cabins of struggling settlers. One wrote, "I had a far better time of it than in many of the small smothering cabins along the road, where bugs and fleas are your night long associates."

Some sections of the country were too rugged for horses. In these places the preachers used canoes to follow the streams and rivers. One preacher in the Northwest Territory wrote:

This was the most uncertain, precarious, laborious itineracy a Methodist preacher ever attempted. Now dashing down foaming and eddying cascades, where the wrong scant of an Indian's paddle-blade by a single inch would shoot the canoe like a catapult against some beetling crag or submerged rock; now wading up the ice-cold stream and wearily tugging at the cordel-rope for hours to make a single mile, or now pulling at the paddle hour after hour to cross miles of river or bay against winds and tides was the most real and least ideal of any itineracy ever attempted. Nightfalls found no house or home; only a camp under a fir tree, or under the lea of some great basaltic cliff. No gathered congregation, large or small, would welcome the weary itinerant... only the still, awful quietude of mighty forests, or the more awful solitude of the mighty plain.

Most of the circuit preachers labored without the support of a wife or family. The preachers and laity alike regarded marriage to be a hindrance to the itinerant ministry. Many regarded the marriage vow "forsaking all others" as a commitment that weakened a preacher's ability to give himself fully to his work. The conference, however, did not forbid marriage. Practical considerations, though, made it difficult for preachers to marry and continue an itinerant ministry. Travel was always difficult and sometimes dangerous. The circumstances rendered it unwise, even perilous, for wives to brave the wilderness. Also, the people on the circuits did not want the "burden" of hosting a preacher's wife. Many lay people objected to

weeks to cover. He ministered to the spiritual needs of more than a thousand Methodists, preaching to them and meeting with them privately and in classes. Finley never hesitated to confront those who disturbed his meetings, shaking them or pitching them out the door. At the same time, his contemporaries reported that "his discourses [were] full of pathos and his friendships the most tender and lasting."

Robert Paine told of beginning a journey across the Alleghenies with Bishop McKendree: "Just at nightfall, near the foot of [a mountain] we found

James B. Finley (1781-1856).

Finley was known as "the war horse" because of his great physical strength and his "terror to the ill-behaved." In 1809 he began serving as a Methodist circuit rider and for a time served as a missionary to the Wyandott Indians. Finley wrote accounts of his ministry that give us insight into early nineteenth-century Methodism. A typical account tells of his preaching in Detroit: "This night will be remembered in eternity. Such were the cries for mercy, that my voice was drowned. More than forty came forward to be prayed for, and several experienced the pardon of their sins, while many others resolved never to rest till they found redemption in the blood of the Lamb. This city seemed now to be visited with a cloud of mercy, and it appeared the next day as if all business was suspended. I went from house to house, and exhorted all to turn to Christ. I went into the bar racks, among the officers and soldiers, and preached to them Jesus and the resurrection. I prayed in every house which I visited, and there was an awful shaking among the dry bones. About sixty joined the Church, as the fruit of these meetings; and, if I could have staid (sic), I have no doubt that many more would have joined; but it was imperiously necessary for me to return home."

providing a financial allowance for spouses. Those holding this view contended that it was "unreasonable that they should raise money for a woman they never saw." Thus, most circuit riders remained single. In 1809 the Virginia Conference had 84 preachers, of which three were married. The first five Methodist bishops were bachelors.

Although few of these itinerant preachers had much formal education, most read continuously, even on horseback. An educated clergyman once asked Francis Asbury how he could take ordinary folk, lacking college or seminary, and turn them into effective preachers. The questioner acknowledged that the uneducated circuit riders "in a few years...become able ministers of the New Testament, equal, if not superior, to our men trained in collegiate and theological halls." Asbury answered, "We tell one another all we know, and then use it at once. A penny used is better than an idle dollar. You study books, we study men, the Bible, the hymn book, and Mr. Wesley's sermons, and are instant in season and out of season."

An early Methodist historian declared that these hardy itinerants "without any patronage derived from social position, with an entire abnegation of self and worldly prospects, with the certainty of meeting contempt and persecution at every step, with hardly 'scrip or purse' for immediate necessities, cast themselves on the care and favor of God, and with only their native genius, and guided by the Spirit Divine, began a work, the greatness of which the world has not fully conceived, and the glorious end of which the world shall never see."

Jason Lee (1803-1845).

In 1834 Lee crossed the "Stony Mountains" (Rocky Mountains) in a daring mission to take Methodism into America's Northwest Territory. That year, he delivered the first Protestant sermon ever preached west of the Rocky Mountains. His text was "Whether therefore ye eat or drink, or whatsoever ye do, do all to the glory of God." This occasion marked the beginnings of Protestantism in that vast territory.

Lee was instrumental in the United States' taking possession of the disputed territory south of the forty-ninth parallel called the "Oregon Territory." As well, he helped found the Oregon Institute, now Willamette University—the oldest college on America's Pacific Slope. His published letters on the value and desirability of the territory inspired settlers from many states to move to the Northwest. Jason Lee's role in the religious and political development of America's great Northwest was determinative for its development.

The stated goals of the early Methodist preachers were the conversion of the lost and the formation of holiness in every believer. To this end, the preachers prayed long hours. The early Methodist Disciplines counseled the circuit riders to spend two 1-hour periods a day praying, meditating, and reading—at 4:00 AM and 6:00 PM. As well, the *Discipline* advised spending the entire morning in study. Asbury scheduled a significant amount of time for prayer at the preachers' conferences.

Frequently, the circuit riders fasted and prayed for God's wisdom and enabling for their ministries. It has been remarked that the circuit riders left both horseshoe prints and the marks of human knees across the American frontier. With Bibles in hand they called sinners to repentance and believers to holiness of heart and life. These preachers proclaimed both the reality of judgment and the optimism of grace. They thundered the message that God can reconstruct the least and the lowest into new creations that are utterly transformed by the power of God's love. An often-repeated couplet described the Methodist message:

> *Free salvation for all men;*
> *Full salvation from all sin.*

In 1805 Francis Asbury, the ceaseless itinerant, wrote that he was "happy to find [that] one spirit animates the whole, for 1700 miles, the same Hymns, prayers & language, salutes my Ears & heart."

Francis Asbury at prayer.

This original painting by Dorothy McKain is located at Asbury Theological Seminary in Kentucky. In this scene, Asbury is praying in the snow. In the background his traveling companion, Harry Hosier, is preparing the evening meal. Photograph by Dave Henderson.

Francis Asbury and Thomas Coke, American Methodism's first two bishops, fulfilled their ministries in different ways. Almost as soon as the Christmas Conference concluded, Coke departed to take Methodism to the West Indies. And for the rest of his life he journeyed often and for long periods to distant mission fields. By contrast, Asbury remained in America for the rest of his long ministry. All America was his circuit. His life of homeless itineracy brought him grinding toil, extreme poverty, harsh privations, and unending hardships. As a bishop, Asbury sent no preacher into any territory, however remote or difficult, that he did not himself visit.

The following extract from Asbury's Journal contains no self-pity, but in plain words describes the context in which he often ministered. "I too have my sufferings, perhaps peculiar to myself—no room to retire to; that in which you sit common to all, crowded with women and children, the fire occupied by cooking, much and long-loved solitude not to be found, unless you choose to run out into the rain, in the woods. Six months in the year I have had, for thirty-two years, occasionally, to submit to what will never be agreeable to me; but the people, it must be confessed, are the kindest souls in the world. But kindness will not make a crowded log cabin, twelve feet by ten, agreeable; without are cold and rain, and within six adults, and as many children, one of which is all motion; the dogs, too, must sometimes be admitted. On Saturday I found that among my other trials I had taken an uncomfortable skin disease; and, considering the filthy houses and filthy beds I have met with ... it is perhaps strange that I have not caught it twenty times. I do not see that there is any securing against it, but my sleeping in a brimstone shirt."

Henry Boehm, Asbury's traveling companion in his final years, said of the sainted bishop, "Bishop Asbury possessed more deadness to the world, more of a self-sacrificing spirit, more of the spirit of prayer, of Christian enterprise, of labor, and of benevolence, than any other man I ever knew. He was the most unselfish being I was ever acquainted with. Bishop Whatcoat I loved, Bishop M'Kendree I admired, Bishop Asbury I venerated."

Methodist Meeting Houses

The Methodists built houses of worship as soon as stable congregations developed. Those early meeting houses—simple structures, without ornamentation—were constructed to accommodate as many people as possible. The founding conference of 1784 put into the new church's first *Discipline*, "Let all our chapels be built plain and decent; but not more expensive than is absolutely unavoidable: otherwise the necessity of raising money will make rich men necessary to us. But if so, we must be dependent upon them, yea; and governed by them. And then farewell to the Methodist discipline, if not doctrine too." In 1816 the New England Conference resolved, "It shall be the duty of every preacher belonging to this conference to use his influence against constructing expensive meeting houses."

The rationale supporting plain meetinghouses was that expensive churches required money that could be used for better purposes. Also, the early Methodists feared that extravagantly constructed churches would lead to pride and vanity, which would lower the spiritual tone of the churches. Most of the early Methodists were poor, and the poor could not afford, nor feel at home in, elaborate buildings. Even as late as 1860, Methodist historian Abel Stevens wrote, "Our mission has been chiefly to the poor; our chief glory will depart when we lose sight of this our chief historical distinction." He went on to say that inexpensive meetinghouses "should be the rule, not the exception, with us."

Methodist chapel in the Virginia wilderness.

Many settlers on the frontier lived in one-room log cabins, and they could not afford lumber or nails. They constructed meeting places such as this one, using logs, wooden pegs, and split timber for seating. This eighteenth-century shelter had no walls or floor.

Log meeting house.

Shiloh Meetinghouse was built in Missouri around 1810, and it was the first Methodist church in the area. Some of the early log churches had dirt floors and no means of heating.

Colfax Chapel.

This sod meetinghouse was built in 1872 about twelve miles north of Vermillion, South Dakota. It was the second Methodist building in the Dakota Territory. The chapel's name derives from Schuyler Colfax, the Vice President of the United States, who donated $50 to the Methodist society that built this structure. A center post upheld round beams fanning out to the sod walls. Willow poles and brush supported the sod roof. At one time, Susan B. Anthony preached here.

John R. Bonney immortalized the sod church in a poem. One of the stanzas reads:

God meets his chosen people here/ In this his temple lowly,/ And human hearts are made to feel/ That every place is holy./ The Spirit from on high descends/ Upon his glorious mission./ To work in unregenerate hearts/ Repentance and contrition.

In the period following American independence, Methodism launched a western expansion. This crusade into the wilderness produced a great number of meeting houses in remote places. Some of these chapels, constructed of logs, were little more than posts supporting a roof. These wooden buildings were built by and intended for frontier people. Timber grew in abundance, and sharp axes quickly produced logs for homes and chapels. Many of these frontier meetinghouses had dirt floors because it required equipment and time-consuming hand labor to saw planks. There were few pews; most meetinghouses had benches without backs.

As the congregations spread into the Great Plains, they sometimes built their meetinghouses out of sod. Timber was scarce, and the settlers used the abundant turf so readily available on the vast prairies. Sod homes and churches were cool in the summer and warm in the winter. Grass grew on the roofs and the north walls, and wild flowers often sprouted on them as well. Sod buildings, however, had drawbacks. The roofs leaked, the interiors were dark, and mice and bed bugs thrived. The more prosperous congregations added shingles to ward off the rain and melting snow.

The first Methodist *Discipline* required that men and women sit in separate sections. Meeting-houses had either a dividing center section or a hip-high partition separating the males and females. Many churches had two entrances, and the men and women entered the building through separate doors.

Heating stove in an early Methodist Protestant chapel.

Because many of the early Methodists were poor, some of the meetinghouses had no stoves. During wintertime, congregations often met in cold buildings. In time, however, they added stoves. Lighting consisted of tallow candles or lard-oil burners, resulting in dingy dimness during evening services. Critics spoke contemptuously of Methodist chapels as "barns."

Ohio Chapel.

This Methodist church, built in 1856, was typical of those structures that replaced the log chapels of frontier Methodism. Between 1850 and 1860 the Methodists built 6,603 churches—more than the number of new churches built by the Baptists, Roman Catholics, Episcopalians, and Presbyterians combined.

Stone church.
Photograph by Darlene V. Shoop.

This New Jersey church, named Mount Bethel, was constructed in 1844 in a community visited by Francis Asbury. As the nineteenth century unfolded, stone and brick churches replaced the log and frame churches so common in first generation American Methodism. Note the separate entrances for men and women.

From Chapels to Churches

Following American independence, a few Methodist congregations in the settled parts of the East built churches in the Federal style—a revival of Roman architecture made popular by Thomas Jefferson. However, not many congregations erected such costly buildings.

During the 1850s the Methodists began replacing their log meetinghouses with churches of framed lumber, brick, and stone. By 1860 Methodism had almost 20,000 houses of worship, and virtually every community in America had at least one Methodist Church. The majority of these new churches were simple frame structures. These relatively inexpensive churches enabled the Methodists to establish a presence in small towns, logging camps, cattle country, agricultural areas, mining communities, and timber operations in the west. Many of these wooden structures were intended as temporary churches. Yet they often endured for many decades. Congregations built larger buildings, while leaving the older ones to serve additional congregations. The multiplication of churches helped establish Methodism's dominant presence in America's villages, towns, and cities. As congregations grew, brick and stone increasingly became popular building materials. Despite differences in style, common to most Methodist churches was the communion rail, a feature that reflects both the Anglican sacramental heritage and the revivalist concern for penitent prayers.

The communion rail.

This picture shows the interior of a nineteenth-century Methodist Church. The communion rail has always been an important part of Methodist church architecture. The altar rail served two purposes: a kneeling rail to receive the Lord's Supper and a holy place to pray.

It was not always easy for the unrefined frontier Methodist preachers to adjust to the church's formal communion ritual. In 1834 Rev. James Gilruth wrote in his journal, "I felt Myself in an awkward situation just at the commencement of the Administration of the sacrement (sic) by reason of accidently (sic) touching one of the tumblers & spilling a part of the consecrated wine. But instantly reflecting that it was accidental I calmed My Mind & proceeded with the service as tho nothing had happened."

Shortly before the Civil War, America experienced a revival of the Gothic style of architecture. This period lasted well into the twentieth century. As the Methodists became financially able, they built larger and more costly buildings, moving away from the earlier determination to build simple churches. Scores of these magnificent edifices remain to this day. The Metropolitan Memorial Methodist Episcopal Church in Washington, D.C., typifies Gothic design. The Methodists wanted to construct quality churches of great beauty, as symbols of enduring religious values. Thus, the Gothic style dominated that era.

The nineteenth century Methodist Episcopal Church became America's largest Protestant denomination. After the middle of the nineteenth century, the saying was common that "There are more Methodist Churches in America than Post Offices." Perhaps the most visible leader of Methodist expansion in that era was Charles C. McCabe. Prior to becoming a bishop, McCabe served for sixteen years as Secretary of the Methodist Extension Society. In that role, his enthusiasm for planting new churches made him famous throughout Methodism. The famed agnostic Robert G. Ingersoll claimed, "The churches are dying out all over the land; they are struck with death." Ingersoll's declaration found its way into newspapers throughout America. McCabe read the quote while traveling by railroad. At the next stop, he wired Ingersoll, "Dear Robert: 'All hail the power of Jesus' name.' We are building more than one Methodist church for

Gothic revival architecture.

The Metropolitan Memorial Methodist Episcopal Church, Washington, D.C. was dedicated February 28, 1869 by Bishop Matthew Simpson, in the presence of a large assembly of people from across the nation. The church has been called "the church of the Presidents." In 1890 in this church, Dr. John Fletcher Hurst proposed a plan to establish American University.

Charles Cardwell McCabe (1836-1906).

During the Civil War C. C. McCabe served as a chaplain in the 122nd Ohio Infantry. He was captured and sent to Libby Prison. After the war his service as Secretary of the Methodist Extension Society took him to numerous churches, where he inspired congregations to give money to start new churches. He often attracted crowds by announcing that he would speak on "The Bright Side of Life in Libby Prison." The subject attracted hordes of people to hear him talk about being in a Civil War Prison. During his address, he would turn to the subject of church extension. His noble cause, irresistible singing voice, and enthusiasm for planting new churches made him a leader in church expansion. In 1896 the church elected him to the episcopacy.

McCabe's famous reply to Robert Ingersoll's prediction, that the churches were dying, inspired Alfred J. Hough to write a song, of which the first stanza reads:

> The infidels, a motley band,
> In council met, and said:
> The churches die all through the land,
> The last will soon be dead.
> When suddenly a message came,
> It filled them with dismay:
> 'All hail the power of Jesus name!'
> We're building two a day.

Methodists across the nation sang this song, and church extension became a crusade.

John Wesley.
The original of this portrait of John Wesley, painted by Frank O. Salisbury, is in the World Methodist Museum in Lake Junaluska, NC, and it is used here by permission of the museum. Photograph by Dave Henderson.

One month before he died, John Wesley wrote a letter to Ezekiel Cooper, an American Methodist preacher: "Those that desire to write or say anything to me, have no time to lose; for time has shaken me by the hand, and death is not far behind. But I have reason to be thankful for the time that is past: I felt few of the infirmities of old age for fourscore and six years. It was not till a year and a half ago that my strength and my sight failed. And still I am enabled to scrawl a little, and to creep, though I cannot run. Probably I should not be able to do so much, did not many of you assist me by your prayers.... Lose no opportunity of declaring to all men, that the Methodists are one people in all the world; and that it is their full determination so to continue, though mountains rise, and oceans roll, to sever us in vain. To the care of our common Lord I commit you; and am your affectionate friend and brother."

John Wesley

every day in the year and propose to make it two a day. C. C. McCabe."

During the latter third of the nineteenth century, American Methodism celebrated two centennials. The year 1866 was the centenary of the planting of Methodism in America, and 1884 marked the one-hundredth anniversary of American Methodism's becoming a church. The 1866 centennial stated as its purpose "the spiritual improvement of our members, and especially by reviewing the great things God hath wrought for us, the cultivation of feelings of gratitude for the blessings received through the agency of Methodism." The church challenged its members to raise a large sum of money for the needs of local congregations and for "connectional" projects. Local churches responded magnificently. Congregations raised and distributed funds for a variety of local needs. Large connectional funds were also raised for ten educational purposes, including the Student Loan Fund of the Board of Education. The church set a goal of two million dollars, and it raised over $8,700,000. Throughout America today there are numerous "Centenary" United Methodist Churches that trace their history back to the nineteenth-century centennial celebrations.

American Methodism also celebrated another centenary in 1919, the one-hundred-year anniversary of the formation of the Methodist Missionary Society (later to become the Board of Missions, and now the Board of Global Ministries). For the first time, the church used modern advertising, and 100,000 "Minute Men" worked to make the 1919 centenary a success. The campaign culminated in a Methodist World's Fair in Columbus, Ohio. In connection with this celebration, the church established a Missionary Centenary Fund for home and foreign missions. The eight-day campaign in

May 1919 exceeded goals by generating pledges and donations of almost $150,000,000. The centenary funds went to build new churches and strengthen the church's missionary work at home and abroad. American Methodism was at this time the most influential church in America. As such, it helped shape the nation's religious outlook and cultural values.

Methodism's remarkable achievements were possible because its message and methods brought so many millions of individuals to a personal encounter with Jesus Christ. The church's structures equipped these people to serve God in their daily lives. The church lived out its doctrinal confession and provided significant leadership for the nation's religious, educational, medical, and social needs. Methodism was a connectional church consisting of a network of people and structures bound together by common theological and missional commitments. The structure of Methodism places all its members under the same discipline. Church membership vows call for participating faithfully in the church's ministries by prayers, presence, gifts, and service.

To be sure, conflicts and differences nagged at the church and at times divided it. Still, despite setbacks, the church in fair measure demonstrated the proud claim of John Wesley that "the Methodists are one people." Historic Methodism accomplished much because God gave favor to a people whose faith rested in him, whose hope rested in his divine promises, and whose love inspired their hearts and hands in service to God and neighbor. In less than a century, Methodism grew from humble beginnings to the most important force in the religious life of America, profoundly influencing the morals and morés of the nation.

5 *Nurturing the Saints*

The heritage of American Methodism includes a rich tradition of Christian nurture. If John and Charles Wesley stressed the importance of evangelism, they gave equal attention to helping Methodist converts grow in the grace and knowledge of God. The Wesleys believed that the Christian mission entailed both winning converts and maturing disciples. Methodism's message emphasizes that Christ calls us to "be perfect, as the Father in heaven is perfect." In response to that call, John and Charles Wesley developed a number of structures aimed at nurturing the saints. These means of grace proved wonderfully effective, and they constitute a lasting legacy to Methodism and to the church universal.

From the Wesleyan perspective, evangelism is not an end, it is a beginning. George Whitefield was one of Methodism's most effective evangelists. His powerful sermons brought more people to Christ than did the preaching of John Wesley. Whitefield was, by most estimations, one of the best preaching evangelists in Christian history. Yet, in some important ways, his ministry differed sharply from that of the Wesleys. Whitefield was a "Calvinistic Methodist" who believed that, once converted to Christ, a person could not fall from grace or forfeit salvation. Therefore, he focused almost entirely on evangelism. He neglected, however, to organize and nurture his converts. Some of them fell by the wayside. In later life Whitefield said, "My brother Wesley acted wisely. The souls that were awakened under his ministry he joined in class [meetings], and thus preserved the fruit of his labour. This I neglected, and my people are as a rope of sand."

The Wesleys taught that the regenerating work of God readies one for a lifetime of growth in grace, ever advancing in holiness of heart and life. In sum, justification must move toward sanctification. John Wesley insisted that the work of Christian ministry is "not only to bring souls to believe in Christ, but to build them up in our most holy faith."

George Whitefield.

As an effective evangelist, Whitefield remains unparalleled in American history. Thousands became Christians under the power and eloquence of his inspired preaching. Whitefield helped perpetuate the First Great Awakening that so revitalized religion in America.

Moreover, the Wesleys took seriously the biblical warnings to believers to guard against falling away from Christ and making shipwreck of their faith. From experience, they had seen converts make a good start in the Christian life but later drift away and return to their former sins. Methodism insisted that persons are not fully evangelized until they become established within a Christian community, grounded in their faith, and set on a path of sanctification. John Wesley declared, "How grievously are they mistaken... who imagine that as soon as the children are born they need to take no more care of them! We do not find it so. The chief care then begins."

Wherever Wesley preached, he organized. Always, he gathered his converts into classes, provided them with preachers, and secured chapels for them. In 1750 Wesley wrote in his journal, "Through all Cornwall I find the societies have suffered great loss from want of discipline. Wisely said the ancients, 'The soul and body make a man; the Spirit and discipline make a Christian.'" Wesley developed methodical means to assist Methodist converts to mature in grace, knowledge, and obedience to Christ. Where discipline was lacking, the societies declined; where discipline was in effect, the societies thrived.

Discipline in the Methodist Tradition

In America, most of those present at the 1784 founding conference of the Methodist Episcopal Church were influenced by Wesley's views on Christian nurture. It was natural that these preachers would have a comparable regard for a disciplined life. Their approach to church order was reflected in the title of the new church's guidelines: *Discipline for the Ministers, Preachers and other Members of the Methodist Episcopal Church in America*. Methodism is *methodical*, and discipleship requires *discipline*.

Methodism's General Rules

Methodism's *Discipline* includes a document that John and Charles Wesley published in 1743 and named *The Nature, Design, and General Rules of the United Societies*. The aim of these "General Rules"

Title page of the 1743 edition of Methodism's General Rules

The intention of the General Rules was to provide helpful descriptions of godly living. The General Rules assume that (1) there are specific things that Christians should not do, (2) there are specific things that Christians should do, and (3) a faithful use of the means of grace is necessary for Christian nurture.

THE NATURE, DESIGN, AND GENERAL RULES, OF THE United Societies, IN London, Briſtol, King's-wood, and Newcaſtle upon Tyne.

NEWCASTLE UPON TYNE, Printed by JOHN GOODING, on the Side. [Price One Penny.] MDCCXLIII.

was to provide the Methodists with biblically prescribed guidelines for godly living. These guidelines do not impart merit to us for our human efforts. Apart from *God's* working, they were in Wesley's words "poor, dead, empty things." The General Rules are not *ends*—they are *means*.

Methodism's General Rules fall under three headings: (1) doing no harm, (2) doing good, and (3) attending upon all the ordinances of God. We sometimes refer to these categories as the Christian Negative, the Christian Positive, and the Christian Dynamic. There are things Christians should *not* do, things they *should* do, and scriptural means that lead to inward and outward holiness.

Included in the General Rules are five so-called "instituted means of grace"—instituted, because Christ established them. These means of grace are (1) *prayer*, (2) *searching the scriptures*, (3) *the Lord's Supper*, (4) *fasting*, and (5) *Christian conference*. These means of grace should not be seen as Christ's *commands*, but as his *gifts*.

▶ *Prayer* links us with God and makes his presence real in our lives. John Wesley observed that without prayer we easily fall into a "wilderness state" that renders us confused and powerless. Prayer gives us clarity of mind and develops the life of the spirit.

The "New Room" at Bristol.
This chapel, built in 1739, rebuilt in 1748 and restored in 1930, is the oldest Methodist building in continuous use. John and Charles Wesley preached here, and the New Room was a center of great revivals of religion.

Charles Wesley wrote a twenty-three verse hymn, "The Means of Grace," to communicate the conviction that the means of grace are *instruments,* not *ends.* Although that hymn was never published in our hymnals, its message sheds light on Methodism's General Rules. Five of the stanzas follow:

Oft did I with th' assembly join
And near Thine altar drew;
A form of godliness was mine,
The power I never knew.

I see the perfect law requires
Truth in the inward parts,
Our full consent, our whole desires,
Our undivided hearts.

But I of means have made my boast,
Of means an idol made;
The spirit in the letter lost,
The substance in the shade.

I rested in the outward law,
Nor knew its deep design;
The length and breadth I never saw,
And height of love divine.

Where am I now, or what my hope?
What can my weakness do?
JESUS, to Thee my soul looks up,
'Tis Thou must make it new.

Francis Asbury.

This portrait by Polk, painted in 1794, was restored when it was recovered. Heat from a stovepipe had burned through Asbury's right hand. The painting was restored again in 1934, and it now hangs at Baltimore's Lovely Lane Museum.

In nurturing the saints, Bishop Asbury maintained a balance between grace and freedom on the one hand and accountability and duty on the other hand. He believed that apart from God's enabling, we can not succeed in our calling and apart from our obedient response to God's revealed purposes, he will not enable us to succeed in our calling.

▶ *Searching the scriptures* exposes us to God's revelation, which the Holy Spirit uses to enlighten our understanding of God's will. Religious truth is grounded in the Bible, not in human reason or public opinion.

▶ *The Lord's Supper* constitutes a continuing sacramental means, instituted by Christ, through which he promises to feed us with his living presence.

▶ *Fasting* helps us detach ourselves from earthly things and focus more clearly on spiritual reality. Following the tradition of the ancient church, the early Methodists fasted every Friday.

▶ *Christian conference* refers to the importance of the Christian community. In fellowship with others, we benefit from mutual accountability, witness, and growth.

The Wesleyan emphasis on discipline flows from the conviction that Christians have a responsible role in their own sanctification. John Wesley declared that God works through the instituted means of grace to impart prevenient, saving, and sanctifying grace "according to our several necessities."

In 1784 the newly formed Methodist Episcopal Church in America adopted the General Rules and required that preachers read them to their congregations at least quarterly. In 1808 the church adopted Restrictive Rules forbidding the repeal or alteration of the General Rules. American Methodism has printed the General Rules in every edition of the *Discipline* to the present time.

When Thomas Rankin returned to England in 1778, Francis Asbury assumed the leadership of American Methodism. Asbury was determined to maintain discipline among the Methodists, and he was successful in his endeavor. Toward the end of his life, Asbury wrote, "'Tis order, 'tis system— under God—that hath kept us from schism, and heresy, and division."

Methodism's General Rules assume the importance of staying "in connection" with other serious-minded Christians. John Wesley insisted that Christianity is a social religion, not a private matter only. He declared,

'Holy solitaries' is a phrase no more consistent with the gospel than holy adulterers. The gospel of Christ knows of no religion, but social; no holiness but social holiness. 'Faith working by love' is the length and breadth and depth and height of Christian perfection. 'This commandment have we from Christ, that he who loves God, love his brother also;' and that we manifest our love 'by doing good unto all men; especially to them that are of the household of faith.' And in truth, whosoever loveth his brethren, not in word only, but as Christ loved him, cannot but be 'zealous of good works.'

Wesley believed that Christian disciples need regular fellowship with other believers to develop such Christian virtues as patience, gentleness, and peacemaking.

In 1798 Bishops Thomas Coke and Francis Asbury wrote, "The *social principle* is one of the

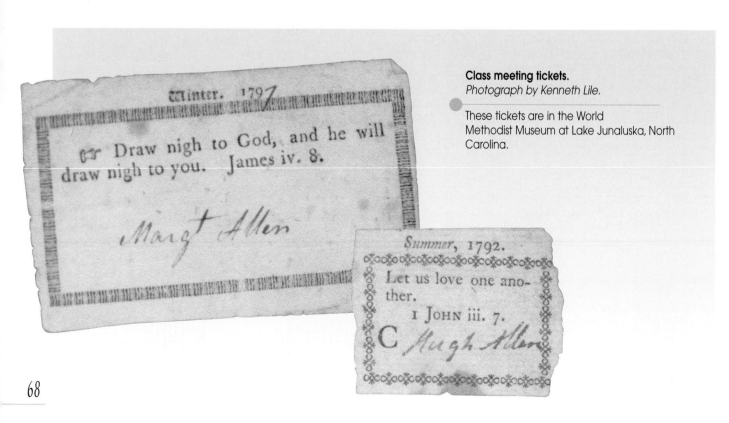

Class meeting tickets.
Photograph by Kenneth Lile.

These tickets are in the World Methodist Museum at Lake Junaluska, North Carolina.

Winter. 1797

☞ Draw nigh to God, and he will draw nigh to you. James iv. 8.

Marg.t Allen

Summer, 1792.
Let us love one another.
1 John iii. 7.
C Hugh Allen

68

grand springs in the soul of man. It was not the design of Christianity to annihilate this principle, but the very contrary—to improve it, to spiritualize it, and strengthen it…. We have made many remarks in the course of our work on the necessity of Christian fellowship: but this cannot be carried on to any considerable advantage without stated solemn times of assembling…. We call ours *Class-meetings*." The Methodist principle of being "in connection" echoes the biblical principle that "iron sharpens iron."

Class Meetings

In the Methodist tradition, Christian nurture began *prior* to one's conversion to Christ. When seekers were "awakened" to God's claim on their lives, they typically joined a class. Class members gathered weekly under a class leader, often a lay person. As societies grew, they added separate classes for men and women. These class meetings constituted the basic units of Methodism. They may be compared to a honeycomb, with individual cells making up the whole. The interconnected structure was astonishingly strong.

Membership in a Methodist society did not require seekers to profess Christian conversion. The stipulations for becoming a member "in society" were: (1) the "desire to flee from the wrath to come, and to be saved from their sins" and (2) the commitment to attend a weekly class meeting. Because the classes admitted only those who were serious about religion, members received class meeting tickets that required quarterly renewal by the minister. The class meetings resulted in numerous conversions to Christ. Indeed, more conversions occurred in class meetings than in public preaching services.

Class meeting activities included singing, prayer, and the sharing of spiritual struggles and victories. The leader would first speak about his or her spiritual state. Then, in turn, he or she would ask each class member questions about his or her spiritual life. In these groups the members shared their hopes, fears, temptations, failures, and victories. The members responded by praying, admonishing, clarifying, and encouraging. John Wesley observed that the members of the Methodist classes "began to bear each other's burdens and naturally to care for each other." Members learned to share freely, without embarrassment or concern about gossip. Class members were expected to follow an important rule: "Let nothing spoken in this society be spoken again."

In instances when a class member was the only Christian in a household, the members of the class constituted a spiritual family. With deep emotion they sang,

> And if our fellowship below
> In Jesus be so sweet,
> What heights of rapture shall we know
> When round His throne we meet!

The Methodists banded together to assist each other with housing, employment, loans, and

First Methodist meeting-house in Ohio, 1801

To the early Methodists, the chapel, class meeting, and special religious services constituted an environment that conditioned all other phases of daily life. The chapel and its activities provided a network of intimate social relationships, a community of caring support, and a secure environment for spiritual nurture.

The class leaders kept abreast of their class members, visiting those who were ill and organizing assistance for those who needed help. The Methodists did business at each other's shops and assisted each other with housing, employment, and interest-free loans. Early Methodist chapels sprang up across the land, signs that Methodism was becoming one of the most vital religious forces in America. One commentator wrote that early Methodism was not only a church within a church, it was almost a nation within a nation.

work. As stated, early American Methodism deemed attendance in a class meeting as essential, and one's failure to continue faithful constituted grounds for expulsion. The Methodist *Discipline* continued to include instructions for class meetings until the 1930s.

After the circuit preacher, the next most important worker in early Methodism was the class leader, who essentially served as a lay pastor. These class leaders ministered to the members of the societies in the absence of the itinerant preachers, whose large circuits required constant travel. The class leaders visited new families, sick people, and, of course, the class members—especially those persons whose spiritual zeal began to cool. Class leaders were often instrumental in reclaiming those who tended to drift away. The close-knit classes guaranteed that no member would slip away from the society for the lack of a caring fellowship.

The classes provided a social structure in which people gained confidence in their abilities. Edwin Tiffin's class meeting experience gave him self-confidence and prompted him to seek a license to preach, which Francis Asbury granted him. Tiffin became Ohio's first governor and later a member of the United States Senate. Numerous national leaders traced their growth in self-assurance and self-worth to the early class meetings where grace, humor, pathos, wisdom, and love flowed so abundantly into their lives.

The class meetings also served as workshops for developing church leaders. The classes identified and developed those who demonstrated spiritual maturity and special aptitudes for Christian ministry. The class meetings gave many persons their first opportunities to speak publicly and thereby test their calls to preach. Gifted class members advanced to become class leaders, teachers, circuit riders, and bishops. Bishops Coke and Asbury wrote, "Through the grace of God our classes form the pillars of our work, and... are in a considerable degree our universities for the ministry."

Around the middle of the nineteenth century, the class meetings declined, even if numerous voices lamented the trend. Several factors contributed to their decline. The circuit riders began to settle into parish ministries as resident pastors.

As the pastors became more readily available to the people, the need for class leaders diminished. Furthermore, the growing emphasis on education caused the class meetings to give way to Sunday school classes. Listening to teachers expound

John Wesley statue, Arthur J. Moore Methodist Museum.
This nine-foot statue stands in the rotunda of the library and museum at Epworth by the Sea, St. Simons Island, Georgia. Photograph courtesy of the museum.

During John Wesley's time in America as a missionary to the Georgia colony, he came to know the Moravian Christians. In fellowship with them, he participated in his first love feast, a ceremony of sharing bread and water with one another and talking about spiritual concerns. This practice derives from the ancient Agape meal of the primitive church.

biblical passages became more popular than participation in class meetings in which members were expected to share their spiritual journeys. The class meetings also declined as the fires of revival waned. As area-wide religious awakenings declined, class meetings tended to become perfunctory, with class members sometimes reiterating the same experiences over and over again. By the beginning of the twentieth century, the class meetings had all but ceased.

The Love Feast

In 1737, while serving as a missionary in Georgia, John Wesley attended his first love feast. It was with the Moravians who lived in the colony. He observed that this love feast was "celebrated in so decent and solemn a manner as a Christian of the apostolic age would have allowed to be worthy of Christ." Soon after John Wesley's heartwarming experience at Aldersgate Street, he established the practice of observing love feasts in the growing Methodist movement. He explained:

In order to increase in them [the Methodists] a grateful sense of all God's mercies, I desired that… we might together 'eat bread', as the ancient Christians did, 'with gladness and singleness of heart'. At these Love-Feasts…our food is only a little plain cake and water. But we seldom return from them without being fed, not only with the 'meat which perisheth', but with 'that which endureth to everlasting life'.

Explaining the love feast, John Wesley wrote:

Great and many are the advantages which have ever since flowed from the closer union of the believers with each other. They prayed for one another, that they might be healed of the faults they had confessed, and it was so. The chains were broken asunder, and sin had no more dominion over them… They were built up in our most holy faith. They rejoiced in the Lord more abundantly. They were strengthened in love and more effectually provoked to abound in every good work.

In 1770 Joseph Pilmore introduced the love feast to the American Methodists. He reported in his journal, "It was indeed a time of love. The people behaved with much propriety and decorum, as if they had been for many years acquainted with the economy of the Methodists. Perhaps this favorable beginning will encourage the people to wish for such a season again, and may help to prepare them to eat bread together in the Kingdom of God."

Methodist love feasts were not the same as the Lord's Supper. Holy Communion is a sacrament; the love feast was a fellowship observance. Only ordained clergy conduct the services of Holy Communion, but any Christian could conduct a love feast. Early Methodists in England and America observed the love feast by sharing bread and water as a symbolic fellowship meal. Worshipers sat in a circle or around a table. The participants shared a common loaf and passed a two-handled cup of water. Those present contributed to an offering for the poor, after which the

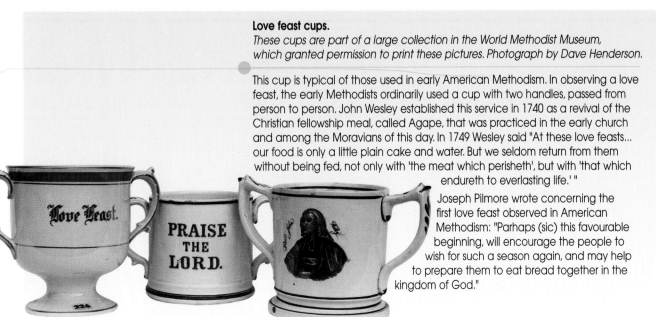

Love feast cups.
These cups are part of a large collection in the World Methodist Museum, which granted permission to print these pictures. Photograph by Dave Henderson.

This cup is typical of those used in early American Methodism. In observing a love feast, the early Methodists ordinarily used a cup with two handles, passed from person to person. John Wesley established this service in 1740 as a revival of the Christian fellowship meal, called Agape, that was practiced in the early church and among the Moravians of this day. In 1749 Wesley said "At these love feasts… our food is only a little plain cake and water. But we seldom return from them without being fed, not only with 'the meat which perisheth', but with 'that which endureth to everlasting life.' "

Joseph Pilmore wrote concerning the first love feast observed in American Methodism: "Parhaps (sic) this favourable beginning, will encourage the people to wish for such a season again, and may help to prepare them to eat bread together in the kingdom of God."

Love feast cup.
Photograph by Kenneth Lile.

Thomas Ware explained the American Methodist love feast in his memoir: "We met early for love-feast. All that had obtained peace with God, and all who were seeking it, were invited, and the barn was nearly full. As few present had ever been in a love-feast, Mr. Mair explained to us its nature and design, namely, to take a little bread and water, not as a sacrament, but in token of our Christian love, in imitation of a primitive usage, and then humbly and briefly to declare the great things the Lord had done for them in having had mercy on them."

members of the society were invited to "relate their religious experience." These meetings lasted about two hours.

The 1789 Methodist *Discipline* made it the duty of ministers to conduct regular love feasts, and the love feast became a much loved and frequently used institution in early American Methodism. In 1806 William Watters published an account of his experiences and labors. Describing a love feast, he wrote:

> *Heaven above will differ more in quantity than in quality. Never did I hear such experiences before. Our eyes overflowed with tears, and our hearts with love to God and each other. The holy fire, the heavenly flame, spread wider and wider, and rose higher and higher. O! happy people whose God is the Lord, may none of you ever weary in well doing.*

Historian Nathan Bangs wrote that Methodism's love feasts were "peculiarly profitable to the souls of God's people."

Those who champion the love feast point to Jesus's sharing meals with his disciples. They also

Wilderness scene

Lacking roads, the early frontier Methodist preachers depended on landmarks, faint trails, and the sun and the stars for guidance to their next preaching appointments. In time, the preachers' horses learned the way, and the circuit riders could read while their horses took them to their next stop.

In January 1790 Richard Whatcoat traveled through a dense forest to attend a love feast. He wrote in his journal, "Sacrament and Lovefeast (was held) half past Nine it was A precious Time some profest the Lord had Santified their Souls it was A General quicking Bror Asbury preachd..."

The Church Fellowship Supper.
Photograph by Dave Henderson.

The congregational fellowship meal is believed by some scholars to be a lingering reminder of the love feast once common among Methodists. This cup and saucer were once used for church fellowship meals in a United Brethren church.

point out the rich fellowship that earlier generations of Methodists enjoyed at their love feasts. The love feasts were occasions to meet together and informally to give and receive expressions of friendship, regard, and esteem.

Today, some Annual Conferences, Charge Conferences, and Covenant Discipleship Groups are reinstituting the love feast. These services provide opportunities for Christians to share what God has been doing in their lives and to celebrate the love of Christ and fellow Christians. United Methodism's current *Book of Worship* contains a love feast service. One of the suggested hymns for use at a love feast is Charles Wesley's "Blest Be the Dear, Uniting Love."

> *Blest be the dear, uniting love*
> *That will not let us part;*
> *Our bodies may far off remove—*
> *We still are one in heart....*
>
> *But let us hasten to the day*
> *Which shall our flesh restore,*
> *When death shall all be done away,*
> *And bodies part no more!*

Watch Night Services

Early in church history, Christians held vigils during the evenings before church festivals. These vigils, or watch night services, seem to have been inspired by Jesus's example of praying all night about important decisions. The night before Jesus went to the cross, he asked his disciples to watch with him in prayerful vigil. Christians in the ancient church were also impressed by the parable of the Ten Virgins whom the Bridegroom found watching and praying when he arrived at midnight. Throughout history, Christians have at times held watch night vigils prior to launching new projects or starting fresh ministries.

Methodism's watch night services began in 1740 when John Wesley revived this neglected practice of ancient Christianity. As was Wesley's custom, he established a means of nurture in response to a specific need. In his day, coal miners had a long-standing practice of watching the old year end and the new year begin by engaging in revelries and drunkenness. And they often spent Saturday nights the same way. Wesley met this situation head on by establishing a monthly watch night service as an alternate way to spend Saturday night. After their conversion to Christ, those who once had spent Saturday night at the alehouse now spent that evening preparing for Sunday worship and "watching" for the Lord's coming.

John Wesley, of course, was familiar with the *Anglican Book of Common Prayer* which calls for sixteen vigils during the year. Although the eighteenth-century Anglican Church neglected these vigils, John Wesley took seriously his church's provision for these watches on special occasions. He explained:

> *We commonly chose for [the watch night] service the Friday night nearest the full moon... that those of the congregation who live at a distance may have light to their several homes. The service begins at half an hour past eight and continues a little after midnight. We have often found a peculiar blessing at these seasons. There is generally a deep awe upon the congregation.*

Some church officials criticized the Methodists for holding watch night services. They worried that this Methodist practice would draw people away

George Washington at Prayer.

"The Prayer at Valley Forge" is painted by Arnold Friberg, RSA and is used by permission of Friberg Fine Art, Inc.

When George Washington and his half-starved soldiers camped at Valley Forge, Washington entreated a banker, Robert Morris, to send $50,000 to help alleviate the desperate situation. It is also a matter of record that before daylight on January 1, 1777, Morris visited friends, rousing them from sleep, and gathered the money, which he sent to General Washington. Robert Morris reported to his friends that he had just come from an all-night watch night service at St. George's Methodist Episcopal Church in Philadelphia. During this service the Methodists had prayed that God would open up the hearts of the people to provide the money needed to pay the troops at Valley Forge, so that the Colonial cause would prevail.

Washington's papers show that he was a subscriber to Cokesbury College, founded by the newly formed Methodist Episcopal Church. Records reveal that the Methodists prayed regularly for Washington. Four weeks after Washington's election to the presidency, the conference of the Methodist Episcopal Church met at Wesley Chapel in New York City. The conference adopted a "Congratulatory Address," delegating Bishops Coke and Asbury to take it to President Washington. Washington received the bishops along with several other leading Methodist preachers, and with dignity Asbury read the address. Deeply moved, Washington responded, "I shall always strive to prove a faithful and impartial patron of genuine vital religion, and I must assure you, in particular, that I take in the kindest part the promise you make of presenting your prayers to the throne of grace for me, and that I likewise implore the Divine benediction on yourselves and your religious community."

from the established church. Wesley answered this faultfinding: "You charge me with holding 'midnight assemblies.' Sir, did you never see the word 'Vigil' in your Common Prayer Book?... It was customary with the ancient Christians to spend whole nights in prayer. Therefore, for spending a part of some nights in this manner, in public and solemn prayer, we have not only the authority of our own national Church, but of the universal Church in the earliest ages."

Charles Wesley wrote hymns for watch night services to be sung by converts who had found new life in Christ. For example:

> *Suffice that for the season past*
> *Hell's horrid language filled our tongues,*
> *We all Thy words behind us cast,*
> *And loudly sang the drunkard's songs.*
>
> *But oh, the pow'r of grace divine!*
> *In hymns we now our voices raise,*
> *Loudly in strange hosannas join,*
> *And blasphemies are turned to praise.*

In November 1770, the American Methodists began holding watch night services at St. George's Church in Philadelphia. Francis Asbury recorded in his *Journal*, "The people gave serious attention; very few left the solemn place until the conclusion. Towards the end, a plain man spoke, who came out of the country, and his words went with great power to the souls of the people."

On December 31, 1770, Joseph Pilmore wrote, "We had our Watch-Night. The Mob had threatened great things, but the terrors of the Lord made them afraid, and we continued till after midnight, that we might end the *old*, and begin the *New Year*, in the service of God... At present I *feel* the obligations I am under for his favours, and, I hope, I shall never forget, how much I am indebted to the Lord my God for his boundless goodness."

The Methodists in America enjoyed these services and found them highly edifying. John Hagerty reported to Bishop Whatcoat the results of a watch night service: "The Lord condescended to visit us! Several were 'born again.'"

John Wesley.
This large oval portrait was painted by John Jackson and given to the World Methodist Museum by Dr. Charles Coolidge Parlin. It is printed here by permission of the museum. Photograph by Dave Henderson.

In 1783, John Wesley wrote in his journal, "There was an Ordination at St. Patrick's. I admired the solemnity wherewith the Archbishop went through the Service: But the vacant faces of the ordained showed how little they were affected thereby. In the evening (at a Methodist chapel) multitudes met to renew their covenant with God. But here was no vacant face to be seen, for God was in the midst, and manifested himself to many; particularly to a daughter of good William Pennington."

The Covenant Service

John Wesley introduced the Covenant Service to Methodism in 1755. The Methodists found this service profoundly worthwhile, and Wesley's *Journal* contains numerous references to the spiritual blessings that attended its use. On one occasion he wrote, "At six in the evening we met at the church… to renew our covenant with God. It was a blessed time; the windows of heaven were open, and the skies poured down righteousness." He wrote about another Covenant Service: "I do not know that ever we had a greater blessing. Afterwards many desired to return thanks, either for a sense of pardon, for full salvation, or for a fresh manifestation of His graces, healing all their backslidings."

In designing the Covenant Service, John Wesley adapted a liturgy by a Puritan clergyman, Richard Alleine, and added words of his own. The invitation in this liturgy begins with these words:

Commit yourselves to Christ as his servants.

Give yourselves to him, that you may belong to him.

Christ has many services to be done.

Some are more easy and honorable, others are more difficult and disgraceful.

Some are suitable to our inclinations and interests, others are contrary to both.

In some we may please Christ and please ourselves.

But then there are other works where we cannot please Christ except by denying ourselves.

It is necessary, therefore, that we consider what it means to be a servant of Christ.

The Covenant Service calls persons to surrender themselves to God and live out their lives in faithful obedience to his will. The spirit of the Covenant Service is captured in the following prayer of commitment:

O God, you know that I make this covenant with you today without guile or reservation. If any falsehood should be in it, guide me and help me to set it aright. And now, glory be to you, O God the Father, whom I from this day forward shall look upon as my God and Father. Glory be to you, O God the Son, who have loved me and washed me from my sins in your own blood, and now is my Savior and Redeemer. Glory be to you, O God the Holy Spirit, who by your almighty power have turned my heart from sin to God. O mighty God, the Lord Omnipotent, Father, Son, and Holy Spirit, you have now become my Covenant Friend. And I, through your infinite grace, have become your covenant servant. So be it. And let the covenant I have made on earth be ratified in heaven.

Over time, revisions of the original Methodist Covenant Service have deleted material from Wesley's pen, altering the service to make room for more congregational participation. The Covenant Service is found in United Methodism's *Book of Worship*. Today, the service is most often observed on New Year's Eve, sometimes in conjunction with a watch night service.

As we have seen, spiritual nurture in the Wesleyan way is not rooted in a narrow reduction of Christianity into legalism. Rather, the heritage of American Methodism lies in its *principles*. It is true that Methodism's General Rules contain specific guidelines that some may regard as "legalistic." However, the standards of behavior contained in the General Rules are specifically taught in scripture and throughout the centuries have been accepted by all branches of Christendom.

Today's United Methodist *Discipline* outlines the duties of the pastor as "overseeing the total ministry of the local church in its nurturing ministries and...fulfilling its mission of witness and service in the world...[by] giving pastoral support, guidance, and training to the lay leadership in the church, equipping them to fulfill the ministry to which they are sent as servants under the Lordship of Christ...." The *Discipline* also charges the bishops of the church with the responsibility "to guard, transmit, teach, and proclaim, corporately and individually, the apostolic faith as it is expressed in Scripture and tradition, and as they are led and endowed by the Spirit, to interpret that faith evangelically and prophetically." Thus, Christian nurture lies at the heart of the mission of the church.

On the global stage, the stated mission of the World Methodist Council, of which American Methodism is a part, is to nurture the saints and expand the Wesleyan witness across the globe. This council, organized in 1881, serves the family of Methodist churches in over 108 countries with a constituency of 65 million people. The stated mission of this fellowship of Methodist denominations is to strengthen international ties, clarify theological and moral standards, and identify priorities for the worldwide Methodist community. Among the council's primary aims is to bring persons to faith in Christ and to nurture them in their faith and witness to the world. Christian nurture lies at the heart of this mission.

The Wesleyan emphasis on Christian nurture reflects the truth that God changes the world by changing individuals. At the heart of the Methodist message is the conviction that Christ calls his covenant people to the lifetime process of sanctification. John Wesley stated that the theological doctrine of "Christian perfection" is the grand depositum that God has lodged with the

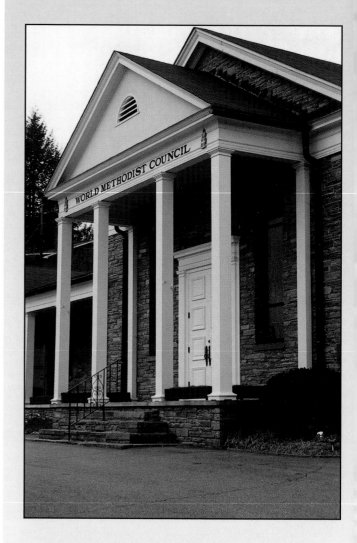

The World Methodist Council Building, Lake Junaluska, North Carolina. *Photograph by Kenneth Lile.*

The World Methodist Council represents all branches of Methodism. The council is an association of the churches in the Methodist tradition throughout the world. It does not legislate for these churches. Rather the council "exists to serve them and to give unity to their witness and enterprise." This building contains the offices of the council, along with a 4,000 square foot World Methodist Museum. The museum contains artifacts, rare letters, prints, paintings, and a large collection of commemorative pottery pertaining to world Methodism.

people called Methodists. Sanctification moves toward its completion through the work of the Holy Spirit who comes to us as we diligently use the means of grace. American Methodism's rich heritage points to the demonstrated reality that the disciplined use of the means of grace can transform any person or renew any church regardless of time or circumstance.

6 The Evangelical United Brethren Legacy

The Church of the United Brethren in Christ and the Evangelical Church both began in the 18th century as spiritual renewal movements among German-speaking Americans. In common with the Methodists, the United Brethren and Evangelicals held to the centrality of biblical authority, justification by faith, the church as a nurturing body, sanctification, and the application of Christianity to the social context. All three movements made use of itinerant preachers, class meetings, love feasts, camp meetings, and enthusiastic congregational singing. They attended each other's revival meetings and for a time considered uniting. The spiritual kinship between these three movements was so pronounced that some referred to the United Brethren and Evangelicals as "German Methodists."

At the time, the American churches were not adequately addressing the spiritual needs of German immigrants. German-speaking congregations needed spiritual renewal and renewed vision. Furthermore, many of the German immigrants to America had settled on the frontier where churches were few and moral standards were low. In numerous instances, their former churches had failed to lead them into Christian conversion, and they were not prepared to meet the moral challenges they faced.

The United Brethren and Evangelical movements arose to minister to these spiritual needs among the German Americans. The preachers sermonized passionately about Jesus Christ who changes the heart and transforms persons into new creations in Christ. The impact of these revival movements was so significant that both movements eventually became churches. The accounts of their rise and development stand among the most remarkable dramas in American religious history.

The Church of the United Brethren in Christ

The United Brethren Church had two principal founders—William Otterbein and Martin Boehm. Both men had significant ties to the Methodists: Otterbein was present at Methodism's founding conference and, with others, laid hands on Francis Asbury at his consecration as a Methodist bishop. Asbury often preached in Otterbein's church, and the two men consulted extensively prior to the formation of the United Brethren Church. Martin Bohem's son, Henry, became an itinerant preacher in the Methodist Episcopal Church, to which he contributed effective leadership. Both Otterbein and Boehm embraced Methodism's theology, method, and spirit. And both men made distinct contributions to early Methodism.

Philip William Otterbein (1726-1813).
This photograph is of the original oil portrait by Frank O. Salisbury. The painting hangs in the World Methodist Council Museum in Lake Junaluska, North Carolina, and is used here by permission. Photograph by Dave Henderson.

Otterbein began his ministry in America as a pastor in the German Reformed Church. While serving as pastor at York, Pennsylvania, Otterbein attended a revival meeting in progress at Isaac Long's barn. Martin Boehm, a Mennonite layman who held evangelistic meetings, was preaching the sermon. That very day, Otterbein began a friendship with Boehm that was to last a lifetime. Their mutual ministries led in 1800 to the formation of the Church of the United Brethren in Christ.

Philip William Otterbein

Philip William Otterbein was born in 1726 in Germany, into a German Reformed parsonage family. The family's six sons all became ordained ministers, and the one surviving daughter married a minister. From infancy, the children in this family benefited from having godly parents who were German Pietists. Pietism was a religious renewal movement in eighteenth-century Germany. It promoted Bible study, prayer, personal conversion, holiness, evangelism, and service to others. From childhood, Philip William Otterbein was thoroughly grounded in the evangelical distinctives of German Pietism, and he experienced in his heart what he understood in his head.

In 1751, Michael Schlatter, a German missionary to America, returned to his homeland to enlist pastors for German-speaking congregations in America. Schlatter looked for candidates who could read the Bible in Greek and Hebrew and who were persons of intellectual excellence and spiritual warmth. He called for young men who were "orthodox, learned, pious and of humble disposition, diligent, sound in body and eagerly desirous not after earthly but heavenly treasure, especially the salvation of immortal souls."

Philip William Otterbein, a twenty-six-year-old pastor, met these qualifications. He readily volunteered to minister in America. After a thorough examination by the synod, Otterbein landed in New York in 1752 and accepted a pastorate in Lancaster, Pennsylvania. His ministry there was so successful that the congregation soon built a new church to accommodate the new members. Over the years, Otterbein served several other German Reformed pastorates, including the Otterbein Church in Baltimore, a city of 6,000. Otterbein stressed the importance of Christ dwelling with us and in us. "Nothing less than a new creature in Christ Jesus will be acceptable in the sight of God," he declared. Contemporaries referred to his preaching as having "energy and power" and as being "zealous and reformatory." The following paragraph is lifted from one of Otterbein's sermons:

> *What will happen when we finally face death and the judgment—when the blood which now calls for forgiveness will then call for vengeance? What treasures of wrath one stores up for himself for eternity by such reckless abuse of the goodness of God! For the sake of God, take note. Listen to me. If you want to be heard by God, why are you so unconcerned, why so stubborn?... Is there any hope for the unconverted man? No, God's Spirit denies this to him. Unconverted—a child of wrath—a curse—an unsaved worm in hell—all of these*

William Otterbein's church in Baltimore.

Otterbein began his pastorate in Baltimore in 1774, when he was almost 48 years old. In 1785 the congregation built this building of brick and stone. The sanctuary and nearby parsonage cost $6,000. Otterbein remained pastor of the church until he died in 1813, having served the congregation for thirty-nine and a half years. This church is the oldest house of worship in Baltimore.

saying your names are written down in the book of life! It is the way of repentance that can lead you to this. Come then to the One who can help you.

Otterbein spoke plainly, and people had no difficulty understanding what he meant.

Some felt that his preaching voice lacked "musical notes." Yet others found his preaching to be compelling, and thousands came to Jesus Christ under his ministry.

Around 1774 Otterbein joined with like-minded pastors and lay people who wanted to promote holiness and revival throughout a wider area. At first, these people did not intend to start a new church. They wished only to work as an association of praying Christians to "leaven the whole lump," by which they meant promoting spiritual renewal in all the churches. Their endeavors were successful, producing religious revival throughout the Middle Atlantic States.

Although Otterbein continued to serve as the pastor of a congregation, he traveled extensively as an evangelist and held a number of "Great Meetings." These advertised ecumenical services brought hundreds of seekers to a personal knowledge of Jesus Christ as savior. To conserve the fruits of these revivals, Otterbein selected qualified lay people to lead societies after the pattern of the Methodist class meetings. Clergy critics denounced Otterbein and other leaders of the association for approving lay leadership for these new societies. Many of these clergy, refusing to recognize the legitimacy of lay people in ministry, stopped supporting the renewal efforts. Even so, the revivals and class meetings continued.

things express the same thing. Your wretchedness is undescribably [sic] great; you are definitely going to be lost.... What then is the best thing to do? It is clearly indicated for you: Repent and believe the gospel; search the Scriptures. There is no other way.... To be a redeemed one of the Lord, what a wonderful blessing! What a joy there will be when God sends the message to one or another of you,

First printing press of the Church of the United Brethren.

This press printed notices of the "Great Meetings" that were such an important part of the early United Brethren movement. These assemblies were neither camp meetings nor protracted meetings. They typically lasted two days and featured preaching; sometimes the Lord's Supper and love feasts were observed.

In 1802 Christian Newcomer wrote, "Nineteen great meetings were held during this year.... The holding of these meetings formed... another link in the chain of reformation. It was a new measure, but one which was productive of much good, and resulted in the best of consequences. They afforded an enlarged field of action, and a wider spread of the knowledge of true religion; and a fit opportunity to enforce the practice of its moral precepts. Hundreds, and we may say thousands, by these means, came to hear, who, in the ordinary way of holding religious or divine worship, would not have been brought under the saving influence of this dispensation of life."

Otterbein was the natural leader of this growing revival movement. In a time when ecumenical cooperation was seldom seen, his German-speaking ministry reached across denominations to include people in Mennonite, Reformed, Amish, and Lutheran Churches. Otterbein avoided sectarianism; he wanted to be "united with all the brethren." This ecumenical emphasis continued throughout his life. In his final days, a Lutheran pastor ministered to him; a Methodist and a Lutheran preached at his funeral; an Episcopalian rector conducted his graveside service. In a memorial service for William Otterbein, Francis Asbury said, "Forty years have I known the retiring modesty of this man of God: towering majestically above his fellows in learning, wisdom, and grace, yet seeking to be known only of God and the people of God."

Martin Boehm

In 1767, another leader in this renewal movement emerged—a farmer named Martin Boehm. Boehm's religious awakening began when, as a member of a Mennonite congregation, he became dissatisfied with his spiritual life. Although he was a lay speaker in the church, he admitted to himself that he had no vital relationship with Christ. His spiritual disquiet turned to anguish. One day, while plowing a field, he dropped to his knees and cried out, "Lord, save me, I am lost." He recalled the words of Christ, "For the Son of man is come to seek and to save that which was lost," and he found peace with God. Later, he described this experience: "In a moment, a stream of joy was poured over me." Boehm dashed home to tell his wife about his dramatic conversion. Soon, she also experienced the assurance of her salvation.

Boehm's Chapel.

Martin Boehm gave a new Methodist society a portion of land on which it built the first Methodist church in Lancaster County, Pennsylvania. This chapel became a historic United Methodist shrine. At the age of twenty-five, Martin Boehm's son, Henry, was converted to Christ and became a Methodist preacher. Henry Boehm's ministry continued for the ensuing seventy-five years.

Martin Boehm (1725-1812).

Boehm was closely associated with William Otterbein in leading the movement that became the Church of the United Brethren in Christ. Prior to Otterbein's famous first meeting with Boehm, Boehm had already spearheaded a religious revival among German-speaking people in eastern Pennsylvania. The youngest of his eight children, Henry Boehm, became a prominent leader in the Methodist Episcopal Church.

Isaac Long's Barn.

In 1767 William Otterbein, a German Reformed pastor, went to a "Great Meeting" in this barn, in Lancaster County, Pennsylvania. The preacher was Martin Boehm, a Mennonite farmer. Otterbein was so strongly impressed with the preaching that after the sermon he rushed forward and embraced Boehm, declaring, "We are brethren."

meeting was held on the threshing floor of Isaac Long's barn, now a historic United Methodist landmark. Contemporaries reported that God's presence in this ecumenical meeting was powerfully evident. Many were converted, and a sense of unity pervaded the gathering.

Otterbein was greatly moved by the fervent preaching of Martin Boehm. He was impressed with Boehm's theology and his emphasis on conversion—the principal theme of the association which Otterbein helped lead. When Boehm finished his sermon, and before he could resume his seat, Otterbein rushed forward to greet the dynamic Mennonite preacher. He embraced Boehm and in a loud voice declared, *"Wir sind Bruder"* ("We are brethren"). The touching scene deeply moved the congregation; some praised God

William Otterbein and Martin Boehm.

This picture of the co-founders of a new denomination for German-speaking Americans shows them in Isaac Long's barn, where they met and discovered their theological and spiritual kinship. Otterbein's declaration "We are brethren" found its way into the name of the new church—The Church of the United Brethren in Christ.

The Sunday following Boehm's religious conversion, he shared his experience with the congregation. Boldly, he called upon his listeners to repent and ask Christ to relieve them of the burden of sin. Many of those present burst into tears; some shouted joyfully; several were converted. When other Mennonite congregations heard of these happenings, they invited Boehm to preach in their churches, homes, and barns. He accepted these invitations, and his preaching spread a revival of religion throughout the Mennonite churches in his area and beyond.

People from miles away flocked to Boehm's "Great Meetings." They brought provisions with them because the meetings usually lasted two days. Preachers of different denominations attended these assemblies and exhorted the crowds to "trust in the Lord." Rural people took advantage of the opportunities to hear the gospel while also enjoying the social contacts with others of like mind. The Great Meetings were conducted in German, although some English-speaking Methodists attended as well.

An event of lasting significance took place in 1767 when William Otterbein attended one of Martin Boehm's Great Meetings. This particular aloud; and many broke into tears. This meeting marked the informal beginning of the United Brethren movement. Boehm and Otterbein became close friends, and later they worked together as co-founders of the Church of the United Brethren in Christ.

The contrasts between Boehm and Otterbein were almost humorous. Boehm wore plain Mennonite garments; Otterbein dressed in clerical attire. Boehm lacked formal education; Otterbein was a classically trained theologian. Boehm was a layman and a farmer; Otterbein was an ordained minister and pastor of a large and highly respected Reformed church. Boehm, small of stature and wearing a long beard, was of an unassuming appearance. Otterbein, tall and clean-shaven, was a man of impressive bearing. However, their denominational, educational, and cultural differences seemed insignificant in the light of their unity of spirit. Reports of Martin Boehm's work have survived in the writings of Francis Asbury, Christian Newcomer, Henry Spayth, and Martin's son Henry Boehm. Newcomer, an overnight guest in Mr. and Mrs. Boehm's home, related a touching account of the conversion of Boehm's son:

> *After family prayers, when we were just about to retire to bed, a son of Br. Boehm's, who lives about nine miles distant, arrived at the house of his parents. He had lately embraced religion, had found the pearl of great price, was yet in his first love, of course very happy, so much so, that he expressed himself in extacy [sic] of his enjoying heaven and the smiles of his Saviour and Redeemer here on earth. His mother, sister Boehm, was so rejoiced at the happiness of her youngest son, that she could not help shouting and praising God for the blessings; the father also got happy, and so we had a blessed time of it, till after midnight: glory to God;—O! that many children may be the cause of such joy to their parents.*

This youngest son in the family of eight children was Henry Boehm, who became a Methodist preacher and confidant of Bishop Francis Asbury. At the age of 91, Henry Boehm wrote his *Reminiscences*, a book that tells us about the life and times of his father, Martin. This book traces how the fellowship of united brothers and sisters grew into a movement and, finally, into a church.

Henry Boehm (1775-1875).

Henry Boehm's father was Martin Boehm, who with William Otterbein co-founded the United Brethren Church. His mother had become a Methodist, and the Boehm household often entertained Methodist preachers. Henry Boehm preached fluently both in English and German, and at Bishop Asbury's request Boehm supervised the translation of the Methodist *Discipline* into the German language. For five years he traveled with Asbury, visiting throughout the Methodist connection and preaching in German in about 14 states.

In his later years Boehm occupied major pulpits in Pennsylvania and New Jersey. His *Reminiscences* give sketches of numerous Methodist preachers as well as the story of the 1875 Methodist centennial celebration of his Newark Annual Conference. Even after he passed his one-hundredth birthday, he retained his intellectual powers. He continued to preach until a few days prior to his death.

The Founding of the Church of the United Brethren in Christ

Most denominations began as movements and gradually became organizations. Over the years, the followers of William Otterbein and Martin Boehm became increasingly aware that God had blessed their *Brudershaft* (brotherhood). God had used the movement to bring spiritual life to a large number of German Americans who for years had been nominal church members. No one knew how many people had attached themselves to this movement. It was clear, though, that some organization was needed if the movement was to continue. Otterbein and Boehm began to license preachers to work within the revival movement. The idea to form a new denomination developed gradually. It did not stem from a doctrinal revolt. Rather, the plan arose out of what the united brethren sensed was the leading of God's Spirit. From their viewpoint, they believed that they could best carry forward their evangelical work by establishing a new church. In 1800 about fourteen German preachers, associates of William Otterbein and Martin Boehm, gathered for a conference for the purpose of carrying forward a plan to start a new denomination. The conference was held in the home of Peter Kemp, about two miles west of Frederick City, Maryland. The assembled preachers agreed on the following resolution:

Resolved: that yearly a day shall be appointed when the unsectarian preachers shall assemble and counsel how they may conduct their office more and more according to the will of God and the mind of God that the Church of God may be built up, and sinners converted, so that God in Christ may be honored.

This conference marked the formal beginning of the United Brethren Church. The persistent theme of the church was "We are brethren," a motto reflecting the movement's denominational diversity. It included people from Mennonite, Lutheran, Tunker (Dunkard), Amish, and Reformed backgrounds.

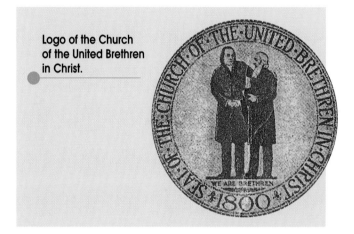

Logo of the Church of the United Brethren in Christ.

The preachers at the organizing conference of the Church of the United Brethren named Otterbein and Boehm their *Eldesten* (meaning superintendents or bishops). Henry Boehm, present at the meeting, later confirmed, "They elected bishops for the first time. William Otterbein and

Peter Kemp Home.

This residence was the site of the 1800 General Conference of the followers of William Otterbein and Martin Boehm. At this conference, the preachers organized themselves into a new denomination, the Church of the United Brethren in Christ.

83

Martin Boehm (my father) were unanimously chosen."

A year earlier the preachers had agreed on five doctrinal points:

- That the Father, Son, and Holy Spirit as Trinity "created heaven and earth and all that in them is, visible as well as invisible, and sustains, governs, protects, and supports the same."

- That Jesus Christ is "very God and man, Saviour and Redeemer of the whole world;

Pleasant Hill United Brethren Church.

This early UB Church was typical of the log meeting houses built by the early Church of the United Brethren in Christ.

that all men through him may be saved if they will."

- That the Holy Spirit "proceeds from the Father and the Son; that we through him must be sanctified and receive faith, thereby being cleansed from all filthiness of the flesh and spirit."

- That "the Bible is the word of God; that it contains the true way to our souls' well-being and salvation; that every true Christian is bound to acknowledge and receive it, with the influences of the Spirit of God, as his only rule and guide."

- That "the doctrine which the Holy Scriptures contain, namely, the fall in Adam and salvation through Jesus Christ, shall be

preached and proclaimed throughout the whole world."

The 1800 conference of preachers set as a requirement for membership an "inward spiritual experience." Also, at that conference the preachers reported to their peers on their "progress in the divine life, [and] their success and industry in the ministry." This practice continued in the yearly conferences.

At the time of the organization of the Church of the United Brethren, its leaders felt themselves compatible with the Methodists. Informal fellowship developed into conversations about possible union. Henry Spayth, a United Brethren preacher, wrote, "In the year 1808 commenced a friendly correspondence between the Methodist Episcopal Church and our Church…. This treaty, if we may so call it, of amity and friendship rested on the conviction…that a Christian people who had all the essential and important elements of our holy religion, in doctrine, in faith experience, and practice…should have some bond of union, some fraternal relations." Asbury, in turn, maintained fraternal relationships with the United Brethren. Referring to Otterbein, Bishop Asbury wrote, "There are very few with whom

Bonnet Schoolhouse.

This structure, located about one mile east of Mount Pleasant, Pennsylvania, was erected in 1810. In 1815 the first General Conference of the United Brethren Church met here. Nearly all the delegates at this conference had come into the ministry under the influence of William Otterbein, and they recognized and honored him for being the wise leader he truly was.

I can find so much unity and freedom in conversation as with him." The two men sometimes conferred about the work of their churches, and they remained confidants.

In 1815 representatives of the church's nine districts met for the first General Conference of the Church of the United Brethren. They held that conference in the historic Bonnet Schoolhouse, located near Mount Pleasant, Pennsylvania. This conference was the first to be held without Otterbein and Boehm because Boehm had died in 1812 and Otterbein in 1813. The 1815 conference needed to elect new bishops, and the preachers chose Christian Newcomer and Andrew Zeller. Henry Spayth recalled, "The conference agreed to humble themselves before God in prayer; and such a prayer-meeting your humble servant never witnessed before, nor since! Brethren, with streaming eyes, embraced and thanked God! From that hour to the end, unanimity and love smiled joyously on that assembly." When the conference dismissed, the church had two new bishops and a growing sense of denominational identity. With renewed vigor, the preachers fanned out to minister to the German-speaking Americans.

Christian Newcomer

Christian Newcomer became the most outstanding leader of the Church of the United Brethren during the nineteenth century. He was reared in a devout Mennonite home, but as a teenager he alternated between religious hope and despair. At the age of 21, he found a satisfying assurance of his salvation and thereafter enjoyed peace with God. In his journal, he described his experience:

> In a moment the peace of God and pardon of my sins was manifested to my soul, and the spirit of God bore witness with my spirit, that God for Jesus' sake had taken away the burden of my sins, and shed abroad his love in my poor unworthy heart.... If at the time I could have called a thousand lives my own, I would have pledged them all, every one of them, to testify to the certainty of my acceptance with God.

He soon sensed a call to preach, but a minister advised him that he might be misguided. This counselor felt uncomfortable with talk of dramatic conversions, so he distrusted Newcomer's ac-

Christian Newcomer (1749-1830).
No known portrait of Newcomer exists. Based on descriptions of his appearance, this drawing represents what he is thought to have looked like.

In 1771 Newcomer experienced a spiritual conversion and in 1777 began preaching. He soon became a friend of William Otterbein and Martin Boehm. Newcomer's abilities moved him into leadership in the movement led by Otterbein and Boehm. Following the deaths of Otterbein and Boehm, Newcomer became the senior leader in the United Brethren Church. In 1815, as a new bishop, he led in organizing the movement's first General Conference. That conference approved the printing of a Confession of Faith and a church *Discipline*. He traveled extensively throughout the conferences, and his influence dominated the first decades of the United Brethren Church.

Newcomer was an itinerant United Brethren bishop, spending over half a century as a travelling preacher and denominational leader. His *Journal* contains over 125 references to the Methodists, with whom he felt entirely comfortable. He often urged union with the Evangelical and Methodist Episcopal Churches. That dream was finally realized in 1968, one hundred and thirty-eight years after his death, when the Evangelical United Brethren and Methodist Churches united to form the United Methodist Church.

count of his Christian experience. The minister's counsel caused Newcomer to doubt his call to ministry, and he became discouraged.

Newcomer tells that while in this state of uncertainty, he met William Otterbein and other United Brethren preachers:

> I heard them preach in my own vicinity, their preaching making lasting impression on the hearts of their hearers. They insisted on the necessity of a genuine repentance and conversion to God, in the knowledge and pardon of

sins past. Their preaching appeared to be owned of God. Many were awakened from their sleep of sin and death, were brought from darkness to light…. These they formed into societies, and for the time being, were called by some, "Otterbein's people." Whereas, these men preached the same doctrine which I had experienced, and which, according to my views and discernment, perfectly agreed with the doctrine taught by Jesus Christ and his apostles; therefore, I associated myself with them, and joined their society, and was blessed.

After attending United Brethren meetings, Newcomer felt confirmed in his call to preach, and he entered the ministry. Thereafter, he maintained a steady course.

In 1815, Newcomer became the third bishop of the Church of the United Brethren in Christ (after Otterbein and Boehm). It is difficult to overestimate the importance of his influence during the early years of the developing church. At the time, a number of the early United Brethren preachers wanted a church without rules or regulations. In their view, liberty in Christ meant freedom from church laws. They preferred, as they stated, "the free and easy fellowship of unsectarian revivalism." Newcomer, however, understood the dangers of a church without stated doctrine and polity. Accordingly, he spoke forcibly in favor of adopting a church *Discipline*. Due to his inspired leadership, the General Conference of 1815 ordered the printing of a *Discipline*, which the preachers studied for two years. Then, in 1817 the General Conference voted to accept it as the law of the church. That conference ordered the publishing of the *Discipline* in German and English. It provided guidelines that enabled the Church of the United Brethren to maintain its unity and accomplish the work for which it gained national renown.

One of Newcomer's strengths was his administrative ability. He assumed the responsibility for organizing converts into classes and supervising the progress of the denomination. At the time he became a bishop, the new church very much needed leadership. Indeed, Bishop Asbury's main reservation about the early United Brethren Church had been its lack of organization. In 1803 Asbury had written, "There are now upwards of twenty German preachers somehow connected with Mr. Philip Otterbein and Martin Boehm; but they want authority, and the Church wants discipline." Christian Newcomer deserves credit for bringing stability and organization to his church. He possessed superior skills as a presiding bishop, and almost every preacher admired and respected him. His administrative work took him through large areas of Pennsylvania, Maryland, and Virginia.

Pfrimmer's Chapel.

John George Pfrimmer (1762-1825) was a minister in the United Brethren Church, and he played an important role in establishing his denomination in what is now the Midwest. Around 1808 he organized a congregation near Corydon, Indiana. The congregation built a log meetinghouse, the first United Brethren church constructed west of Ohio.

In this building Pfrimmer started the first Sunday school in the Church of the United Brethren. The United Brethren Board of Christian Education stated as its objective "that all persons be aware of God through his self disclosure … and that they respond in faith and love to the end that they may … grow as (children) of God rooted in the Christian community, love in the spirit of God in every relationship, fulfill their common discipleship in the world, and abide in Christian hope."

A series of entries in Newcomer's *Journal* give us insight into the way he lived and thought:

An uncommonly large congregation had this day collected; I preached [in German] with great liberty... I was followed by a brother in the English language; a vast number came to the Lord's table, and we had a melting time. At night I preached again at John Buck's; here we again had a soul-reviving meeting; nearly every person present melted into tears; some cried for mercy, others shouted and praised God.... This forenoon we held our Love-feast; we had truly a day of Pentecost: all the glory be to our God.... This forenoon the session of our Conference commenced; upwards of twenty preachers were present; poor unworthy me was elected their president [bishop]. The Conference continued until the 28th; all things were done in brotherly love, and the greatest unanimity prevailed throughout the session: bless the Lord, O my soul! For all his mercy.

Until the end of his life, Newcomer remained unflagging in his labors. When 61 years old, he developed a circuit that ran from his home in Maryland through West Virginia, across the southern part of Ohio, into Kentucky as far south as Lexington, to Louisville, into southern Indiana, through north central Ohio, to Pittsburgh, and back to his home. He rode this circuit nineteen times, continuing this travel until he reached eighty years of age. In addition to this long circuit, he covered three additional circuits several times a year, lodging in homes or sleeping on the ground. In addition to excelling as a bishop, he preached evangelistic messages, wrote on the subjects of doctrine and church order, and established ecumenical relationships with other Christians. His episcopal leadership was uncommonly effective among the courageous and hard-working United Brethren pioneer pastors.

Albright's People: The Evangelical Association

Parallel to the developments among the United Brethren, another movement was emerging among the German-speaking followers of Jacob Albright. Whereas several persons were active in the forma-

Jacob Albright (1759-1808).

Albright was the founder and first bishop of the Evangelical Association. He was the son of German immigrants and at the age of 17 served in the militia during the American Revolution. After the war he married and settled in Lancaster County, Pennsylvania. There he farmed and developed a profitable tile-making business. The deaths of several of his children caused him to conclude that God was punishing him for his spiritual indifference. After seeking spiritual counsel from William Otterbein and Martin Boehm, he was converted to Christ. Albright joined a Methodist class and soon began to hold evangelistic meetings. He preached in the German language, which he found more comfortable than English. Around 1800 he organized his converts into classes, patterned after the Methodist class meetings.

tion of the United Brethren Church, Jacob Albright was the sole early leader of the Evangelicals.

Jacob Albright's parents had immigrated from Germany to America in 1732, and Jacob was born here in 1759. Although his family was nominally Lutheran, he later reported that he was reared without significant religious influence or instruction: "We knew nothing of conversion; there was no trace of prayer-meetings, Bible study, family prayers, Sunday-schools or revivals. Hardly a show of godliness remained. The power thereof was outlawed as fanaticism. The salt had lost its savor." He married at the age of 20 and supported his family by manufacturing brick and tile from the high-quality clay deposits on his farm. He earned a reputation as "the honest brick-maker."

In 1790 an epidemic resulted in the deaths of several of his children. This tragedy caused him great anguish, and he began thinking seriously about religion. A preacher of the Reformed Church, Anton Haut, conducted the funerals of Albright's children, and Haut's messages deeply moved this grieving young father. Albright felt that he had come under conviction for his sins, and he began to pray earnestly. Through the help of a Christian friend, he came to a personal knowledge of Jesus Christ. He wrote of his conversion in glowing terms:

> In place of a worldly-minded spirit I was filled with a holy love for God and his word and for his true children. All depression of spirit was removed; sweet comfort and deep peace permeated my being; the Spirit of God witnessed that I was a child of God; one wave of joy after another swept over my soul and such ecstasy [sic] thrilled me as can not be described. In comparison with this all sinful pleasures and enjoyments were emptiness and vanity. My prayer was answered. My soul was filled with gratitude and praise to God, the Giver of every good and perfect gift.

Almost immediately after his conversion, he joined the Methodist Episcopal Church. Albright was especially attracted to Methodism because he admired its doctrine, discipline, worship, and spiritual vitality.

The Methodists soon granted Albright an exhorter's license, and later a local preacher's license. Albright carried a burden for the spiritual welfare of German-speaking Americans, whom the Methodists were not reaching in great numbers. He wrote:

> I frequently cast myself upon my knees and pleaded with hot tears that God might lead my German brethren to a knowledge of the truth as it is in Jesus, and might send them faithful leaders, who should preach to them the gospel in power, awaken lifeless professors of religion, and lead them to a life of true godliness, so that they might be made partakers of the peace of God and of the inheritance of the saints in light. Thus I prayed daily.

In 1796 Albright began preaching among his neighbors. He emphasized the need for repentance and the possibility of receiving the assurance of a personal religious conversion to Jesus Christ. This message brought tears of joy to many of his hearers because many of the ministers in their churches insisted that claims to a sure knowledge of salvation were presumptive, or even prideful.

Albright also stressed the importance of disciplined living. He preached that formal religion consisting only of outward ceremonies was powerless to bring salvation. "We must place complete trust in Christ alone, if we would be saved," he cried. Albright's effective preaching earned him a wide reputation as a gifted evangelist. He preached out-of-doors as well as in barns, market places, private homes, and churches. Multitudes flocked to hear him, and his sermons led many to Christ.

Albright's preaching stirred up opposition among certain nominal church members. His detractors slandered and even beat him. On a few occasions small gangs almost killed him. This opposition did not deter him, and he kept preaching in local churches and at the Great Meetings, where large crowds gathered.

In the meantime, Methodism's leaders believed that the use of the German language would soon cease in America, and they continued to direct

The first preacher's license of the Evangelical Association.

The translation of this license reads, "Upon the authority of the Newly-Formed Methodist Conference, which has given John Dreisbach a good testimony, and is willing to receive him as a minister into our association; I the undersigned, give him the permission to serve in the office according to our regulation, and he is also appointed thereto, as a preacher for one year on trial, if he conducts himself as is meet according to the Word of God. Jacob Albright, November 14, 1807."

Albright Memorial Chapel.

This Evangelical Church shrine memorializes Jacob Albright, the founder of the Evangelical Church. It is located near Kleinfeltersville, Pennsylvania. In 1808 Albright became seriously ill in Harrisburg, and he headed home on his horse. He reached the home of George Becker in Muehlbach, some 20 miles from where he lived. He died there, and the Becker family buried him in the family cemetery. This memorial church stands in Albright's memory.

attention to those who spoke English. Albright, however, sensed a divine call into a different harvest field—a ministry to the German Americans. Still, the principles of Methodism remained with Albright and the church he was to found.

In 1803 Albright and his assistants gathered for a meeting that marked the beginning of a new denomination. At this conference Albright's followers pronounced themselves an independent ecclesiastical organization. They adopted the Bible as their rule of faith, and the preachers ordained Albright as their chief elder. The denomination adopted the position that the church should consist only of committed Christians. "Seekers" could join only after a conversion experience. During the next few years, with Albright appointing the preachers to their rounds, the new church grew steadily.

In 1807 Albright's people held their first annual preachers' meeting. At that time, the twenty-eight Christian workers adopted the name "The Newly Formed Methodist Conference." The preachers bestowed on Albright the title of superintendent, or bishop, with the authority to ordain. The preachers rejected the theory that only a bishop had the authority to ordain. They believed that so long as they were faithful to "the doctrines and fellowship of the apostles," they had a right to claim ordination. Because they saw no need to secure a bishop to ordain Jacob Albright, they ordained him.

Following the 1807 conference, Albright's health began to decline rapidly, and he realized that he had only a short time to live. Five months later, on Easter Sunday in 1808, Albright attended his last conference. He assigned the preachers to their circuits and bade them farewell. His parting advice to his preachers has been preserved:

> In all that you do, or think of doing, let your object be to promote the glory of God and the operation of his grace, as well in your own hearts as among your brethren and sisters, and be faithful co-workers with them in the manner which God has shown you, in which endeavor he will also give you his blessing."

Jacob Albright died in the home of George Becker, at Muehlbach, Pennsylvania, May 18, 1808. He was forty-nine years old. Reports tell that his death scene was radiant with the presence of God. A large number of Christians attended his funeral, which was the occasion of the conversion of many. A simple marble slab marked Albright's grave, and later a small church was built at the site.

In 1816 the preachers met for an important annual conference and elected a new bishop—John Seybert. The men met in a barn in Union County, Pennsylvania, and adopted the name "The Evangelical Association." For doctrinal standards, the preachers approved a German translation of the Methodist Articles of Religion, with the addition of an article on the Last Judgment. They also voted to compile a collection

Eyler's Valley Chapel.

This United Brethren church, built in 1857, illustrates the growing trend of the nineteenth-century Methodists, United Brethren, and Evangelical Churches to build churches with towers and bells. However, during this building time, some church leaders frowned on the trend to build more and more elaborate structures.

The Evangelical Church, St. Paul, Minnesota.

Toward the end of the nineteenth century the Evangelical, United Brethren, and Methodist Churches built large and imposing cathedrals, in contrast to the simple and undecorated log, frame, brick, and stone structures of earlier times. In 1871 the conservative *Evangelical Messenger* objected to building elaborate edifices. "Colored windows… affect the nervous system most painfully and induce an almost intolerable headache during public worship, to say nothing of the dreariness and gloom spread over the whole audience room."

of hymns. At that conference, the Evangelical Association considered uniting with the Church of the United Brethren, and delegates from the Association arranged a "social meeting" with delegates from the United Brethren Church. Merger talks, however, did not result in union. The merger of these two churches would not take place until 1946.

John Seybert

After Albright's death, John Seybert, the church's second bishop, assumed the leadership role in the Evangelical Association. Seybert was not outwardly impressive: he lacked superior oratorical skills, he wore plain, sometimes threadbare, clothing; his manner was modest and retiring. He had no desire for power or recognition. Yet his colleagues saw him as a person of intelligence, constancy, executive ability, humility, and spiritual maturity. At the time of his election as bishop, he wrote in his journal, "I felt disposed to submit myself to God and to my brethren, and formed the determination to serve the church in the faithful performance of the important duties of the office, and to labor for the glory of God and the welfare of my fellow pilgrims to eternity."

As bishop, Seybert traveled almost continuously. In 1841 he reached South Bend, Indiana, and his horse became deathly sick. Seybert led the animal to a grove outside the city and tried unsuccessfully to revive it. There was no hope that the now prostrate horse could be saved. The bishop dropped to his knees, and with upturned face he tearfully pleaded with God to restore his horse. Seybert concluded his prayer, "Thou hast often helped me in marvelous ways, and Thou canst help me also in this time of need." On arising, he looked toward his horse; the animal was on its feet, grazing quietly as though it had not been ill. Bishop Seybert led his horse back to the city, fed it, and soon resumed travel.

In 1842 he wrote in his diary:

> O God! What shall I render unto Thee, or what offering shall I bring, for all the goodness which Thou hast shown me! Thou hast caused me to experience Thy great love, all the years, months, weeks, days, hours, minutes and seconds of my life. O God! I am pained at

John Seybert (1791-1860).
John Sartain of Philadelphia created this engraving.

Seybert was the second bishop of the Evangelical Association. He had a strong interest in reaching German-speaking Americans with the Gospel. Accordingly, he traveled extensively from Pennsylvania to the Rocky Mountains and into Canada. A tireless worker, he freely expended his time, energy, and money to supply the western settlements with Christian literature in the German language. Seybert's diaries reveal that he traveled 175,000 miles by horseback and one-horse wagon, making over 46,000 pastoral visits and distributing thousands of books from the Evangelical Publishing House.

the thought of having done so little for Thy glory and for Thy kingdom. Oh, give grace and strength that I may dedicate my future life wholly to Thee, and that I may spend all my future days joyfully in Thy service, through Jesus Christ. Amen.

Bishop Seybert preached sermons designed to convert the unbelievers and help believers grow in holiness. He made it a practice to speak well of others. In one of his sermons he spoke about the sin of slander:

The slanderer has three swords on his tongue, with which he kills three persons with one stroke, namely himself, the one whom he slanders, and the one who listens attentively to his words. Sometimes slanderers do not even let the dead alone. Lying and murder are inseparable, and Jesus says of the devil, that he is a liar and a murderer from the beginning. The slanderer is no better. For one thing he has the devil's nature and disposition, and then he is a tool of the devil. Nobody is safe from the devil, and much less from the slanderer's tongue. No one can tame the devil, neither can the backbiter's tongue be tamed, which is set on fire of hell. Consider this, you who speak bold lies against your neighbor.
You are a devil.

Once, a congregation of only three people came to hear him. At first, he did not want to preach to such a small number. Then, on reflection, he prayed for forgiveness for his reluctance. He preached to the small assembly with "excellent results." Once, a prominent citizen came to one of Seybert's meetings, intending to start a fight. Seybert wrote that God enabled him to preach with such liberty on the love of God in Christ that "our moral persecutor was struck by the Word of the Lord and began to melt like wax [until he] fell upon his knees in great distress of soul." Seybert, a lifelong bachelor, served his church from 1820 to 1860, and during those forty years he gave of himself sacrificially. His eighteen-volume diary reveals that he traveled on horseback and by one-horse wagon over 170,000 miles, preached almost 9,900 sermons, made approximately 46,000 pastoral visits, held about 8,000 prayer and class meetings, and visited at least 10,000 sick people. Always, he carried books and literature in German, which he shared with settlers along the way. Under his leadership, the church grew from one to eight conferences. Toward the end of his life, he said, "My time is short, and I want to improve it as well as possible, and I guess God will help me through." Malaria and the toils of travel took their toll. Seybert died away from his home and was buried on his circuit.

The Evangelical United Brethren Church

The doctrines and aims of the United Brethren and the Evangelicals were compatible. From the start both denominations had similar missions, and each was strongly influenced by Methodist spirit, doctrine, and practice. Throughout the

First United Brethren Church, Johnstown, Pennsylvania, 1946.

In 1946 the United Brethren Church and the Evangelical Church merged their separate denominations to form the Evangelical United Brethren Church. In this building the United Brethren delegates met and approved the union. Concurrently, a few blocks distant, the delegates of the Evangelical Church also met to consider the proposed merger. After each conference approved the merger, the delegates met in what is now the First United Methodist Church in Johnstown to seal the merger of these two churches.

Bishop Stamm and Bishop Clippinger, representing the two communions, shook hands as a symbol of the unity of the new church.

In 1968, the Evangelical United Brethren Church united with the Methodist Church to form the United Methodist Church. The EUB Confession of Faith continued as a standard of doctrine for the new church, alongside Methodism's Articles of Religion and John Wesley's *Sermons* and *Notes Upon the New Testament*. This merger brought together three great traditions that had sustained fraternal relationships from the latter third of the eighteenth century.

Both the United Brethren and Evangelical Churches were born in rural Pennsylvania among German Americans. The heritage of these churches flowed out of the simple yet profound faith of ardent seekers after God. The preachers and lay people were humble Christians, for the most part without wealth or position. Those who helped make their church such a powerful spiritual force had turned their backs on the ways of the world to serve God with a full will. They were persons of integrity, and the holiness of their lives imparted to them the compelling strength of quiet power. God honored their faith and obedience—and they left a lasting legacy.

It is natural that outward strategies and institutional forms can and should change. Successive generations develop new wineskins for the dynamic wine of truth. Yet core values remain. The Evangelical United Brethren legacy continues to remind us of the importance of biblical authority, human worth, salvation by grace through faith, and the application of religion to the social context. These values abide as a permanent heritage that neither begins nor ends with any Christian denomination or historical context.

nineteenth century and the first half of the twentieth century, delegates of the Evangelical Church and the United Brethren Church came together periodically to talk about a possible merger. In 1926 United Brethren Bishop William Bell proposed that the two Churches begin working on a plan of union. In 1934 both churches officially declared their desire to merge the two denominations. By 1942 a Basis of Union plan was ready. The proposed name for the new denomination was the Evangelical United Brethren Church. The merger of the two churches occurred on November 16, 1946.

This historic union took place in the First United Brethren Church in Johnstown, Pennsylvania. Delegates packed into the church at 9:00 AM. Those present reported that the atmosphere was optimistic and glowing. Evangelical Church Bishop John S. Stamm and United Brethren Bishop Arthur R. Clippinger led the delegates in the union ceremony. The delegates confirmed the merger of the two Churches by singing "Blest Be the Tie That Binds," and all shared in the sacrament of Holy Communion.

Uniting Conference Logo.

On April 23, 1968, in Dallas, Texas, the Evangelical United Brethren and Methodist Churches united to form the United Methodist Church. At the climax of the service EUB Bishop Reuben H. Mueller and Methodist Bishop Lloyd C. Wicke declared, "Lord of the Church, we are united in Thee, in Thy Church, and now in The United Methodist Church." This union of churches resulted from merger conversations between these two denominations that from their beginnings had similarities in doctrine, ethos, and mission.

7 Methodism and the Black Experience

During John Wesley's sojourn in America in the 1730s, he saw firsthand the evils of slavery. Thereafter, he vigorously opposed all forms of human bondage. He was among the first in England publicly to denounce slavery, a practice he described as "that execrable sum of all villainies." Wesley took the view that God will judge slave owners for the monstrous crime of enslaving others. He declared forthrightly that it was every person's duty to free his or her slaves and that holding others in slavery would result in the loss of one's soul. Methodism's *General Rules of the United Societies* clearly forbade "the buying or selling the bodies and souls of men, women, and children, with an intention to enslave them."

In 1774 John Wesley published a tract, *Thoughts Upon Slavery*, in which he wrote, "Give liberty to whom liberty is due, that is, to every child of man, to every partaker of human nature. Let none serve you but by his own act and deed, by his own voluntary choice." One week before his death, Wesley penned an elegant letter to British parliamentarian William Wilberforce, urging him to continue his work to abolish slavery: "O be not weary of well doing! Go on, in the name of God and in the power of his might, till even American slavery (the vilest that ever saw the sun) shall vanish away before it."

The early Methodists in America continued Wesley's anti-slavery stance. Robert Strawbridge's first Methodist society in Maryland contained African-American charter members. In New York black worshipers belonged to Philip Embury's first

John Wesley. *In 1789 John Wesley sat for a portrait by George Romney. This painting has been regarded as the best of Wesley in his later years. The original painting hangs in the Great Hall of Christ Church College, Oxford.*

In 1774 John Wesley wrote a tract, *Thoughts Upon Slavery,* which had a wide circulation in England and America. Wesley declared, "I absolutely deny all slave-holding to be consistent with any degree of natural justice, mercy, and truth.... Liberty is the right of every human creature."

Throughout his long ministry, John Wesley remained active in the antislavery campaign in England, speaking against slavery and supporting lawmakers who opposed this great evil. Following the sentiments of Wesley's *Thoughts Upon Slavery*, eighteenth-century American Methodists considered it an act of honor and a demonstration of virtue for slaveholders who became Christians to free their slaves. However, early in the nineteenth century Methodism began to relax its opposition against slavery to "avoid controversy" and "to keep the peace of the church."

Methodist society. In 1768 Thomas Taylor wrote John Wesley to inform him of a new Methodist society on Long Island: "Within six months, about twenty-four persons received justifying grace. Near half of them whites, the rest Negroes." As Methodism spread to Philadelphia and beyond, the number of black class members equaled or exceeded that of white members.

The journals of Joseph Pilmore and Francis Asbury contain references to black Christians in the Methodist societies. Pilmore's journal, for instance, states, "I met the Negroes apart, and found many of them very happy. God has wrought a most glorious work in many of their souls, and made them witnesses that He is no respecter of persons." In 1813 Asbury reported on a camp meeting which attracted 3,000 people. He wrote, "The poor Africans, abandoned by all sects to us, were greatly engaged."

Methodism's Appeal to African-Americans

It is clear from the records that Methodism held an especially strong attraction for America's black community, whether free or slave. The Methodist message was one of hope for all people—especially the poor, disadvantaged, and enslaved. For those who saw no real hope for better circumstances in this life, God's promise that his children would someday rule and reign with Christ gave slaves comfort for the present and hope for the future. Black worshipers thrilled to the Methodist message that "Whosoever will, may come." Methodism's enthusiastic worship services offered an exhilarating contrast to the dreary lives the slaves endured. The Methodists clapped their hands, shouted for joy, and expressed exuberant worship. They welcomed black worshipers as fellow citizens in the kingdom of God. Membership in Methodism's societies was not dependent on material means, social status, or race.

The early Methodist Episcopal Church appointed black class leaders and licensed black preachers. These Methodist preachers included Harry Hosier, traveling companion to Bishop Asbury; John Stewart, missionary to the Wyandott Indians; and Henry Evans, a brilliant speaker and organizer. John Thompson, a southern slave, wrote that Methodism "brought glad tidings to the poor bondsman; it bound up the broken-hearted; it opened the prison doors to them that were bound, and let the captive go free. As soon as it got among the slaves, it spread from plantation to plantation, until it reached ours, where there were but few who did not experience religion."

Methodism's first two bishops, Francis Asbury and Thomas Coke, worked to abolish slavery in America. Asbury visited President George Washington and the Governor of North Carolina to plead for the end of slavery. Asbury also petitioned the legislature of Virginia to stop the slave trade. The first *Discipline* of the Church stated, "We view it [slavery] as contrary to the Golden Law of God.... We think it our bounden duty, to take immediately some effectual method to extirpate this Abomination from among us." The

Harry Hosier (c. 1750-1805). *This photograph appears with the permission of the Arthur J. Moore Museum, St. Simons Island, Georgia.*

Hosier was an itinerant traveling companion of Bishop Francis Asbury. Many contemporaries considered Hosier to be one of the best preachers in America. With Richard Allen, Harry Hosier helped found Zoar AME Church in Philadelphia, the first black Methodist church in America.

first *Discipline* asked, "What shall be done with those who buy or sell Slaves, or give them away?... They are immediately to be expelled; unless they buy them on purpose to free them."

This policy, however, was difficult to implement. During the 1780s, slaves were worth £30-£40 each, and emancipation was costly for slaveholders. A number of Methodists convinced themselves that kindness toward their slaves was a satisfactory substitute for granting them freedom.

The Specter of Racial Prejudice

Despite the anti-slavery position of America's churches, the mood of the nation was to segregate whites and blacks. Mobs railed against Bishops Asbury and Coke for preaching emancipation; angry people threatened them with clubs. Eli Whitney's invention of the cotton gin in 1792

William Capers (1790-1855).

Capers founded the Methodist Episcopal Church's mission to slaves and served as the mission's superintendent. He also ministered as a presiding elder, professor, and editor in the ME Church. Capers was a member of the General Conference of 1844, which divided Methodism into northern and southern branches. At its first General Conference in 1845 the MEC, South, elected William Capers a bishop. As bishop, Capers labored diligently and effectively, supporting evangelism among the slaves.

made cotton growing highly profitable, increasing the demand for slaves to work the plantations. Also, landowners needed slaves to cultivate and harvest southern indigo plants that produced a highly prized blue dye used in the manufacture of clothing.

As the years unfolded, some Methodists began buying slaves to work their land. Also, the specter of segregation began to surface in Methodist societies. As early as 1772, Joseph Pilmore reported that the white members of a Methodist congregation "appointed men to stand at the doors to keep all the Negroes out until the white persons were in." In the 1780s Methodist congregations began to install balconies to accommodate people of color. Voices within the church began to challenge Methodism's official stand against buying and selling slaves. Despite its admirable beginnings, the church began backing away from its strict opposition to slavery.

In 1808 a turning point came when Methodism's 1808 General Conference Committee on Slavery reported, "We deem it improper further to agitate the subject." The General Conference struck out of the *Discipline* the prohibition against buying and selling slaves. Annual Conferences were instructed to form their own regulations regarding the issue of slavery.

The Bishops' Pastoral Address to the 1808 General Conference exhorted the church "to abstain from all abolition movements and associations." The reason for this admonition was fivefold: (1) Some of the abolitionist groups lacked a religious base. (2) Many abolitionists stridently demanded the immediate release of every slave in America, ignoring the social chaos that would

follow. (3) Concern for states' rights created opposition to passing federal slave laws that limited the sovereignty of the states. (4) Abolitionism was threatening to divide the church. (5) A growing number of Methodists wanted to own slaves because they were economically profitable. Some within the church went so far as to defend slavery as a social good. Many of the ministers who opposed slavery did not stand against it because they wished "to keep peace in the church."

The growing controversy about slavery eventually led to the formation of three major black Methodist denominations: (1) In 1816, the African Methodist Episcopal Church (AME) formed in Philadelphia. (2) In 1820, the African Methodist Episcopal Zion Church (AMEZ) formed in New York City. (3) In 1870, the Colored Methodist Episcopal Church (CME) [now the Christian Methodist Episcopal Church] formed in Jackson, Tennessee.

THE AFRICAN METHODIST EPISCOPICAL CHURCH

The first black denomination in America began in Philadelphia under the leadership of Richard Allen. The occasion for starting this new church was the tension that developed between the black and white members of Philadelphia's St. George's Church. There, on April 12, 1787, the congregation's black members met to protest slavery and discuss the discrimination they experienced at the worship services. This meeting set in motion a chain of events that led eventually to the official formation of the African Methodist Episcopal Church.

Richard Allen

Richard Allen was converted to Christ under the ministry of Freeborn Garrettson. Describing this experience, Allen wrote,

> I was awakened and brought to see myself, poor, wretched and undone, and without the mercy of God must be lost.... I cried unto Him who delighted to hear the prayers of a poor sinner, and all of a sudden my dungeon shook, my chains flew off, and glory to God, I cried.

Soon after his conversion, he joined St. George's Methodist Episcopal Church.

Allen's owner permitted him to work at an extra job for pay. With the money he earned for

Richard Allen (1760-1831).

At the age of seventeen Richard Allen was converted to Christ and joined a Methodist society. When he was twenty-two years old, he became a local preacher, and under the supervision of Bishop Francis Asbury, Allen began to travel widely in a preaching ministry. Growing tensions between black and white Methodists in Philadelphia and elsewhere led Allen in 1816 to organize sixteen black Methodist congregations into a new denomination—the African Methodist Episcopal Church. The organizing conference elected Allen its first bishop, and he led the church until his death fifteen years later.

this work, Allen purchased his freedom. In 1783, six years after his conversion, he began to preach, and his speaking and leadership skills soon became apparent. St. George's Church granted him a license to preach and gave him regular preaching assignments. By his own initiative, he expanded his ministry, preaching where and when he could. He wrote, "I frequently preached twice a day, at 5 o'clock in the morning and in the evening, and it was not uncommon for me to preach from four to five times a day." Allen enjoyed such respect as a Methodist preacher that he and Harry Hosier, a black traveling companion of Francis Asbury, were both invited to attend the 1784 Christmas Conference.

In 1787 Richard Allen and Absalom Jones helped found the Free African Society, the first black organization in America established to improve the circumstances of African Americans. Allen's religious and civic leadership drew criticism from some of the white members of St. George's Church. In addition, these members were disturbed that the congregation's black members outnumbered the whites. In 1786 a group of white members persuaded the congregation to require black worshipers to sit near the walls of the sanctuary, occupy back seats, and commune last at the Lord's Table. Eventually, the church constructed a balcony for persons of color, excluding them from the main floor of the sanctuary.

In the meantime, Allen had organized 42 of the church's black members into a class meeting. They sat together in the balcony during worship services at St. George's Church and also held separate prayer meetings and class meetings. On a Sunday morning in November 1787, Richard Allen, Absalom Jones, and other black worshipers arrived at St. George's Church after the singing had already started. The sexton directed these worshipers to the gallery. Before they could ascend the steps, the minister began the congregational prayer.

Allen recorded what happened next:

> We had not been long upon our knees before I heard considerable scuffling and low talking. I raised my head up and saw one of the trustees, H—M—, having hold of the Rev. Absalom Jones, pulling him up off of his knees, and saying, "You must get up—you must not kneel here." Mr. Jones replied, "Wait until prayer is over." Mr. H—M— said "No, you must get up now, or I will call for aid and force you away." Mr. Jones said, "Wait until prayer is over, and I will get up and trouble you no more." With that he beckoned to one of the other trustees, Mr. L—S—to come to his assistance. He came, and went to William White to pull him up. By this time prayer was over, and we all went out of the church in a body, and they were no more plagued with us in the church.

Allen maintained a charitable spirit toward the white members who treated him unfairly. He devoted himself to shepherding his flock, and it grew into what amounted to a new Methodist congregation.

Allen wrote that a few white preachers tried to undermine his work:

[They were] much opposed to an African church, and used very degrading and insulting language to us, to try and prevent us from going on. We all belonged to St. George's church.... We felt ourselves much cramped; but my dear Lord was with us, and we believed, if it was his will, the work would go on, and that we would be able to succeed in building the house of the Lord. We established prayer meetings and meetings of exhortation, and the Lord blessed our endeavors, and many souls were awakened; but the elder soon forbid us holding any such meetings; but we viewed the forlorn state of our colored brethren, and that they were destitute of a place of worship.

Allen remained steadfast in his purpose and maintained a gentle spirit, answering hostile charges with soft replies. He wrote, "We were filled with fresh vigor to get a house erected to worship God in."

Shortly after walking out of St. George's Church, Allen and his followers made plans to secure their own meetinghouse. In 1793, Allen used his own money to buy an abandoned blacksmith shop for $35, and with a team of ten horses, he moved it to a lot he had purchased with his own money. This building became the new congregation's place of worship. Allen and his followers drafted a declaration of their reasons for establishing their own chapel:

Whereas, from time to time, many inconveniences have arisen from white people and people of color mixing together in public assemblies, more particularly in places of public worship, we have thought it necessary to provide for ourselves a convenient house to assemble in separate from our white brethren.

Bishop Asbury supported Allen and his followers in their work to secure their own building. He and John Dickins, pastor at St. George's Church, helped the congregation dedicate its new house of worship. Dickins prayed that the building might become "a Bethel to the gathering in of

Jarena Lee (1783-1850).
This portrait was painted in 1844, and it shows Mrs. Lee at the age of sixty.

In the beginning, there were more women than men in the AME Church. The denomination, however, did not ordain women. A few women did have public ministries, despite their not being permitted to serve in leadership positions. Black preachers such as Jarena Lee, Zilpha Elaw, and Julia A. Foote stood out as examples of women who were highly effective speakers.

Lee was converted under the preaching of Richard Allen, and she became the first female preacher in the AME Church. Her journal, published in 1849, tells of her conversion: "That day was the first when my heart had believed and my tongue had made confession unto salvation. The first words uttered, a part of that song which shall fill eternity with its sound, was 'Glory to God!' For a few moments, I had power to exhort sinners and to tell of the wonders and of the goodness of him who had clothed me with his salvation."

Although Bishop Richard Allen would not ordain Jarena Lee, he permitted her to hold prayer meetings and to exhort as she "found liberty." Her journal tells that her exhortations won a great number of men and women to Jesus Christ.

thousands of souls." This prayer inspired the name of the building—Bethel Church. In 1794 Asbury ordained Allen a deacon, and in 1799 Allen became an elder, making him the first person of color to receive ordination in the Methodist Episcopal Church.

At the time of Bethel Church's beginning, it was under the administration of St. George's Church. Allen's congregation even accepted a white pastor, because Allen was not yet ordained. However, disputes over salary and oversight increased the tension between the Bethel congregation and the parent church. Dissatisfaction with white supervision prompted Allen to sue through the Pennsylvania courts to procure Bethel Church's legal autonomy. In 1816 Bethel Church gained its independence, and its official relationship with the Methodist Episcopal Church ended.

Daniel Coker

Daniel Coker, a colleague of Richard Allen, was an important co-leader in the rise of the AME Church. Because he was permitted to attend school as a companion to his master's son, he acquired an education, which he improved throughout his lifetime. As a young man he experienced Christian conversion and soon began to teach and preach. In time, Coker gained the confidence and bravery to run away from his master. He fled to Baltimore where a Methodist preacher purchased his freedom. Coker joined a Methodist church in Baltimore and successfully taught classes for black students.

In Baltimore, toward the end of the 18th century, relationships between the races had become seriously strained. These tensions affected Baltimore Methodism, causing the leadership at Lovely Lane and Strawberry Alley ME churches to rule that persons of color must sit in galleries and receive communion after white members had been served. In response to these decisions, Coker led the black Methodists in starting separate worship services in these churches, at times when the whites were not meeting.

Concurrently, other black Methodists in the Middle Atlantic States met with frustrations similar to those encountered by Allen's followers in Philadelphia and Coker's followers in Baltimore. They were also breaking away from Methodist churches and establishing independent congregations. In 1816 Richard Allen invited all the black Methodist congregations to send delegates to Philadelphia for a general convention of black Methodists. Many black congregations responded to the invitation and sent delegates. At one of the sessions, Stephen Hill moved that the churches represented by the assembled delegates "become one body under the name and style of the African Methodist Episcopal Church." The convention approved Hill's motion, and he deserves credit for the name of the new denomination—the African Methodist Episcopal Church.

Daniel Coker (dates uncertain).

Coker was converted under the ministry of Robert Strawbridge, and became his protégé. Later, Bishop Francis Asbury ordained Coker, who became an effective preacher in the Methodist Episcopal Church. Coker gained the benefits of education, and in 1810 he wrote a piece titled "Dialogue between a Virginian and an African Minister." Under Coker's leadership the black Methodists of Baltimore joined with Richard Allen in forming the African Methodist Episcopal Church.

In the early nineteenth century, the intellectually gifted Coker took his place as a leader in the AME Church. Daniel A. Payne, the renowned AME bishop, evaluated Coker as "a man of uncommon talent, (who) possessed more information on all subjects than usually fell to the lot of colored men of his day. Those living who had the happiness of hearing him, inform us that he was a powerful and eloquent preacher. It was through his counsel that our people withdrew from the ME Church. He was not only their leader in this great movement, but also their able and successful defender against the slanderous attacks of their enemies." Coker also served as a missionary, and in 1820 he organized the first AME churches in Liberia and Sierra Leone.

The new AME Church adopted the Methodist Episcopal Church's Articles of Religion and General Rules and elected Richard Allen its first bishop. Allen, a former slave, was now a bishop of a new denomination. Similarly, seven of the first eight bishops of the AME Church had been slaves. To witness to their non-militant spirit, the conference participants adopted the maxim, "God our Father, Christ our Redeemer, Man our Brother." This motto is presently inscribed over the front of the sanctuary of Mother Bethel AME Church in Philadelphia.

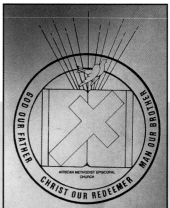

First Seal of the AME Church.

In 1856 the African Methodist Episcopal Church authorized Bishop Daniel Payne to order a seal for the church. The resulting design was a prominent view of an open Bible and the cross of Christ. From the Bible radiates the light of God; the dove represents the Holy Spirit. On the border of the seal is the maxim "God our Father, Christ our Redeemer, Man our Brother."

Morris Brown (1770-1849).

Brown became the second bishop of the African Methodist Episcopal Church. He assisted Richard Allen at Bethel Church, Philadelphia, and was also instrumental in establishing the AME Church in the West and in Canada. Bishop Brown lacked even a primary education, and he was not noted as an eloquent speaker. Yet his ministry was effective and far-reaching as he worked tirelessly in the cause of Christ. Brown traversed vast territories on horseback and planted his church as far west as the Mississippi River.

In a sermon preached in 1844, Brown exhorted, "Don't deceive yourselves as you may deceive others, but be honest before God. And you, my brethren in the ministry, set a good example before the people. Oh, that God would let these few broken remarks rest upon your hearts, and bring us all to heaven, for Christ's sake." A line from Morris Brown's obituary reads, "As a Bishop in the AME Church, he endured much hardship, privation and suffering in the discharge of his itinerant duties over thirteen states in the union, pursuing a course of conduct which was entirely free from arrogance, pride and tyranny, accomplishing much good in the cause of the Redeemer."

Daniel Alexander Payne (1811-1893).

Payne was a renowned African Methodist Episcopal bishop and educator who gave invaluable leadership to his church. He became an AME elder in 1843 and was the earliest advocate of an educated AME ministry. In 1852 the AME Church elected him bishop. As the first historian of his church, he wrote one of the first histories of American black people, *History of the AME Church* (1891). Payne also wrote and published poetry.

As a bishop, he served the longest tenure in his church—41 years. He organized three Annual Conferences (New England, 1852; Missouri, 1855; Kentucky, 1868). Following the Civil War, Payne was instrumental in planting his church in southern states. He declared that the AME Church was a "refuge for the hated race." In a venture of historic significance, Payne negotiated his church's purchase of Wilberforce University in Ohio in 1863. At the time Payne took charge of Wilberforce University, most other schools in Ohio (with the exception of Oberlin College and two or three others) denied admission to black students. Wilberforce University became the first institution of higher education in the world founded by persons of color, and Payne became the first black person to be elected a college president.

"Father" Peter Spencer (1782-1843).

Spencer's teachings and example did much to further the well-being of the black community. In a day when most African Americans were poor, Spencer bought property, established a home, and operated a successful business. He advised the people to pay their debts, deal fairly with everyone, support fellow black Christians in business, and practice the virtues of industry and thrift. Spencer, a contemporary of Richard Allen, chose not to join the African Methodist Episcopal Church. Instead, Spencer founded the African Union Methodist Protestant Church.

Following his death, the *Delaware State Journal* paid tribute to his life and ministry in the following notice: "Few persons vested with the authority which he held would have walked so humbly and exercised so tender and liberal a sway over those under his direction. He was influential yet not proud; he was powerful but not dictatorial or tyrannical; he was wise, kind, and parental; giving his superior energies to the amelioration of his associates and the advancement of his church."

Today, the declared mission of the AME Church is "to find and save the lost and to serve those in need through preaching, caring for the needy, sick, and elderly, and encourage economic advancement." The denomination is committed to missions and to providing education for its members. The church sponsors seven colleges and universities and two seminaries. Over thirty percent of the church's congregations sponsor local housing, schools, and facilities for the aged.

After the Civil War, the membership of the AME Church exploded dramatically. Between 1866 and 1876 the church grew from 70,000 to 391,000. Today, the AME Church has more than 8,000 churches worldwide and more than 3,500,000 members. The basic requirement for membership in the church is "saving faith in the Lord Jesus Christ."

Present day Mother Bethel African Methodist Episcopal Church in Philadelphia.

This building is the fourth house of worship for Mother Bethel Church, and it is the successor to the original wooden blacksmith shop that Richard Allen moved to this site with a team of ten horses.

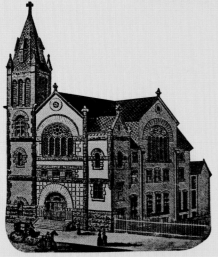

Mother Bethel AME Church, Philadelphia, former building.

In 1916 the AME Church General Conference met in this church, called "Mother Bethel," to celebrate the centennial of the founding of the AME Church.

Wilberforce University.

Wilberforce University traces its beginnings to 1847 when the Ohio Conference of the Methodist Episcopal Church established Union Seminary. In 1856, the Cincinnati Conference of the ME Church opened Wilberforce University in Xenia, Ohio, for the education of black men and women. In 1862 AME Bishop Daniel A. Payne arranged for his denomination to purchase these two schools. Union Seminary merged with Wilberforce to become a strong school under the administration of African Americans. Wilberforce University was the first institution of higher education in the world founded by African Americans.

THE AFRICAN METHODIST EPISCOPAL ZION CHURCH

By the end of the eighteenth century, the subject of slavery fueled vigorous discussions throughout Methodism. Although the Methodist Episcopal Church had granted licenses to a number of black preachers, the church customarily allowed them to preach only to black assemblies. African Americans in New York City were experiencing the same prejudice as those in Philadelphia who, under Richard Allen, had organized the AME Church. J. W. Hood recorded an extreme example of the demeaning treatment some blacks received:

> When a minister finished baptizing white children, he looked into the balcony and declared, "Now you niggers can bring your children down." A black woman presented her child for baptism, and when the minister said, "Name this child," the mother replied, "George Washington." The minister glared at her and said, "George Washington, Indeed! Caesar's his name. Caesar, I baptize thee..."

New York City mandated that black people be interred in separate cemeteries. The leadership at John Street Methodist Episcopal Church required persons of color to sit in balconies and to receive communion after white members. After suffering a series of indignities, the black Methodists in New York took steps to establish a separate society. In 1796 these Christians entreated Bishop Asbury to allow them to hold separate meetings. He granted the request, and the black members organized their own Methodist society. This small beginning eventually led to a new denomination.

Peter Williams

One of those who conferred with Asbury about separate services for blacks was Peter Williams, the black sexton of John Street ME Church. Williams, born in slavery, had been converted under the preaching of Philip Embury and Thomas Webb. As sexton of the church, he often assisted visiting preachers, such as Francis

Peter Williams (175?-1823).

Friends of Williams purchased his freedom, and through the tobacco trade he became one of the most prosperous black men in New York City. Williams felt a deep concern for the welfare of those of his own color. Largely through his efforts and generosity, black members of John Street ME Church obtained a separate meetinghouse. This structure was the first church edifice built expressly for people of color in New York City.

Peter Williams and his wife provided an excellent education for their two children, and their son, Peter, Jr., became one of the first ordained black clergy persons in the Episcopal Church. Nineteenth-century Methodist historian J. B. Wakeley wrote, "Christianity elevated Peter, ennobled him; it raised him from a bond-slave to become God's freeman.... All Peter Williams was on earth, and all he hoped to be in heaven, he owed to the religion of the cross."

Asbury, Richard Whatcoat, and Thomas Coke. Williams' friends purchased his freedom, and he became a businessman and property owner. He was motivated by a desire to see all black people experience the same joy and fulfillment in Christ that he knew. As well, he wanted all African Americans to enjoy social equality. Williams stepped forward to lead these black Methodists in securing a house, which they converted into a chapel. This newly formed black congregation thrived, and the members named their building Zion Church. The congregation adopted Articles of Agreement requesting Bishop Asbury to supply them with an ordained minister. This arrangement stipulated that the Zion congregation would remain in the Methodist Episcopal Church, with the benefit of regular preaching and sacraments to be provided by ME preachers. Bishop Asbury assigned a white preacher to the church. The property, however, was under the control of black trustees. To keep friction to a minimum, this black congregation timed its meetings to avoid conflict with the services at John Street ME Church.

Soon, Zion Church outgrew its building. Peter Williams spearheaded a successful drive to raise money to construct a building on the corner of Leonard and Church Streets. This structure was the first church in New York City built explicitly for a black congregation. In 1813 some of the members of the Zion congregation asked Bishop Asbury for permission to start a second society in another location. He granted the request and provided the new congregation with a minister. The worshipers named their chapel Asbury Church. By 1818 the two congregations, Zion and Asbury, had a combined membership of almost 800.

William Stillwell and Division

In 1819 Bishop Asbury appointed William Stillwell, an ordained white preacher, to serve Zion Church. The following year, Stillwell suddenly announced to the Zion congregation that he and about 300 persons had withdrawn from the Methodist Episcopal Church. He alarmed the Zion congregation (still under Bishop Asbury's supervision) by telling the people that the parent church could take their property and their liberty if they remained under Bishop Asbury. In a state of anxiety, the members of the Zion congregation repudiated any further relationship with the ME Church and asked Stillwell to remain their pastor.

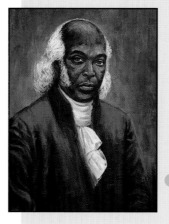

James Varick (1750-1827). *This original oil painting by Don Miller is located in the World Methodist Council Museum in Lake Junaluska, North Carolina. This copy appears here by permission of the museum. Photograph by Dave Henderson.*

Varick's name derives from a Dutch family of that name who had slaves in New York State. Early in his life, James Varick had a deep devotion to God and an eager desire to know the Bible. He was converted under the preaching of Philip Embury and Thomas Webb, and he joined the famed John Street Church in New York City. In response to the racial discrimination he endured there, in 1796 he led about 30 black Christians to form the first African-American church in New York City. In 1820 this church and others joined together to form the African Methodist Episcopal Zion Church. The new church elected Varick its first general superintendent, or bishop.

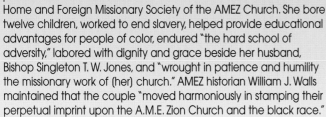

Mary Jane Talbert Jones (1831-1895).

Jones served as the founding president of the Woman's Home and Foreign Missionary Society of the AMEZ Church. She bore twelve children, worked to end slavery, helped provide educational advantages for people of color, endured "the hard school of adversity," labored with dignity and grace beside her husband, Bishop Singleton T. W. Jones, and "wrought in patience and humility the missionary work of (her) church." AMEZ historian William J. Walls maintained that the couple "moved harmoniously in stamping their perpetual imprint upon the A.M.E. Zion Church and the black race."

The congregation appealed unsuccessfully to Richard Allen of the AME Church to ordain a minister for Zion Chapel. The members of the Zion congregation then asked the Protestant Episcopal Church to ordain a black minister for them. Its bishops also declined the request. Next, a committee appealed to Methodist Bishop William McKendree to assist the Zion and Asbury congregations by ordaining black ministers. Methodist Church law did not permit this action.

Following the advice of William Stillwell (their white pastor), delegates from the Zion and Asbury Churches elected their own elders—James Varick and Abraham Thompson. On October 25, 1820, the Zion and Asbury congregations met together to adopt a Discipline patterned after that of the Methodist Episcopal Church. This action marked the official formation of the African Methodist Episcopal Zion Church.

The new denomination still had no ordained ministry. Consequently, in 1821 William Stillwell and two other white ministers, who had also left the ME Church, ordained three black preachers—James Varick, Abraham Thompson, and Leven Smith. A month later, these newly ordained ministers ordained six additional ministers, and the church elected James Varick its first general superintendent.

By 1831 the AMEZ Church had two Annual Conferences and more than 1,600 members. With this modest beginning, the church grew steadily. By 1868, the AMEZ Church had grown to 391,044. In 1920 the church created a Bureau of Evangelism to further its mission: "the chief end of the Gospel—the salvation of souls."

A Legacy of Honor

The African Methodist Episcopal Zion Church has produced a number of noteworthy leaders. One such person was Harriet Tubman who, along with other 19th century leaders, worked to rid the nation of slavery. Tubman was born to a slave mother and torn away from her in early childhood. At the age of five, she kept house, took care of a baby, and labored at other chores. She began working in the fields when she was 12 or 13 years of age. On one occasion, her angry master threw a two-pound weight at her, striking her head and knocking her unconscious. The injury caused her recurring discomfort for the rest of her life. At the age of 29, Harriet Tubman escaped to Pennsylvania.

After gaining her own freedom, she devoted the rest of her life to helping others escape slavery. She declared, "I was free, and they would be free also. I would make a home for them in the North, and the Lord helping me, I would bring them all there." She became an active member of the Underground Railroad, an organization that assisted slaves to escape. Escapees traveled at night to minimize detection, and by day they slept in "stations"—a code word for the homes and buildings made available by sympathizers (called "station masters" or "conductors"). The rigors of escape were frightful, dangerous, and exhausting. Despite the risks, she escorted thousands of slaves to freedom. Tubman encouraged those she helped by telling them, "Children if you are tired, keep going; if you are scared, keep going; if you are hungry, keep going, if you want a taste of freedom, keep going." Harriet Tubman was gifted at raising money, overseeing construction, and organizing projects. One of her last accomplishments was the purchase of 25 acres for an AMEZ home for the elderly. Concerning that land purchase, she wrote:

They were all white folks but me, there, and I was like a blackberry in a pail of milk, but I hid down in a corner, and no one knew who was bidding. The man began down pretty low, and kept going up by fifties. At last I got up to fourteen hundred and fifty, and then others stopped bidding, and the man said, "All done. Who is the buyer?" "Harriet Tubman," I shouted.

She borrowed the money to pay for the property and later deeded the 25 acres and her home to the AMEZ Church, making possible the construction of her Home for the Aged and Indigent.

Another AMEZ hero was William Hamilton, a layman and an original trustee of the Zion congregation in New York. Hamilton worked selflessly to gain dignity for all people of color. He wrote a letter to John Jay, Governor of the State of New York:

I am, dear Sir, one of those whom the generality men call Negroes. My forefathers or ancestors [come] from Africa but I am a native of New York, worthy Sir when I behold many of the sons of Africa groaning under oppression, some laboring with difficulty to get free, and others having to bear the yoke. I cannot help shedding a silent tear at the miserable misfortunes Providence hath brought upon them.... How false and contradictory do the Americans speak when this land, a land of liberty and equality, a Christian country, when almost every part of it abounds with slavery and oppression.... The intent of my writing to you was this. To know whether there can be no measures taken for the recovery of the objects of pity. Is it not high time that the scandal of the country should be taken away that it might be called a free nation in deed and in truth? Is it not time that Negroes should be free Is it not time that robbery should cease Is it not time that the threatening of heaven should be taken away.... May heaven diffuse its choicest blessings on your head. May you open your mouth and judge righteously and plead the cause of the poor and needy. May your family be blessed from above.

In addition to working in his church, Hamilton helped found organizations such as the New York African Mutual Relief Society and the Wilberforce Benevolent Society. He was a gifted speaker who gave inspiring addresses. In 1834 he spoke to a large assembly:

The hitherto strong-footed, but sore-eyed vixen, prejudice, is limping off, seeking the shade. The Anti-Slavery Society and the friends of immediate abolition, are taking a noble, bold, and manly stand, in the cause of universal liberty. It is true they are assailed on every quarter, but the more they are assailed the faster they recruit. From present appearances the prospect is cheering, in a high degree.

When Hamilton died in 1837, at the age of 63, *The Weekly Advocate*, a church paper, stated, "In recording the death of Mr. Hamilton, we are aware that we allude to no common man. He was one of sterling virtue and truth, and all his dealings thru life were marked by a strict adherence to truth and justice. 'An honest man is the noblest work of God.'"

Another outstanding example of AMEZ leadership was Christopher Rush. Born a slave, he became a Christian at the age of sixteen. In 1798, after gaining freedom, he went to New York, where he became a member of the Zion congregation. Later, he received a license to preach. Rush studied the teachings of John Wesley and held them in high regard. Reading Wesley's views on slavery and knowing Methodism's original stand on slavery, he became deeply troubled by the racial prejudice he saw in the Methodist Episcopal Church. In 1828 he became the second bishop of the AMEZ Church. During his service as bishop, he saw his church expand to cover a large portion of the United States.

Harriet Tubman (c. 1820-1913).

Tubman was a member of the AMEZ Church and one of its most illustrious daughters. She escaped from slavery and became a leading Abolitionist. Despite large rewards offered for her capture, she demonstrated extraordinary courage and endurance escorting slaves to freedom. Tubman became a leading figure in the "Underground Railroad," a secret network organized to help slaves escape to freedom. She earned the unofficial title, "The Moses of Her People."

Frederick Douglass wrote her, "Most that I have done has been in public, and I have received much encouragement.... You on the other hand have labored in a private way.... I have had the applause of the crowd... While the most that you have done has been witnessed by a few trembling, scared and footsore bondsmen.... The midnight sky and the silent stars have been the witnesses of your devotion to freedom and of your heroism."

Rush also served as president of the Phoenix Society of New York City. The general purpose of that organization was to educate and prepare black people for freedom, unity, equality, and peace. Specifically, the society worked "to promote the improvement of the coloured people in morals, literature, and the mechanical arts." After his death, his church paid grateful tribute to his memory. The conference minutes stated, "His life was marked with filial devotion, to the prosperity of the church and an answering confidence in God, and the spread of the Gospel and the elevation of his race, morally and intellectually, and until the hour of his death, he was an educator and upholder of the principles of Christianity."

Probably the most renowned early AMEZ leader was Frederick Douglass. Douglass was born in Maryland to a slave mother. He showed an early interest in learning, and his master's wife taught him to read. Early in life he demonstrated intellectual promise, and he used the first money he earned to buy a book. When he became an adult, he escaped to the North and joined a Methodist Episcopal Church in New York City. Douglass soon left that church, however, because of its discrimination against people of color. He wrote:

When I came north, I thought one Sunday I would attend communion, at one of the churches of my denomination.... The white people gathered round the altar, the blacks clustered by the door.... [The minister] proceeded till all the white members had been served. Then he drew a long breath, and looking out towards the door, exclaimed, "Come up, colored friends, come up! For you know God is no respecter of persons!" I haven't been there to see the sacraments taken since.

Douglass joined a small black congregation, where he became a leading member. He reflected on the leadership of his minister, William Serrington: "I found him a man of deep piety, and of high intelligence. His character attracted me, and I received from him much excellent advice and brotherly sympathy." Douglass worked diligently in the church, and he gradually discovered and exercised his superb gifts as a thinker, orator, and writer. More and more, he devoted his considerable abilities to elevating the status of people of color. At first, he spoke only to black assemblies, but in time he also spoke to large white audiences. Douglass became an active Abolitionist, and he eventually gained national and international respect for his work. His speaking and writing abilities earned him additional fame.

During the Civil War, Douglass was among the first to suggest the use of black troops by the Union Army; later, two of his sons served with the northern forces. Douglass went on to become Marshal of the District of Columbia in 1877, and subsequently he served as the American Minister Resident and Consul General in the Republic of Haiti. After becoming famous, he wrote about his earlier experiences in Zion church: "My connection with the little church continued long after I was in the antislavery field. I look back to the days I spent...in the several capacities of sexton,

Christopher Rush (1777-1873).

Rush was the second bishop of the African Methodist Episcopal Zion Church. He contributed remarkable leadership in the church as well as in a number of civic and benevolent societies. He spent many decades working for the emancipation of slaves. Because he had gone blind in about 1852, someone had to read Lincoln's Emancipation Proclamation to him. Hearing this proclamation, Rush lifted his hands and exclaimed, "Lord, now lettest thou thy servant depart in peace according to thy word; for mine eyes have seen thy salvation." He declared, "I knew that the justice of God could not sleep forever; he has called, and ever will raise up men to battle against political error, till all unjust laws shall be forever wiped out."

steward, class leader, clerk, and local preacher, as among the happiest days of my life."

From its beginning, the AMEZ Church has been committed to sharing the good news of Jesus Christ as Savior and Lord, promoting justice, and finding ways to improve the lives of African Americans. Membership in the church requires a six-month period of probation "in order that we may not admit improper persons into our Church." During the period of probation, potential members are required to receive instruction in the rules and doctrines of the church. Those finally admitted into membership must give "satisfactory evidence of saving faith in the Lord Jesus Christ." The church has grown steadily over the years. At the end of the twentieth century, the worldwide AME, Zion Church registers over 6,275 clergy, and 1,200,000 members.

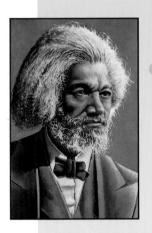

Frederick Douglass (1817-1895).
Picture by Paul Collins.

Douglass, a prominent member of the AMEZ Church, was an escaped slave who, in freedom, discovered that he was gifted with literary and oratorical genius. Douglass became a prominent leader in the Abolitionist Movement, and in 1847 he founded the anti-slavery newspaper *The North Star.* His 1845 autobiography, *My Bondage and My Freedom* (rewritten in 1882 as *Life and Times of Frederick Douglass*) is one of the best-authenticated slave narratives ever written.

One of his last letters, written in 1894, reveals his wit and humor: "I have heard much, and the country has heard much, of what is popularly called the "New South." Please tell me if you have seen any such south in your travels. I fear that the New South is but a slightly revised edition of the Old South. It is said at a town meeting in some remote part a series of resolutions were adopted to build a new jail. The first resolution was,

- Resolved, That we will build a new jail.
- Resolved, 2nd, That we will build it out of material of the old one.
- Resolved, 3rd, That the new jail shall stand on the site of the old jail, and the prisoners shall remain in the old jail until the new jail is built.'

I think there is some resemblance to this in the so-called New South, and shall continue to think so until I hear less of lynch law and lawless violence in general in that section."

James O. Andrew (1796-1871).
Picture supplied by the courtesy of the Arthur J. Moore Museum, Epworth by the Sea, St. Simons Island, Georgia. Photograph by Jay Roberson.

Bishop Andrew was the central figure in the controversy in 1844 that led to a major split in the Methodist Episcopal Church. Bishop Andrew had inherited his deceased wife's young female slave. Even though Georgia law forbade freeing slaves, he gave her the liberty to go to a free state as soon as he could arrange for her financial support. The northern delegates at the 1844 General Conference (the majority), voted to relieve Bishop Andrew of his episcopal duties—even though he had never bought or sold a slave. The southern delegates regarded that action to be a violation of church law. Consequently, that General Conference implemented a Plan of Separation. The following year, meeting in Louisville, the southern Annual Conferences formed the Methodist Episcopal Church, South. In 1939 the two branches of Methodism and the Methodist Protestant Church were again united to form the Methodist Church.

THE CHRISTIAN METHODIST EPISCOPAL CHURCH

Another important African-American Methodist denomination was the Colored Methodist Episcopal Church. The circumstances leading to the formation of this church were related to the Civil War. When that war began, the Methodist Episcopal Church, South, had 207,766 black members, most of whom were slaves. These African Americans met separately from white members and functioned under restrictions imposed by the church. During the war, the majority of the black members of the MEC, South, either transferred to the northern branch of Methodism or joined the AME or AMEZ Church. Consequently, by the end of the Civil War, black membership in the southern branch of Methodism had fallen to about 78,000. Most of these remaining members did not wish to continue as members of the Methodist Episcopal Church, South.

In 1866, these black members of the southern branch of Methodism asked the church for permission to form a separate denomination. Out of respect for the parent body, however, they wanted to remain under the supervision of the southern church. Isaac Lane, a leader of these black Christians, envisioned a new church that was fraternally related to the MEC, South, but "patterned after our own ideas and notions."

A Plan of Separation

The 1870 General Conference of the Methodist Episcopal Church, South, met in Memphis and considered the report of a committee charged with drafting a response to the proposal of the black Methodists. During the 1866-1870 quadrennium, an all-white committee had formulated a plan of separation. The committee's report recommended that the black members organize into a new denomination, completely separate from the Methodist Episcopal Church, South. The General Conference accepted this recommendation

Bishop William Henry Miles (1828-1892).
This original oil painting by Gary Blair is located in the World Methodist Council Museum in Lake Junaluska, North Carolina. This copy appears here by permission of the museum. Photograph by Dave Henderson.

Miles was born a slave and freed by his owner at her death. A contemporary newspaper said of him, "He was distinguished for his fidelity, integrity, and intelligence—qualities which were so highly appreciated that, while (others) were hired for $100 per year, he readily commanded $200, and sometimes as much as $250."

As a young man Miles experienced a profound conversion to Christ. Of this experience he wrote, "If ever I was happy, it was that night in the old Methodist church in Lebanon (Kentucky). Since that time I have had my bitter trials and my sweet experiences ... but thank the Great Head of the Church, I am still pulling for the shore and expect to make the landing after awhile, when my work is done." In 1855 Miles joined the Methodist Episcopal Church, and two years later received a license to preach. He became a superior preacher and an effective evangelist. When the CME Church was formed in 1870, Miles was elected his church's first bishop, and he served as senior bishop for twenty-two years.

Bishop Robert Paine | **Bishop Holland N. McTyeire**
(1799-1882) | **(1824-1889).**

In 1870 the General Conference of the Methodist Episcopal Church, South, agreed to the petition of its black members to form for themselves a separate church for persons of color. The parent church deeded over property and supplied funds to help establish the new denomination, which chose the name Colored Methodist Episcopal Church. (In 1954 the church changed its name to the Christian Methodist Episcopal Church.) Bishops Paine and McTyeire of the MEC, South, presided over the organizing conference of the CME Church which met December 15, 1870, at Jackson, Tennessee. Paine and McTyeire also ordained clergy for the new church and consecrated its first two bishops—William H. Miles and Richard H. Vanderhorst.

and offered to help the black members form an autonomous church.

The Methodist Episcopal Church, South, agreed to ordain black ministers for the new denomination and to deed over properties occupied by black congregations. The MEC, South, assigned two bishops—Robert Paine and Holland N. McTyeire—to assist in organizing the black Methodists into a new church. Also, Paine and McTyeire would ordain a ministry for the new church. The church was formed in Jackson, Tennessee, on December 15, 1870. Its name was the Colored Methodist Episcopal Church. (CME).

The MEC, South, continued financially to assist the CME Church, especially with the establishing and support of Lane and Paine Colleges. The founding conference of the CME Church elected two new bishops—William Henry Miles and Richard H. Vanderhorst. Paine and McTyeire consecrated these new bishops. The CME Church adopted the Discipline of the MEC, South. In 1954, the denomination changed its name to the Christian Methodist Episcopal Church.

The CME Focus

The CME Church's second General Conference began March 19, 1873, at Trinity Church in Augusta, Georgia, and the delegates elected three additional bishops—Isaac Lane, Lucius H. Holsey, and Joseph A. Beebe. By 1874 the new church had fifteen Annual Conferences, with 600 ordained ministers and about 75,000 members. Today the CME Church in America reports over 800,000 members, about 3,000 churches, and 34 Annual Conferences.

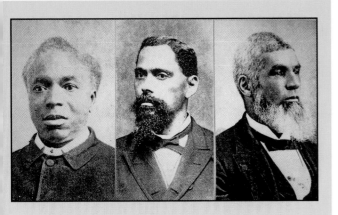

Bishops Joseph A. Beebe (1832-1903), Lucius H. Holsey (1842-1920), and Isaac Lane (1834-1937), the third, fourth, and fifth bishops of the Colored Methodist Episcopal Church.

Isaac Lane's autobiography gives us insight into the difficulties of the early episcopacy in the Colored Methodist Episcopal Church. He wrote about his first year as a bishop in 1873: "This was a large Conference; and although asked to raise three hundred and eighty dollars for the support of the bishop, they reported only fifty-seven dollars. When we called the attention of the brethren to the importance and necessity of raising the small amount asked for the support of the bishops of the Church, the brethren seemed to have been surprised to know that they would be expected to bring money for the bishops instead of the bishops sending money to them... With the adjournment of this Conference my first year as a bishop came to a close. I had worked hard during the year and had but little financial help. On my salary the Church had paid me only one hundred and sixty dollars and fifteen cents during the year, and my expenses necessarily carried me far into debt. My wife and children had a crop of cotton. This I sold, and with the money I paid the debt and took up the note. I then worked hard to replace this money. I cut wood and hauled it to town and sold it, making enough money thereby to buy such things as clothing and other provisions that were needed by me and my family."

Lane Institute.

The Christian Methodist Episcopal Church has always stressed education for its youth. In 1882 Bishop Isaac Lane founded Lane Institute, and in 1895 the school changed its name to Lane College. This nineteenth-century drawing of a building at Lane Institute represents the type of architecture used in the early years of the school. Presently, the CME Church supports Phillips School of Theology, Lane College, Paine College, Miles College, and Texas College.

Israel Metropolitan Colored Methodist Episcopal Church, Washington, DC.

The founders of the CME Church declared that they would stand "aloof from politics." The first *Discipline* of the church stated that "church-houses" shall not be used for political speeches and meetings. Bishop Lucius H. Holsey explained: "While exercising their rights as citizens, they endeavor to keep their religious assemblies free from that complication with political parties which has been so damaging to the spiritual interests of the colored people."

Seal of the Christian Methodist Episcopal Church.

Wiley College, Claflin College, and Bethune-Cookman College.

The United Methodist Church supports twelve historically black institutions of higher education: Bennett College, Bethune-Cookman College, Clark College, Claflin College, Dillard University, Gammon Theological Seminary, Huston-Tillotson College, Meharry Medical School, Morristown College, Paine College, Philander-Smith College, Rust College, and Wiley College. These schools are affiliated with the United Methodist Church.

Each school began during a period when most colleges did not admit black students. The northern and southern branches of Methodism began these colleges to provide training that embodied the aspirations of the African-American community. These schools continue as historically black institutions for several reasons: they are excellent schools with quality programs, about half of America's black college students prefer to attend historically black schools, and these colleges help preserve black culture.

From the beginning, the CME Church emphasized the evangelization of people of color, primarily through preaching and education. Numerous CME Churches functioned as houses of worship on Sunday and elementary schools during the week. Black children received instruction in religion, music, and basic academic subjects. This educational emphasis has continued in the CME Church. The denomination also developed a strong missionary program, especially in Africa, Haiti, and Jamaica. At the end of the twentieth century, the worldwide church has approximately one million members.

The Heritage of Black Methodism

African-American Methodism in America is now in its third century. During the first century, it struggled for freedom and dignity. This struggle led to new denominations, each with schools, colleges, seminaries, and publishing houses. The second century saw black Methodism develop

missionary outreach into regions beyond America. During this period there emerged a national leadership that worked for equality and justice. Today, black Methodism faces the evangelistic challenge presented by Islam and by a growing number of black émigrés to America.

The United Methodist Church is, of course, a racially integrated denomination. It has a large number of congregations made up of predominantly black members. In addition, United Methodism maintains fraternal relationships with the historically black denominations in the Methodist family of denominations. As fraternal members of the World Methodist Council, these churches meet for discussion and explore ways to engage in shared ministries. Presently, conversations are under way regarding possible mergers with United Methodism in the early years of the twenty-first century.

Vitally Wesleyan and Truly Methodist

The traditionally black Methodist denominations in America are vitally Wesleyan, in that they hold to the vision of equality for people of all races and social circumstances. African-American Methodists have sought to balance evangelism and social action as twin expressions of the Wesleyan way. Black Methodism's doctrines demonstrate faithfulness to the teachings of the Wesleys and to Methodism's polity and ecumenical vision. Particularly in its commitments to justice, human dignity, and the optimism of grace, black Methodism continues to model for all Methodists important fundamental aspects of the Wesleyan heritage. A phrase in the Discipline of the CME Church echoes the spirit of black Methodism: "We have descended regularly from the very father of Methodism."

Gammon Theological Seminary.

This seminary was founded in 1875 in Atlanta on the campus of Clark University. In 1883 a generous gift from Elijah Gammon enabled the school to gain a charter, under the auspices of the Methodist Episcopal Church. Gammon Theological Seminary became the principal center for educating black ministers.

8

Knowledge and Vital Piety

The eighteenth-century Wesleyan revival brought to England and America a new era of spiritual vitality. This religious renewal was profound and sweeping. Methodism also fostered an intellectual awakening which led to profound social changes—particularly among those for whom education had not been a priority. In America, this intellectual renewal found expression in new concepts of education, which led to the founding of a number of important Methodist schools, colleges, seminaries, and universities.

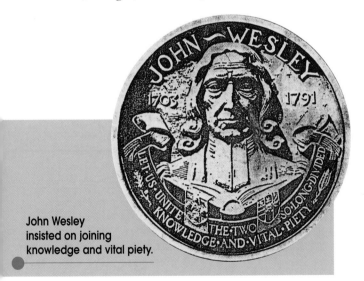

John Wesley insisted on joining knowledge and vital piety.

These educational impulses were grounded in three principles that characterized the Wesleyan concept of education: (1) The search for knowledge must be linked with a quest for vital piety. (2) Learning must be available to all people. (3) The purpose of gaining knowledge is to equip the learner for a life of service.

From the Wesleyan perspective, the first principle of learning is that we must combine knowledge and religious devotion. John Wesley wrote a tract, *To All Parents and Schoolmasters*, in which he addressed the matter of educating children: "If the fear of the Lord is the beginning of wisdom, then it is certainly the very first thing they should learn. And why may they not be taught the knowledge of God, and the knowledge of letters, at the same time?" Wesley insisted that attempts to separate knowledge from vital piety dwarf the human spirit and lead to grievous consequences.

Making the point that secular education can do more harm than good, Wesley wrote:

> [Some] were sent to school, and learned at least to read and write; but they learned all kind of vice at the same time: so that it had been better for them to have been without their knowledge than to have bought it at so dear a price.... At length I determined to have them taught in my own house, that they might have an opportunity to learn to read, write, and cast accounts (if no more), without being under almost a necessity of learning heathenism at the same time.

Wesley often asserted that the informed mind is not necessarily an enlightened mind, because knowledge in itself cannot give wisdom.

Second, John Wesley affirmed that all people are deserving of education. He lived in a day when education was reserved almost entirely for a privileged few. There were some eighteenth-century

John Wesley.
This original watercolor was painted by an unknown artist who apparently worked from a painting of John Wesley that Thomas Horsley completed in 1790, a year before Wesley's death. The picture appears here by permission of its owner, the Reverend Walter Price.

Wesley was keenly interested in the education of children, particularly through Sunday schools. In a revealing passage, he wrote, "I ask, then, for what end do you send your children to school? 'Why, that they may be fit to live in the world.' In which world do you mean,—this or the next? Perhaps you thought of this world only; and had forgot that there is a world to come; yea, and one that will last for ever! Pray take this into your account, and send them to such masters as will keep it always before their eyes.

Otherwise, to send them to school (permit me to speak plainly) is little better than sending them to the devil. At all events, then, send your (children), if you have any concern for their souls, not to any of the large public schools, (for they are nurseries of all manner of wickedness) but a private school, kept by some pious man, who endeavours to instruct a small number of children in religion and learning together."

Anglican clergymen who taught basic academic subjects to the children of their parishes. However, the majority of people—lay and clergy, rich and poor—accepted the notion that children of working families had a duty to begin earning wages as soon as possible. Many regarded it a waste of time and money to educate the children of the poor. This way of thinking assumed that educating the masses tended to render them unfit for their commonplace duties.

Wesley saw the toll that this attitude had taken on people and society, and he took practical steps to educate the neglected segments of society. He declared, "The Methodists may be poor, but there is no need they should be ignorant." His concern was shared by other Methodists. For instance, in

1769 a Methodist woman in England, Hannah Ball, started a Sunday school for children who worked on weekdays. This school taught religion and basic subjects such as reading and writing. Her innovations began fourteen years prior to those of Robert Raikes, the famous champion of British Sunday schools.

Throughout his adult life, Wesley wrote "plain truth for plain people." He published a plethora of tracts and books for ordinary people, at inexpensive prices. To make good literature available to ordinary folk, he edited *The Christian Library*, a 50-volume project containing "Extracts from, and Abridgments of, the Choicest Pieces of Practical Divinity." This series of books included devotional and theological selections from the best Roman Catholic and Protestant writers. Wesley also promoted learning in other ways—by starting a school for children, by preaching in a way that all could understand, and by encouraging literacy and education for every person in England. His educational work in Great Britain helped pave the way for laws that guaranteed elementary education for all children.

The third educational principle which John Wesley taught was that learning was not an end but a means. The aim of education is to prepare us for responsible service. John Wesley's *Collection of Forms of Prayer* contains the following petition: "Bless the Universities with learning and holiness, that they may afford a constant supply of men fit and able to do thee service." During the eighteenth century, many educated people used their learning chiefly for personal gain and self-promotion. These people leveraged their educational advantages to promote themselves and to exploit others. Methodism taught that our advantages obligate us to serve others, helping them to achieve dignity and reach their potential.

The Wesleyan legacy emphasizes that apart from God's love we *cannot* love others, and with God's love we *will* love others. Preaching on Christ's Sermon on the Mount, Wesley posed these questions:

Are you zealous of good works? Do you, as you have time, do good to all men? Do you feed the hungry, and clothe the naked, and visit the fatherless and widow in their affliction? Do you visit those that are sick? Relieve them that are in prison? Is any a stranger, and you take him in? Friend, come up

Rules for Life

Do all the good you can,

By all the means you can,

In all the ways you can,

In all the places you can,

At all the times you can,

To all the people you can,

As long as ever you can.

Selected from the writings of
John Wesley, founder of Methodism

John Wesley's Rules for Life.

higher!… Be thou a lover of God and of all mankind! In this spirit do and suffer all things! Thus show thy faith by thy works; thus "do the will of thy Father which is in heaven!" And, as sure as thou now walkest with God on earth, thou shalt also reign with him in glory!

Wesley never tired of preaching that the fundamental test of true religion is love for God and neighbor. He believed that as faith should lead to works, so learning should lead to service.

The Methodist heritage highlights the need to search for the underlying causes of social ills and develop ways to overcome injustice and oppression in all their forms. John Wesley contended that there is no holiness other than social holiness, by which he meant that we must translate profession into performance. This belief is expressed in United Methodism's Baptismal Covenant for adults: "Do you accept the freedom and power God gives you to resist evil, injustice, and oppression in whatever forms they present themselves?"

Thus, the Methodist view of education links knowledge with vital piety, espouses education for the masses, and calls for dedicated service to neighbor. This Wesleyan educational legacy took root in America, guiding Methodism to become an illuminating influence in the life of the nation.

Education in Early American Methodism

Most of the preachers at the 1784 Christmas Conference lacked formal education and cultural finesse. However, they were intelligent people, filled with devotion to God and a sense of divine purpose. One of their first decisions was to begin a school. Francis Asbury wanted to build an academy (the equivalent of primary and secondary education), but Thomas Coke contended that the new church should found a college. Bishop Coke's influence prevailed. The conference selected Abingdon, Maryland, as the site of American Methodism's first educational institution. In honor of American Methodism's first two bishops, the founders of this school gave it the name Cokesbury College. The school opened on December 6, 1787, with a president, a faculty of two, and twenty-five students.

Cokesbury College.

This picture is a drawing of Cokesbury College in Abingdon, Maryland, as it looked in 1787. The brick building was 108 feet long and 40 feet deep. It stood on the summit and center of six acres of land. The Methodists boasted that Cokesbury College was architecturally equal, if not superior, to any college building in America. The first *Discipline* of the church stated that Cokesbury College was to be a school "where learning and religion may go hand in hand."

A suspicious fire destroyed Cokesbury College in 1795. At the time, the Methodists did not have enough members or wealth to support its rebuilding. During its brief history, Cokesbury College produced preachers, leaders in business and law, two U.S. senators, and one of the founders of Wesleyan University.

The published statement of the college's mission was to form "the minds of the youth, through divine aid, to wisdom and holiness; by instilling into their tender minds the principles of true religion, speculative, experimental and practical, and training them in the ancient way, that they may be rational scriptural Christians." The founders stated their intention to create an environment "where learning and religion may go hand in hand."

During the next few years, Bishop Asbury struggled to raise money for the college. His efforts resulted in donations of more than $50,000, mostly in small sums, from scattered sources. Interestingly, the papers of George Washington reveal that he may have contributed to the school. Regrettably, the life of Cokesbury College was short; fire, thought to be the work of an arsonist, destroyed the building in 1795. The lack of adequate financial support for Cokesbury combined with the calamitous fire to dishearten Bishop Asbury. Subsequently, friends in Baltimore purchased a house, and the college reopened for a short time. This facility also burned. After its destruction, the Methodists built no more colleges for three decades. In a depressed mood, Asbury declared, "The Lord called not… the Methodists to build colleges."

A number of Methodists agreed with Asbury. They worried that concerns with colleges would harm the spiritual vitality of the church. The early Methodists tended to fear anything with the potential to undermine the primacy of "experimental religion." They observed that college-educated preachers in other denominations opposed revivals and revival preachers. Consequently, they regarded colleges with suspicion. A number of the preachers noted that college education sometimes prompted intellectual pride and abetted a drift toward Unitarianism. They argued that when one received God's call to preach, it was unnecessary to spend time *preparing* to preach.

The church's first *Discipline* advised preachers to "read while they rode." In theory, young preachers would learn by themselves, with help from experienced preachers who would coach them along the way. This assumption, though, was not realistic. For one thing, work on the circuits did not allow adequate time for the mentoring process. Also, uneducated mentors could not impart knowledge they did not possess.

In time, it became apparent that the preachers needed a higher level of formal learning. Consequently, in 1816 the General Conference took a first step toward establishing educational requirements for preachers. The delegates authorized the bishops to "point out a course of reading and study proper to be pursued by candidates for the ministry." This plan, however, produced uneven results. The various Annual Conferences did not regard the reading course with equal seriousness. The presiding elders often were too busy to supervise the program of reading, and the examinations were frequently inadequate.

In 1844 the General Conference voted to standardize a denominational course of study for preachers. After a careful selection process was completed, the 1848 *Discipline* published a uniform list of required books for preachers. Presiding elders had the specific responsibility for supervising this program of reading. The "Course of Study" contained a list of books selected to give the preachers a better understanding of scripture, the Christian tradition, and practical tools for ministry. This plan for educating preachers served the church for many decades. As late as 1939, more than half of Methodism's ministers received their theological educations through the Course of Study. Not until 1956 did General Conference make seminary education the norm for ministerial preparation. The Course of Study, although still used, became the exception.

Methodist Academies and Conference Schools

After the failure of Cokesbury College, Bishop Asbury decided that, rather than building colleges, Methodists would build academies. In 1791, he wrote a letter instructing the conferences to erect academies in their areas. He explained that the purpose of these educational institutions would be "to give the key of knowledge in a general way, to your children, and those of the poor in the vicinity of your small towns and villages." Bishop Asbury wanted these schools to nurture both mind and spirit, being free from "any restraints from refractory [perverse] men."

These academies also were called conference schools or seminaries. Whether called academies, conference schools or seminaries, these schools

Cokesbury Conference School.

This building, near Greenwood, South Carolina, was once the home of Cokesbury Conference School. It grew out of Tabernacle Academy, connected with Old Tabernacle Church, begun in 1778. The distinguished leader Stephen Olin was converted while teaching at Tabernacle Academy. He joined the South Carolina Conference and eventually became the first president of Randolph-Macon College. In 1864, Tabernacle Academy was renamed Cokesbury College, evoking a memory of the short-lived Cokesbury College established by Methodism's founding conference in 1784. In 1918 the school closed, and its property became a part of Wofford College. This structure was restored in 1970, as a reminder of an earlier educational era in American Methodism.

provided education on the primary and secondary levels. Asbury personally led in establishing academies in Virginia, North Carolina, Kentucky, South Carolina, and Georgia. For his work in education, he later gained the unofficial and honorary title of the first Commissioner of Education in the United States.

In a forty-year period, the church began an average of five new conference schools and academies per year. Representative early Methodist academies were Ebenezer Academy in Virginia, Asbury College in Baltimore, Wesleyan Seminary in New York, Newmarket Academy in New Hampshire, South Carolina Bethel Academy, and Bethel Academy in Kentucky. However, each of these schools struggled financially, and eventually they all closed. Several factors contributed to their collapse. At the time, many Methodists were not yet convinced of the importance of education. Also, the church did not have enough properly qualified teachers. Most of the academies were built in remote locations where the sparse populations could not sustain them.

The Rise of the Sunday School

Around 1783, in Hanover County, Virginia, Francis Asbury started America's first Sunday school. Because many Methodists had no access to formal education, this Sunday school taught

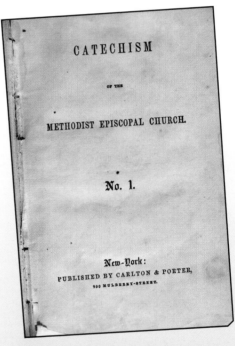

Catechism of the Methodist Episcopal Church, 1852.

In 1787 the American church encouraged the preachers to catechize the young people on their circuits, using a catechism that John Wesley had prepared for children. In 1824, the General Conference required all preachers to use this catechism in Sunday schools. Then in 1848 the church commissioned Daniel Kidder, editor of Sunday school materials, to prepare a new catechism. The 1852 General Conference approved Kidder's work. Both Wesley's and Kidder's catechisms were used for many years.

During the first three decades of the twentieth century, the church gradually moved away from using the catechism, in favor of graded lessons. In 1939, the Curriculum Committee, under the pressure of strong opposition, dropped the catechism. After 1939, the Methodist Publishing House continued for several years to print the catechism. A number of Christian educators, however, did not use them. Their publication ceased.

Methodist Sunday school card.

This pocket-sized edition of the Children's Sunday school series was printed by the Methodist Book Concern for use on December 21, 1919. The lesson on the back of the card emphasizes the importance of seeking and worshiping Christ. The year's supply of 52 cards cost twelve cents.

John Heyl Vincent (1832-1920).

In 1866 Vincent became the General Agent of the Methodist Episcopal Church's Sunday School Union. He introduced Sunday school lessons printed as separate sheets for class members. These popular Sunday school leaflets reached a circulation of almost two-and-a-half million.

In 1888 the church elected Vincent to the episcopacy. After serving as bishop in New York and Kansas, he assumed the episcopal leadership of Methodism's work in Europe. After retiring in 1904, Vincent preached, lectured, and wrote. However, he is most remembered as a creative and indefatigable champion of the Sunday school.

both religion and basic academic subjects. In 1790, the General Conference voted to establish Sunday schools across the entire church. The 1824 General Conference directed each traveling preacher to establish and promote Sunday schools on his circuit. This action reflected John Wesley's view that none were too poor or socially disadvantaged to benefit from learning, and that Methodism had an obligation to provide it.

The 1824 General Conference also commissioned a catechism for young people. The catechism became a popular method of teaching the Bible, Christian doctrine, and Methodism's distinctives. In 1827 the church founded the Methodist Sunday School Union, which by 1830 listed more than 150,000 scholars in Methodist Sunday schools.

The Methodist Episcopal Church's publishing house printed numerous pamphlets, tracts, and books directed at Christian education. Many local churches established libraries.

In 1868 the Church elected John Vincent as secretary of the Methodist Sunday School Union and editor of the church's Sunday school literature. During Vincent's service of twenty years, he introduced numerous educational innovations. He inaugurated the Sunday school quarterly, teacher's guides, and teacher training institutes. His idea of lesson leaflets for Sunday schools became enormously popular, and their circulation reached into the millions. Vincent's introduction of the graded Uniform Lesson system became so successful in Methodism that in 1872 the International Sunday School Convention adopted it for its member denominations. Vincent's innovative methods took root in Methodism and set Sunday school standards for other American churches.

Vincent also founded the Chautauqua Assembly in New York. The Chautauqua Assembly began as a Sunday school teacher's training event and developed into an elaborate series of summer institutes. Many of these institutes took place at Methodist camp meeting sites. At these locations, cottages replaced tents, and sermons gave way to lectures on a variety of subjects. Summer Chautauquas spread across America. Over time they became more elaborate, with impressive buildings, daily papers, and four-

THE GOOD SHEPHERD

Primary Class Sunday school leaflet.

This picture appeared on a four-page Sunday school paper for primary-age children printed in 1943. The lesson, based on Luke 15:3-6, featured a story about a shepherd finding a lost sheep. The memory verse was "The father himself loveth you." A poem at the end of the lesson was titled *Until He Found It*.

"I have lost one sheep," said the shepherd.
"I must look till that sheep is found."
So over the rocky mountains,
And over the thorny ground,
He searched through the night, and he did not sleep
Until at last he found that sheep.

And then, did he scold that silly sheep
That had given such trouble and pain?
Oh no; he so tenderly lifted it up,
And carried it home again.
"Rejoice! he called with a joyful sound,
"Rejoice, for my little lost sheep is found!"

Chautauqua Assembly Grounds.
Photograph by Elizabeth Priset.

John Vincent started the Chautauqua Assembly in New York in 1874. Its purpose was to train Sunday school teachers. Vincent's plan was that experts would deliver lectures on various subjects and that Sunday school teachers would become motivated to study the Bible and relate its teachings to all phases of life. This picture shows cottages for summer occupancy.

Over the years, the Chautauqua Assembly developed into an elaborate series of summer gatherings with courses offered in many subject areas. Chautauqua Assemblies began at other sites in America and around the world. William R. Harper, president of the University of Chicago, wrote glowingly about "the scores of Chautauqua assemblies throughout the United States... the hundreds of thousands of readers who have been connected with the Chautauqua Literary and Scientific Circle, the tens of thousands of homes into which a new light has penetrated as a result of the Chautauqua idea." A number of churches in other countries borrowed the idea and adapted it for their use.

year correspondence courses. The Chautauqua plan called for lectures on a wide range of subjects, both religious and secular. All instruction was to be given from a Christian perspective.

Methodism's Era of College Building

As the first two decades of the 19th century unfolded, Methodist people gained financial stability and moved from log and sod cabins into masonry and frame homes. Better financial conditions allowed many of them to send their children to college. However, the church did not have any colleges. Methodist young people were forced to attend schools of other denominations. Church members began demanding that the church build colleges for their young people. The Methodist Episcopal Church soon responded to the need.

The 1820 General Conference took a decisive step of historical importance. Delegates voted to direct the Annual Conferences to "establish as soon as practicable, literary institutions under their control, in such way and manner as they

Wesleyan University, Middletown, Connecticut, in 1831.

Wesleyan University is the oldest Methodist-founded college still in operation. From its beginning until 1924, all its presidents were Methodist ministers, except for one Methodist layman. Eighteen of its alumni have become Methodist bishops. Up until 1930, twenty percent of Wesleyan University's graduates had become ministers. Due to Wesleyan's high academic standards, its graduates have exerted a particularly strong influence in higher education.

Wesleyan University did not remain a Methodist school. Its charter stated that "subscribing to religious tenets shall never be a condition of admission to students or a cause of ineligibility to the president, professor, or other officers." Despite the millions of dollars given to Wesleyan by Methodists, in the mid-twentieth century the university severed its Methodist connections.

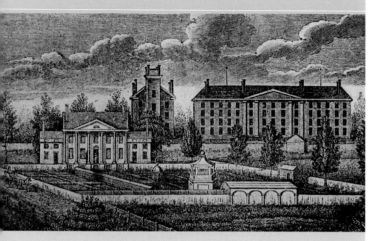

Augusta College.
Original building

Augusta College in Kentucky was Methodism's second college. Cokesbury College had burned in 1795. The Kentucky Conference appointed Commissioners in 1820, the school was chartered in 1822, and this building was constructed in 1825. In 1844 the ME Church split into northern and southern branches. The northern branch of the church no longer supported Augusta College, and it closed. During the school's short life it produced a number of important Methodist leaders, including John G. Fee, who founded Berea College, theologian John M. Miley, Bishop Randolph Foster, and Governor Alexander Donniphan.

Stephen Olin (1797-1851).

Some regard Olin has having had one of the best minds in American Methodism. Olin graduated from Middlebury College with honors, having earned the respect and admiration of his teachers. He became the principal of Tabernacle Academy in South Carolina. Olin boarded with the family of a lay preacher named James Glenn. Mrs. Glenn's asking Olin whether he opened his school with prayer prompted him to begin doing so. He soon experienced a life-changing conversion to Christ. In 1824 he joined the ME Church's South Carolina Conference, and in 1826 the bishop appointed him Professor of English Literature at the University of Georgia.

After becoming a leading professor at the University of Georgia, he received an invitation to become president of the newly founded Randolph-Macon College. This school was established to provide education for all qualified students, regardless of their financial standing. Its founders committed themselves to maintaining a balance between scholarship and religious faith. Accepting the invitation to become president of Randolph-Macon, Olin said, "There is no work to which I so desire to consecrate myself. I have greatly desired to preach but this is now in my view a more excellent way."

In 1842, Olin became president of the prestigious Wesleyan University in Middletown, Connecticut, a position he occupied until his death. His scholarly and intellectual contributions helped set a high standard for those who would lead the educational institutions of the church.

may think proper." That conference also authorized the bishops to appoint Methodist ministers as officers and teachers in these colleges. Up to this time, if a Methodist preacher wanted to serve in one of the church's academies or conference schools, he was required to surrender his credentials and work as a lay person. That policy had contributed to the failure of Methodism's early schools. Now, preachers could serve as professors.

The first Methodist college chartered after the 1820 General Conference action was Augusta College in Kentucky. It was co-sponsored by the Kentucky and Ohio Annual Conferences. In 1825 the college opened in a three-story brick building. During the decade between 1820 and 1830, the Annual Conferences began fifteen colleges in nine different states. Some of these schools closed within a few years. Inadequate funding and a shortage of leadership remained major problems.

However, some of the colleges thrived. One such example was Wesleyan University, established in 1831 in Middletown, Connecticut. Due to the closings of Augusta College in Kentucky and Madison College in Pennsylvania, Wesleyan University is the oldest continuing college started by the Methodist Episcopal Church. Across

Martin Ruter (1785-1838).

During the 1820 General Conference Martin Ruter sponsored the proposal to ask every Annual Conference to develop a college. Conference adoption of this proposal led to a remarkable era of college building during the two decades from 1820 to 1840. From 1815 through 1836, Ruter stood out as the foremost educational leader in American Methodism.

As a child, Ruter evidenced an uncommon thirst for knowledge. He was converted to Christ at the age of 14 and joined the ME Church. Within a year of his conversion he began to serve as a traveling preacher on Methodist circuits. Although he became an effective preacher, his most influential work was in education. Ruter served successively as superintendent of Wesleyan Academy in New Hampshire, president of Augusta College in Kentucky, and president of Allegheny College in Pennsylvania. He also became the Western Book Agent for the church, and he founded the Methodist Book Concern in Cincinnati.

Wilbur Fisk (1792-1838).

As a young man, Fisk became seriously ill to the point of death, and this experience caused him to return to the religious faith he had known as a child but had neglected as a young adult. He recommitted his life to Christ and, following his recovery, left his study of law to join the New England Conference of the ME Church. Fisk became the first college graduate to serve in New England Methodism. His training and native abilities gave him widespread credibility for his ministries of speaking, writing and academic administration.

Fisk served successively as the presiding elder of the Vermont District, principal of Wilbraham Academy, and the first president of Wesleyan University in Middletown, Connecticut. Historian Abel Stevens contended, "No man did more to redeem his Church from the imputation of ignorance, not to say the contempt, with which it had been branded among the trained clergy… Fisk led up the whole Methodism of the East in educational enterprise, ministerial culture, and public influence."

America, a total of 53 permanent colleges were established between 1830 and 1861, the majority by America's churches. Of those successful schools, the Methodists founded thirty-two. Representative Methodist colleges were Randolph-Macon and Emory and Henry Colleges in Virginia; Dickinson and Allegheny Colleges in Pennsylvania; Indiana Asbury University in Indiana; McKendree College in Illinois; and Emory College in Georgia. These Methodist schools, along with others, such as Otterbein College and Albright College, have joined the ranks of excellent American colleges. Indeed, a large proportion of today's better-known American educational institutions, including a number of state-supported schools, began as church-supported colleges.

The ME Church was the first denomination to establish colleges for women. In 1839, in a bold and unprecedented step, the church founded Wesleyan Female College in Macon, Georgia. This school was the first women's college in the world to grant the B. A. degree. Other women's colleges were Greensboro Female College in North Carolina and Cincinnati College for Young Women. With the exception of the Cincinnati school, these women's colleges thrived.

Over the decades, Methodism established more than 1,200 schools, colleges, seminaries, and uni-

Randolph-Macon College (top) Wofford College (bottom).
Original buildings.

The founding of Virginia's Randolph-Macon College in 1832 was followed by the rise of other Methodist colleges in the South. In 1836, Methodists established Emory College in Georgia and Emory and Henry College in Virginia. Wofford College, in South Carolina, followed in 1851. These schools hired a number of Randolph-Macon graduates for their faculties.

Wesleyan Female College at Macon, Georgia.

This school began in 1836 under the leadership of a Methodist minister, Elijah Sinclair. A revival he led in the Mulberry Street ME Church in Macon, Georgia, led to a community desire for a college. Once the college began, its founders expressed an "ardent desire" to place it officially with the ME Church. Accordingly, in 1839 the church assumed control of the school, and it became the first college in the world to bestow the bachelor's degree upon a woman.

Cincinnati College for Young Women.

This school, founded in 1842, was one of Methodism's early colleges for women. The college eventually changed its name to Cincinnati Wesleyan College, and in 1868 moved into the building pictured above. At the time, the building was one of the most attractive structures in Cincinnati.

The interior of Duke Chapel, Duke University.

The United Methodist Church supports a large number of college preparatory schools, two-year colleges, senior colleges, seminaries, universities, and professional schools.

versities. One hundred and twenty-four of them remain today, and some of them rank among America's best schools of higher education. These institutions are an outgrowth of the original vision of the Wesleys—to unite knowledge and vital piety. United Methodism's University Senate defines and evaluates the educational standards of the educational institutions of the church. This agency, established in 1892, was the first accrediting body of its kind in the United States, pre-dating America's regional accrediting organizations.

The Woman's College of Baltimore City.

In 1884, the Baltimore Annual Conference held its 100th session. On the eve of the conference, the Women's Education Association published a supplement to *The Baltimore Methodist*. The piece issued a challenge to the conference: "One hundred and fifty thousand dollars held by the Education Board of the Baltimore Conference for the benefit of its sons and not one cent for its daughters. Is that fair? Is that wise? Not that we love our sons less or our daughters more, but let us give them equal advantages in the business of life."

After three days of debate, the conference unanimously approved a motion to "make the foundation and endowment of a female college the special object of its effort." In 1885, the Baltimore Conference of the ME Church incorporated Baltimore Woman's College as the ninth college for women in the United States. In 1910 the school changed its name to Goucher College, in honor of Dr. John F. Goucher, an early benefactor of the school.

The Development of Theological Seminaries

In the decades following 1820, the Methodists successfully planted a number of colleges. However, there was little support for the idea of building theological schools. Several arguments against seminaries were put forth: (1) The need for preachers was too pressing for Christian workers to spend time in academic seclusion. (2) Schools of theology might become hothouses for heresy. (3) Earlier Methodist preachers did mighty exploits without having attended theological school. (4) Practical experience on a circuit serves as the best training for ministry. (5) Only God can make preachers.

Prior to the 1840s, at least two-thirds of Methodism's preachers opposed starting theological schools. Those in opposition to schools of theology feared that they might produce preachers who lacked evangelistic passion and the willingness to endure the difficulties of riding a circuit. In 1840, a Methodist minister wrote an article in the *New York Christian Advocate* that called for the founding of a theological school. The idea was so alien to common sentiment that the magazine's editor, Thomas Bond, included a disclaimer stating that the *Christian Advocate* disagreed with the article. As late as 1866, Bishop George Pierce, of the ME Church, South, asserted, "It is my opinion that every dollar invested in a theological school will be a danger to Methodism. Had I a million dollars I would not give a dime for such an object."

In the meantime, the Methodist colleges were graduating growing numbers of laity. These graduates chafed under their poorly-educated ministers. They became increasingly intolerant of the poor grammar, lack of theological polish, and unrefined manners of some of the Methodist preachers. Congregations wanted preachers on an equal educational level with ministers in other denominations. Methodism was becoming a large American denomination, but some of its preachers lacked the education adequately to defend Methodist doctrines against the attacks of theological critics.

John Durbin, editor of the *New York Christian Advocate*, stood out as an early champion of graduate theological education. In a ground-breaking editorial, "An Educated Ministry Among Us," published July 18, 1834, Durbin argued in favor of establishing theological schools. The article stated,

The Methodist ministry might share more largely in this great work [of God], if to her first and great foundations, a Divine call and sound doctrine, she should add a suitable education.... Have you no interest in having ministers who are not only good and holy men of God; but such as can circulate freely in every class of society?... Have the people no interest in having a succession of ministers among them, that can be felt in community, and draw the world to Christ?

John Price Durbin (1800-1876).

After serving as a circuit rider in Ohio, in 1826 John Durbin became a professor of languages at Augusta College, at the time a leading college in the Kentucky-Ohio area. In 1831 he served as the chaplain of the United States Senate. Afterward, he became the editor of the New York *Christian Advocate*. As editor, he championed theological education for preachers.

In addition to Durbin's support of theological education, he was a tireless advocate of foreign missions. In 1852 the church elected him to the position of Missionary Secretary, in which position he remained for the rest of his active ministry. During his administration the church greatly expanded its work overseas, and contributions for missions increased almost seven-fold. The nineteenth-century *Cyclopaedia of Methodism* said of John Durbin, "Few men ever equaled him in solid and widespread popularity; few have been his equals in ability, fidelity, tact, and industry. He ranked among the first in the church as a pulpit orator, a pastor, educator, a writer, and an administrator."

Durbin also expressed the view that theological schools should require students to have a divine call to ministry and to receive the endorsement of those who were familiar with their ministries.

Meanwhile, in 1839 the Methodist academy in Newbury, Vermont, added a theological school. In 1847 the school moved to Concord, New Hampshire. As yet, however, the church had not given official denominational approval to begin seminaries. This theological school, at the time, lacked the official sponsorship of the church.

In 1855, Randolph S. Foster published a short book titled *A Treatise on the Need of the Methodist Episcopal Church With Respect to Her Ministry.* Foster argued, "[The church] needs a thoroughly-educated and liberally-informed ministry." He called for Methodism to develop a strong intellectual framework to support its spiritual life and institutional mission. Foster asked:

Bishop Randolph S. Foster (1820-1903).

Foster was converted to Christ at the age of 11, and he eventually became a gifted preacher. He studied at Augusta College in Kentucky, but on the advice of others left before graduation to become a circuit rider. In his pastorate in Cincinnati he gained widespread renown for defending Methodism's beliefs against a critic of Methodist doctrine. Foster's work was published in 1849 as *Objections to Calvinism.* Eventually, he became the president of Northwestern University, then professor of systematic theology and president of Drew Theological Seminary.

Foster's numerous books were influential. His titles include *The Nature and Blessedness of Christian Purity, Philosophy of Christian Experience, Address in Sacred Memories, Beyond the Grave, Centenary Thoughts, The First Hundred Years of Episcopal Methodism, Union of Episcopal Methodisms,* and a six-volume work, *Studies in Theology.* His brilliant intellect gained him numerous invitations to speak on difficult and profound subjects, and Foster was a favorite speaker at the Chautauqua Institutes. In 1872, the ME church elected Foster its twenty-fourth bishop. He reluctantly accepted the office, declaring that he preferred teaching in seminary to the administrative cares of the episcopacy. Nevertheless, Foster served effectively as a bishop for 24 years.

Newbury Biblical Institute.

In 1839, ministers and laity meeting in the Bromfield Street Church in Boston took the first step toward developing a school of theology in American Methodism. They selected a Methodist academy in Newbury, Vermont, as the site for a theological school.

This school, established in 1839, was the genesis of the first Methodist theological seminary in America.

Will a man sit as a learner at the feet of a child? Will he, can he become the docile listener at the lips of one he knows to be his inferior? Whose ignorance shames, and whose inabilities offend him? Will he, especially when, without serious compromise of feeling or principle, he can supply himself and family with the instruction and entertainment which they crave, but which their teacher cannot furnish?... This is precisely the tendency at the present time: a tendency which must increase and produce wide havoc, if we awake not to our responsibility.

A year after Foster's book appeared, the 1856 General Conference of the ME Church approved a plan to begin theological seminaries.

The most prominent figure in starting Methodist theological seminaries was John Dempster. In the early 1830s, while serving as a superintendent in the Oneida Conference

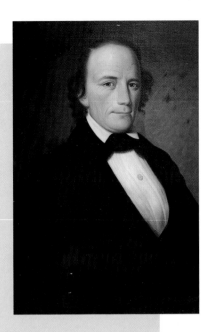

John Dempster (1794-1863).
This portrait is located at Garrett-Evangelical Theological Seminary, and is printed here by permission. Photo by Adolf Hansen.

Dempster was the son of James Dempster, a Methodist missionary that John Wesley had sent to America. Following the younger Dempster's conversion at a Methodist camp meeting at the age of 18, he devoted the rest of his life to faithful study and ministerial labor. From 1818 to 1835, he served as a circuit preacher and a district superintendent. In 1842, after serving as a missionary to South America, he was assigned to a pastorate in New York City. Next, Dempster became president of Newbury Academy in Vermont. In 1847 he helped move this school to Concord, New Hampshire, where it took the name Methodist General Biblical Institute. This school, later moved to Boston (1867), had the distinction of being American Methodism's first graduate theological school.

After serving the theological school in Concord, New Hampshire, Dempster went to Chicago in 1853, where he was instrumental in establishing the church's second theological school, Garrett Biblical Institute. Dempster was a man of tireless energy and was devoted to the cause of theological education. He had laid plans for another theological school on the Pacific coast, but before he could carry out those plans, he underwent surgery, from which he did not recover.

(central New York), Dempster had found that the educated people converted under Methodist preaching often joined other denominations because those churches had ministers who were better educated. He implored Bishop Elijah Hedding to provide him with educated pastors. The bishop was forced to answer, "We have no such men to spare." A crusading fire ignited within Dempster, and he devoted the rest of his life to graduate theological education. His tireless work earned him the appellation "The Father of Methodist Theological Education."

In 1844 Dempster became president of the Methodist Biblical Institute of Newbury, Vermont (later moved to Concord, New Hampshire). He encouraged his students to combine a search for knowledge with a quest for God: "Let your convictions never be shaken of the kindredship of *intellectual* and *moral* improvement. Never sunder these which God has joined together.... Never, then, divorce the highest culture of the mind from the deepest piety of the heart. No more suppose that the intellectual and moral power can be separated in ourselves than in the Almighty which made us."

In 1853, John Dempster moved to Chicago to help found the church's second theological school. At the time, Americans regarded this area as the "Northwest." In planning for the seminary, the trustees agreed that the instructors must be theologically and spiritually "the most fit and proper men." The seminary's charter stipulated that the bishops should take responsibility for approving only those professors who held sound theological opinions. With money contributed by Mrs. Eliza Garrett, the school opened in 1855 in Evanston, as Garrett Biblical Institute, with Dempster as its first president. He addressed the students on the importance of spiritual formation for the ordained ministry: "The whole character calls for a high controlling piety—a living, energetic, all-conquering piety—one that imbues

Eliza Garrett (1805-1855).
This portrait is located at Garrett-Evangelical Theological Seminary, and is printed here by permission. Photograph by Adolf Hansen.

In 1834 Eliza and Augustus Garrett moved to Chicago where Mr. Garrett became a successful businessman. In 1939 the two of them were converted to Christ at Clark Street Methodist Episcopal Church, where they became members. In 1843, Mr. Garrett became mayor of the city. He died in 1848, leaving Mrs. Garrett a large estate. She gave most of her money to found Methodism's second theological school, named Garrett Biblical Institute, now Garrett-Evangelical Theological Seminary.

Dempster Hall at Garrett Biblical Institute.

This frame building, constructed in 1854, was the first educational building on what is now the campus of Northwestern University. The ground floor housed the "boarding department" for students; the second floor had rooms for faculty families, classes, and a chapel; the third floor contained student rooms and the library. When the school opened, it had four students and three faculty members.

the heart, the life, the studies, the habits, the whole man." In honor of Dempster's effective leadership, the seminary named its first building Dempster Hall.

In 1867, the trustees of the Methodist Biblical Institute—first at Newbury, then at Concord—relocated in Boston. After the move, it was renamed Boston Theological Seminary, and William F. Warren became its first president. Warren later became president of Boston University, where he recruited an outstanding faculty. Among those who taught there was Alexander Graham Bell, who invented the telephone while at the university.

Methodism's seminaries gave attention both to academics and to spiritual formation. Garrett Biblical Institute's initial catalog stated, "Every student is required to maintain a spirit and deportment worthy of his profession as a Christian and as a candidate for the Christian ministry; bearing in mind that one great design of the Institution is to aid in forming the character of ministers of Christ." While addressing a graduating class, Dempster talked about the necessity of God's anointing on one's preaching: "That moment the pulpit assumes independent action of God's Spirit, the distance becomes *infinite* between the *means* and the *end*. The simple motion of Moses' rod has as much adequacy in piling in heaps the ocean depths as pulpit eloquence in effecting conversions without the Spirit."

Boston University Theological Seminary.

This picture shows how the school appeared in the nineteenth century. This school was the forerunner of Boston University, of which the seminary is a part.

Northwestern University Woman's College.

Northwestern University, founded in 1851, established a Woman's College in 1873.

Daniel Drew (1791-1879).

Mr. Drew provided money to found Drew Theological Seminary in Madison, New Jersey; Drew Ladies' Seminary in Carmel, New York; a Methodist church at Carmel, New York; and several additional enterprises in the Methodist Episcopal Church.

The Methodist Centenary celebrations of 1866 included fundraising for theological education. This church-wide effort garnered financial aid for Methodism's two seminaries—Boston and Garrett. The campaign also raised funds to establish four additional seminaries (although the one projected for Cincinnati failed to materialize). In 1867, Methodism's third seminary was founded in Madison, New Jersey. This theological school was made possible by a generous gift from Methodist millionaire Daniel Drew. Again, John Dempster's influence was apparent. He had been Mr. Drew's pastor prior to his (Dempster's) leaving the pastorate to devote full time to theological education.

The ME Church established additional seminaries, as did the ME Church, South. The Methodist Protestant, United Brethren, and Evangelical Churches also built theological schools. In 1871, the Church of the United Brethren opened Union Seminary in Dayton, Ohio. This institution later took the name Bonebrake Seminary and in 1954 was renamed United Theological Seminary. In 1876 the Evangelical Church opened Union Biblical Institute in Naperville, Illinois. In 1881 the Methodist Protestant Church started what is now Wesley Theological Seminary. And in 1883 the ME Church opened Gammon Theological Seminary for training black ministers. Today, the United Methodist Church supports 13 theological seminaries. In the order of their founding, they are:

Boston University School of Theology, 1839

Garrett-Evangelical Theological Seminary, 1855

Drew University Theological School, 1867

United Theological Seminary, 1871

Wesley Theological Seminary, 1881

Gammon Theological Seminary, 1883

School of Theology at Claremont, 1885

Iliff School of Theology, 1892

Candler School of Theology, 1914

Perkins School of Theology, 1915

Duke University Divinity School, 1926

St. Paul School of Theology, 1958

Methodist Theological School in Ohio, 1960

Mead Hall, Drew Theological Seminary.
Photograph by Darlene Shoop.

This building was originally the William Gibbons Mansion, constructed in 1832. Daniel Drew purchased this property, along with additional buildings and considerable acreage (including 80 acres of forest), for the site of Drew Seminary. The opening ceremonies on Nov. 6, 1867, drew all the church's bishops, 200 ministers from 24 conferences, church officials, and many guests. Among the speakers was Dr. Daniel Curry, the celebrated editor of the *New York Christian Advocate*. Curry said to the solemn assembly, "Concerning our doctrines there are those which are essentially Methodist, and which ought never to be lost sight of... These we demand that our professors shall inculcate."

Thomas Jackson, one of John Wesley's early biographers, wrote that Wesley's work shows "close connexion between useful knowledge and vital godliness. [His work is] at once designed and calculated, not only to improve the understanding, but also to promote the love of God and man." This joining of head and heart constitutes a major theme running through the symphony of Methodism's grand heritage.

Several other independent seminaries also embrace the Wesleyan heritage and are engaged in preparing men and women for ministry in the United Methodist Church.

The Wesleyan perspective continues to influence higher education at the college, seminary, and university levels. The passionate pioneers who started the church's educational institutions envisioned schools that would transmit the treasures of the Christian faith to successive generations of students.

The intended purpose of education in the Wesleyan way is summed up in the following verse of Charles Wesley:

> Let us unite the two so long disjoined,
> Knowledge and vital piety;
> Learning and holiness combined,
> And truth and love, let all men see
> In those whom up to Thee we give,
> Thine, wholly Thine, to die and live.

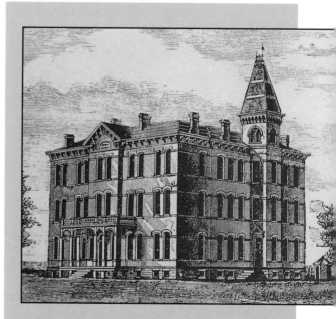

Union Biblical Seminary.

The Church of the United Brethren opened this theological school in 1871 in Dayton. Today, this school is named United Theological Seminary.

9 Worship in the Wesleyan Way

John Wesley was keenly interested in the biblical account of our creation in God's image and likeness. Elaborating on this theme, he concluded: "[Humankind] is capable of God; the inferior creatures [animals] are not.... This is the specific difference between man and brute; the great gulf which they cannot pass over." John's brother Charles agreed. In a hymn calling for repentance, he wrote:

> Let the beasts their breath resign,
> Strangers to the life divine...
>
> You for higher ends were born,
> You may all to God return,
> Dwell with him above the sky;
> Why will you resolve to die?

The unique human ability to commune personally with God stands out as a basic biblical theme and an especially important Wesleyan distinctive. Building on this truth, Methodism developed a rich tradition of worship.

The early Methodists attracted widespread attention because of the joy, freedom, and power so evident in Methodist worship services. These assemblies enabled multitudes of common folk to understand the gospel and experience a personal relationship with Jesus Christ. For many people, Methodist worship in the open fields and rustic chapels had a greater attraction than services in majestic cathedrals where worship had become uninspired and uninspiring. In 1759

"The Sleeping Congregation" *by William Hogarth (1697-1764).*

Hogarth's satirical drawings pointed out the foibles of eighteenth-century English church life. This picture shows an apathetic priest reading the service to a sleepy congregation. Some Anglican priests preached briefly (if at all) and so poorly that the few who attended their services did not expect any inspiration from their sermons.

A number of the priests neglected the laboring classes and spent their time drinking with friends. Some of the priests consumed so much alcohol that their parishioners referred to them as "three bottle men." The lazy and spiritually bereft priests repelled many from the church and created a need for the ministries of Methodism.

In contrast to dull religious services, worship in the Methodist chapels was lively and often profoundly inspiring. John Wesley designed the worship in Methodist chapels to complement Anglican worship, not to replace it. He contended that people could gain from worship in the established church, even if some of its unbelieving priests lived scandalous lives. The words of the liturgy were always valid. Because the sermons in the established church were often poor, preaching assumed an especially important place in Methodist worship. Wesley commented on the preaching and prayers of the Methodist lay speakers as being "artless and unlabored, and yet rational and scriptural."

Rural church in Kentucky.

American Methodism has kept a tension between two modes of worship—free worship and structured worship. Free worship includes extemporaneous prayers, gospel songs, testimonies, and unstructured services. Structured worship makes use of formal prayers, ordered liturgy, hymns, responsive readings, and canticles.

Free worship in Methodism has tended to express spontaneity, individual experience and the impromptu demonstration of emotion. Formal worship tends to emphasize order, corporate devotion, and the awareness of the church's link with historic Christianity. The two forms of worship are not opposed to one another; they are complementary. In general, congregations tend over time to move from informal worship toward structured worship. At the same time, some congregations that cherish ritual discover the values of informality and incorporate it into their traditional ways of worshiping.

John Wesley recorded an incident that highlighted the extraordinary attraction of Methodist worship: "The roads were so extremely slippery, it was with much difficulty we reached Bedford. We had a pretty large congregation; but the stench from the swine under the Room was scarce supportable. Was ever a preaching-place over a hog-sty before? Surely they love the Gospel, who come to hear it in such a place."

John Wesley called for worship that is "both scriptural and rational." He and his brother Charles developed a variety of practices designed to assist the Methodists in the worship of God. In doing so, they established a unique worship tradition that constitutes a treasured aspect of the heritage of American Methodism.

The Dynamic of Wesleyan Worship

John Wesley spoke to the question, "What is it to worship God in spirit and truth?" He defined such worship as directed toward and energized by the holy Trinity:

> [To worship God in spirit and truth] is to worship him with our spirit; to worship him in that manner which none but spirits are capable of. It is to believe in him, as a wise, just, holy Being, of purer eyes than to behold iniquity; and yet merciful, gracious, and long-suffering; forgiving iniquity, and transgression, and sin; casting all our sins behind his back, and accepting us in the Beloved. It is, to love him, to delight in him, to desire him, with all our heart, and mind, and soul, and strength; to imitate him we love, by purifying ourselves even as He is pure; and to obey him whom we love, and in whom we believe, both in thought, and word, and work. Consequently, one branch of the worshipping God in spirit and in truth is, the keeping his outward commandments. To glorify him, therefore, with our bodies, as well as with our spirits; to go through outward work with hearts lifted up to him; to make our daily employment a sacrifice to God; to buy and sell, to eat and drink, to his glory; —this is worshipping God in spirit and in truth.

Wesley emphasized that the only worship acceptable to God is worship with an undivided heart. For instance, in giving directions for hymn singing he wrote, "Above all sing *spiritually*. Have an eye to God in every word you sing. Aim at pleasing *Him* more than yourself, or any other creature. In order to do this attend strictly to the sense of what you sing, and see that your *Heart* is not carried away with the sound, but offered to God continually."

Wesleyan worship focused on God, the source of all the multiplied benefits and blessings provided through Jesus Christ and made personal by the Holy Spirit. Wesleyan worship assumes that if worship centers on anything other than God, it easily moves away from its purpose. Charles Wesley's hymns of worship have endured because they keep us focused on the Creator and our response to his love.

In the days of early Methodism, the services of worship pointed to the divine realities not present to our physical eyes. Once, leading a service at City Road Chapel, John Wesley became caught up into a sublime awareness of being in the presence of God. He stood silently for 10 minutes, as though transported into another realm. A participant in that service later wrote, "His eyes were closed, his countenance devoutly lifted to heaven, and his hands clasped together on the pulpit Bible." The congregation sat almost transfixed, sensing that heaven was touching earth. Then Wesley announced the hymn, which contained the following verses:

> *Come let us join our friends above,*
> *That have obtained the prize,*
> *And on the eagle wings of love,*
> *To joys celestial rise.*
>
> *One family we dwell in Him,*
> *One Church above, beneath,*
> *Though now divided by the stream*
> *The narrow stream of death.*

An eyewitness reported that the people wept and worshiped, singing as though in harmony with celestial choirs.

Wesleyan worship brought the people to an encounter with God which transformed their lives, set them to singing, and motivated them to minister to others. Once, Hester Ann Rogers wrote to John Wesley, "The preaching-house was filled, and God was truly present to bless; many were awakened, and some converted.... The house was truly shaken (I mean every soul therein) by the power of God. I believe none present, preachers or people, will ever forget it. I trust I never shall. It was none other than the ante-chamber of glory to my soul!—the house of God!—the gate of heaven."

Early missionaries brought the spirit and power of Methodist worship to America, where it took root and found appropriate expressions in its new environment. Numerous accounts of Methodism's worship services refer to them as "Pentecostal seasons." The following description of early American Methodist worship is typical.

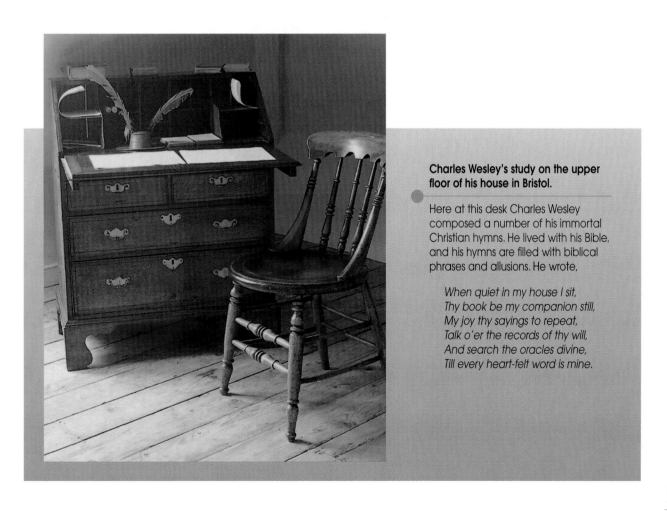

Charles Wesley's study on the upper floor of his house in Bristol.

Here at this desk Charles Wesley composed a number of his immortal Christian hymns. He lived with his Bible, and his hymns are filled with biblical phrases and allusions. He wrote,

When quiet in my house I sit,
Thy book be my companion still,
My joy thy sayings to repeat,
Talk o'er the records of thy will,
And search the oracles divine,
Till every heart-felt word is mine.

It appears in the *Journal of Bishop Richard Whatcoat* (original spellings and punctuation):

At Nine we Gave the Sacrament to Near two hundred people But one of the preachers Mightely Exhort[ed] the people so that the power of God Came Down and interupted in Giving the Elements which Continued Neare two hours at Eleven F asbury preach[d] to Maney More then [than] the house Could Hold at the Close of his Discource the power of the Lord Came Down upon the people So that Maney began to praise the Lord Call upon his Name and Exhort the people &C I hope Meney will Date their Conversion from the Q [Quarterly] Meeting.

Methodism's early preachers often reported that God gave them "liberty" in preaching, as the Holy Spirit anointed their sermons. When God's word entered receptive hearts, Methodist worship services became "melting times," by which it was meant that some were moved to tears of joy. Jesse Lee wrote about Methodism's revivals in 1789: "The word was so accompanied by the energy of the Holy Ghost, that there were few but felt its mighty power. Some of the greatest revilers of the work were constrained to tremble and weep."

John Wesley's statue at Wesley's Chapel, City Road, London.
This sculpture of John Wesley is by Adams-Acton, and it was erected in 1891 on the centenary of Wesley's death. George Dance the younger designed the chapel, regarded as the Mother Church of World Methodism. Wesley described it as "perfectly neat, but not fine." Wesley's tomb is behind the chapel. Picture reproduced by permission of the Trustees for Methodist Church Purposes, Great Britain.

With regard to worship, as with other aspects of the Christian life, John Wesley borrowed from diverse religious traditions and reshaped them to serve his central purpose—evangelism and spiritual nurture. On the one hand, Wesley declared himself to be "a Church of England man." As such, he held a deep appreciation for, and loyalty to, its theology, liturgy and polity. On the other hand, Wesley was not bound by the Anglican tradition. He freely borrowed from such diverse traditions as Roman Catholicism, Eastern Orthodoxy, the Protestant reformers, Moravians and Puritans.

In his unique blending of traditions, he sought to remain loyal to the plain teaching of the Bible and the mission to which God had called him. Always, he sought to communicate clearly. In the preface to his sermons he wrote, "I design plain truth for plain people: therefore, of set purpose, I abstain from all nice and philosophical speculations; from all perplexed and intricate reasonings; and, as far as possible, from even the show of learning, unless in sometimes citing the original (Hebrew or Greek) Scripture." The result of Wesley's eclecticism led to the formation of a creative and highly effective new religious tradition called Methodism.

128

Formal and Informal Worship

Two influences helped shape the development of worship in American Methodism—one formal and the other informal. The formal side of United Methodist worship was based on John Wesley's *Sunday Service*, which he prepared for American Methodism. This liturgy derives from the worship forms of the Church of England. Its influence continues in American Methodism, most notably in its formal services of Baptism, Holy Communion, Marriage, Ordination, and Burial.

The informal side of Methodist worship developed as a complement to the liturgy of the Church of England. John Wesley explained that free worship was not a replacement for Anglican liturgy, but rather an enriching addition. Informal Methodist worship found expression in extemporaneous prayer, preaching without notes, outdoor meetings, lay involvement in worship services, and a variety of spontaneous expressions of worship.

Methodist worship has not been as tradition-bound as Anglican worship or as anti-liturgical as some of the Puritan churches. Instead, Methodist worship has been free to combine both formal and informal modes of worship. Although John Wesley regarded the Anglican liturgy as "possessed of rare excellence," he did not hesitate either to delete or change those parts he believed he could improve. Wesley reported that the Methodists "did not object to the use of forms, [but] they durst not confine themselves to them." He approved both the formal services of the cathedral and the informal services held in homes, modest chapels, and open fields. He publicly read the historic Anglican prayers, and he often prayed extemporaneously. Sometimes

THE WORLD IS MY PARISH

ERECTED WITH FUNDS COLLECTED
BY THE CHILDREN OF METHODISM

WESLEY

he delivered his sermons from a manuscript; at other times he preached without notes. John Wesley combined the use of extemporaneous worship with liturgy. This balance permitted a large degree of freedom in worship, while assuring a measure of order and dignity. In combining formal and informal approaches to God, Methodism has made a historically significant contribution to Christian worship.

The Sunday Service

When John Wesley consecrated Thomas Coke as the first superintendent of American Methodism, he sent Coke to America with a book of worship titled *The Sunday Service of the Methodists in North America With Other Occasional Services.* Wesley had adapted this work from the Church of England's Book of Common Prayer, making appropriate changes for the American Methodists. In doing so, he eliminated most of the Anglican holy days, shortened the services, and omitted phrases he considered "improper for the mouths of a Christian congregation" (e. g., prayers to saints and intercessions for the dead). Throughout the *Sunday Service,* Wesley substituted the word *elder* for *priest,* and changed the title *bishop* to *superintendent.* He replaced the priestly declaration of absolution with a brief prayer for pardon. In the liturgy for the Baptism of Infants, he dispensed with the Anglican practice of signing the infant with a cross, and he struck out the phrase, "It hath pleased God to regenerate this infant with His Holy Spirit." In all, Wesley retained the historic grandeur of the Anglican liturgy.

The founding conference of the Methodist Episcopal Church adopted Wesley's *Sunday Service* as its official Book of Worship. At first, the American Methodist preachers attempted to use this liturgy. Jesse Lee wrote, "In the large towns, and in some country places, our preachers read prayers [from the *Sunday Service*] on the Lord's day: and in some cases the preachers read part of the morning service on Wednesdays and Fridays." For a brief period, American Methodism's bishops and some of the preachers wore gowns and bands, after the manner of Anglican priests. For a short time, Bishop

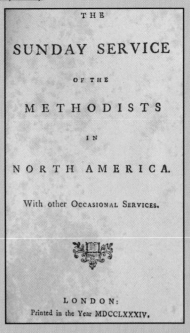

Title page of John Wesley's *Sunday Service* for the American Methodists.

John Wesley's *Sunday Service* has served as the foundation for Methodist worship in America. In 1784 Wesley commended this book of worship to the American Methodists: "I believe there is no Liturgy in the world, either in ancient or modern language, which breathes more of solid, Scriptural, rational piety than the Common Prayer of the Church of England; and though the main of it was compiled considerably more than two hundred years ago, yet is the language of it not only pure, but strong and elegant in the highest degree." Wesley's adaptation of the Book of Common Prayer for the American Methodists is called the *Sunday Service.* Some have called this work John Wesley's last will and testament to the Methodists in America.

Asbury (wearing a white wig) appeared in "full canonical gown, cassock, and bands" and read from the prayer book.

Such formalities, however, did not fit American Methodism. The sturdy homespun garments of the weather-beaten circuit riders suited them better than the embroidered linen of priestly robes. American Methodism soon discontinued the use of Wesley's *Sunday Service* in favor of free and spontaneous worship. In 1810 Jesse Lee, who had originally favored adopting the *Sunday Service,* wrote, "After a few years the prayer book was laid aside, and has never been used since in public worship." For many decades, the Methodists did not print the *Sunday Service.*

Several factors contributed to American Methodism's move away from formal liturgy. Most of the Methodists were farmers and laborers who were unaccustomed to the formal style of the *Sunday Service.* The language of the liturgy reminded them of the (then absent) Anglican priests who had viewed the Methodists as uncultured and uneducated people. Furthermore, the stately language of the *Sunday Service* seemed out of place in American Methodism's simple meetinghouses, humble

COMMUNION WARE

IN ELEGANT DESIGNS
HEAVILY PLATED WITH PURE SILVER

Style 12, as shown in illustration

PRICES

Flagon, 1½ quarts,	$12.50	Goblet, 1 pint,	4.00, gold lined, $5.00
" 2 "	13.50	Plate, 10-inch,	4.50
" 3 "	15.00	" 11-inch,	5.50
Baptismal Bowl,	$8.00, gold lined, 10.00		

Set of 6 pieces

3-pint Flagon, Bowl, 2 Cups, and 2 Plates, . . 37.50
Same, with Cups and Bowl gold lined, . . . 41.50

Write us for special terms to Churches.

150 Fifth Avenue, **METHODIST BOOK CONCERN** NEW YORK

Advertisement for communion ware appearing in the 1898 *Christian Advocate*.

From fermented to unfermented communion wine.

In 1869, the First Methodist Episcopal Church of Vineland, New Jersey elected Dr. Thomas Bramwell Welch as Communion Steward. Welch accepted the position provided that he would be permitted to use grape juice, pasteurized by a new method he had recently discovered. Thus, Welch and his son Charles pasteurized the first bottles of "unfermented sacramental wine" for use at the communion services. This circumstance marks the beginning of the use of grape juice for communion in Methodism. Favorable reaction to Welch's new product was so great that it gave rise to a highly successful new grape juice industry, pioneered by the Welches.

In 1870, the New Jersey Conference organized a Temperance Society "to oppose the manufacture, and use of, and traffic in all kinds of intoxicating liquors as a beverage." In 1875 the New Jersey Conference urged all its churches to use unfermented wine in Holy Communion. Soon, the entire Methodist Episcopal Church began using grape juice for Holy Communion. This practice continues in most United Methodist congregations today.

Interestingly, in 1913 William Jennings Bryan, Secretary of State, startled the world by substituting Welch's grape juice for wine at a full-dress diplomatic function honoring the retiring British ambassador. For months, cartoonists and journalists ridiculed Bryan's action.

In 1914, the Secretary of the Navy, Josephus Daniels, forbade the use of alcoholic beverages on the ships of the U.S. Navy. As a substitute for fermented wine, the navy served Welch's grape juice to all members of the U.S. fleet.

homes, primitive barns, and open-air brush arbors. In ordinary conversation the Methodists did not use such lofty language. The Americans did not feel comfortable reading prepared prayers from a book. They preferred to pray extemporaneously (with eyes closed) about the concerns immediately on their minds. In short, the temperament of early American Methodism was incompatible with the fixed liturgy and formal cadences of the *Sunday Service*.

Despite the preference for informal worship, the 1792 General Conference expressed concern about the lack of order and structure in Methodist worship. The preachers agreed on "the establishment of uniformity in public worship amongst us on the Lord's Day." Accordingly, the bishops prepared public worship guidelines to ensure a common form of worship throughout the church.

In 1824, the Methodist Episcopal Church took further steps toward more formal worship services. The General Conference that year stipulated that when conducting baptisms and administering Holy Communion, the preachers should use the liturgy in Wesley's *Sunday Service*. The 1824 conference also mandated that the preachers' opening prayers in worship services conclude with the Lord's Prayer and that they close their services with a trinitarian benediction. As well, the church adopted the *Sunday Service* rituals for the ordination of clergy and the consecration of bishops. A later General Conference (1864) moved the church toward still more formality in worship. The conference instructed congregations to join the preacher in repeating the Lord's Prayer and in singing the doxology at the end of each worship service.

While making these adjustments, Methodists also retained informal elements of worship. As the nineteenth century unfolded, some continued to punctuate prayers and preaching with exclamations of "Amen," "Hallelujah," and "Praise the Lord." Occasionally, a sister or brother would shout for joy, as the Methodists had done so frequently in earlier times. Many churches retained the use of public testimonies, because they provided opportunities for individual lay people to express themselves in worship services.

The end result of these developments was that Methodism's Sunday morning services became more formal, while Sunday evening services, midweek prayer gatherings, and camp meetings continued to use freer forms of worship. On Sunday mornings the congregations ordinarily sang the Wesleyan hymns from the official Methodist hymnal; at the other services they sang more informal songs from unofficial hymn collections called "songsters." Often, formal and informal worship took place in the same service. This integration of ritual and spontaneity distinguished Methodist worship as unique in American Protestantism.

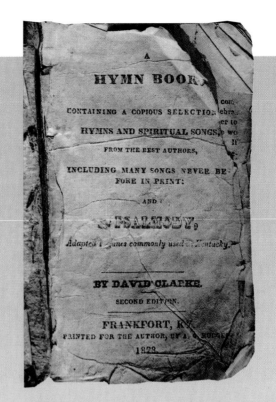

A "Songster" used by Methodists in their camp meetings.

Songsters were unofficial hymnbooks, containing many songs that were not in Methodism's official hymnals. Most of these songs, while sincere, have not survived the test of time. For example, the following song in common meter, "Belshazzar Smitten," was once popular, but it is no longer sung.

> *Poor sinners! Little do they think*
> *With whom they have to do!*
> *But stand, securely, on the brink,*
> *Of everlasting woe!*
>
> *Belshazzar, thus profanely bold*
> *The Lord of hosts defied!*
> *But vengeance soon his hoasts(sic) controll'd;*
> *And humbled all his pride!*
>
> *His pomp and music, guests and wine*
> *No more delight afford;*
> *O! sinner, ere this case be thine,*
> *Begin to seek the Lord!*

Another example of the hymn texts in the songsters illustrates the use of the language of the day to describe those who were turning from darkness to light:

> *Sinners through the camp are falling*
> *Deep distress their souls pervade*
> *Wondering why they are not rolling*
> *In the dark infernal shade.*

American Camp Meeting, 1930s.
This painting by Kenneth Wyatt hangs in the Beeson Center at Asbury Theological Seminary. Photo courtesy of the seminary department of development.

Starting at the end of the eighteenth century, a powerful revival swept through much of America. This religious renewal was called the Second Great Awakening. One of the forms of worship to come out of that revival was the camp meeting. The early camp meetings attracted large crowds. These times of worship, sometimes called "sacramental seasons," contributed significantly to the growth of Methodism and elevated the morality of the frontier.

Hundreds of camp meetings developed across America, and many still continue today. This scene of a camp meeting in the 1930s shows a "ring of prayer." Before the services began, people gathered in a circle to pray. Those who prayed "bound the powers of darkness" and petitioned God for the conversion of sinners, the reclamation of backsliders, and the sanctification of believers. This picture shows all adult males, although these rings of prayer frequently included women and children.

Methodism's Liturgical Revival

In 1826 American Methodism celebrated the semi-centennial anniversary of its beginnings. On that occasion, Freeborn Garrettson's address to the New York Annual Conference set in motion a series of changes in Methodist worship. Garrettson called on the denomination to recover the neglected benefits of Wesley's *Sunday Service*. He lamented, "I have been astonished to see some of our brethren...laying aside such beautiful and expressive compositions [in the *Sunday Service*], and marrying, baptizing, and even administering the Lord's supper, extemporaneously. I am sorry to lose a single sentence or even word of our sacramental forms." Garrettson's exhortation prompted a reconsideration of Methodism's liturgical heritage. Meanwhile, increasing numbers of college-trained preachers moved the church toward more formal styles of worship. Educated church members came to treasure the beauty of liturgy and its centuries-old link with historic Christianity. American Methodist congregations, however, have very seldom, or never, observed the rituals for evensong and special holy days found in Wesley's *Sunday Service*.

In 1866 Dr. Thomas O. Summers of the ME Church, South, persuaded the southern branch of Methodism to reprint Wesley's *Sunday Service* so that it would be available to those who wanted to use it. The 1892 General Conference of Methodism's northern branch authorized the bishops to "promulgate two orders of service, one taken from the order used in England as adapted from John Wesley's [*Sunday Service*]... the other to be an order the bishops judge best." Local churches were free to choose the liturgy best suited to their needs.

In 1896 the Methodist Episcopal Church adopted a new order of public worship and added it to the existing (1878) hymnal. This trend toward formality met with some resistance. As late as 1881, W. McKay had presented a paper at the first "Oecumenical Methodist Conference" on *Possible Perils of Methodism from Formality, Worldliness, and Improper Amusements among our own Members*. Interestingly, McKay

Thomas O. Summers (1812-1882).

In 1845 Summers served as the secretary of the Louisville Convention at which the ME Church, South was organized. Summers became the general editor of books and of the *Christian Advocate* for the southern branch of Methodism. He gave much attention to hymnology, liturgy, theology and worship. He chaired the committee that compiled a hymnal for the ME Church, South. Summers also served as professor of systematic theology and dean of the theological faculty of Vanderbilt University. His six-volume *Ritual of the ME Church, South,* his *Treatise on Baptism,* and his *Catechetical Condition of the Church* successfully argued for the church to develop a greater appreciation for Methodism's liturgical heritage.

placed "formality" alongside worldliness and improper amusements as a danger to the church. Some claimed that there was only one place for "the rags of ritualism"—"in the wastebasket." Still, the trend toward formal worship gathered strength.

In 1905, anticipating an eventual merger, the ME and ME, South Churches published a common hymnal containing a structured order of worship. The liturgy included the Apostles' Creed, the *Gloria Patri*, and responsive readings. Some of the clergy and laity protested that these additions were too formal. Most congregations, however, soon adapted to the new order of worship, and it gained widespread use across the church.

By the 1920s and 1930s, there was a noticeable shift away from emotional demonstrations in Methodist worship services. The church seldom saw the exuberant expressions of worship so common in the early decades of the denomination. Certain leaders expressed embarrassment over lingering informalities in Methodist worship, and they called for public services marked by "decorum, dignity, and decency." Once, Methodist preachers had invited their congregations to "Praise the Lord with a mighty voice" and declared, "Let the redeemed of the Lord say so." Now, a new generation of preachers called for order and formality. Earlier generations of Methodists were known for spontaneous testimonies and shouts of joy; now, worship services used printed liturgies, and observed periods of silence. Pastors began reading prayers, calls to worship, collects, and other fixed forms of liturgy. After almost 140 years of relative neglect, parts of John Wesley's *Sunday Service* regained widespread use in the church.

Concurrent with this move toward formal worship, congregations built more elaborate church buildings. The early Methodists had built houses of worship that were free of architectural embellishments. Now, during the 1840s, the Methodists were erecting large and ornamented churches. Originally, the Methodists had positioned the pulpit at the center, symbolizing the centrality of the Bible and the ministry of prophetic preaching. A new liturgical movement led to "splitting the chancel" and moving the pulpit

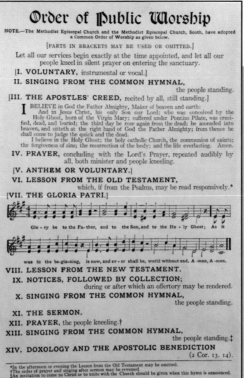

Order of Public Worship from the 1905 Methodist Hymnal.

This hymnal, the work of 22 ministers and lay persons appointed in equal numbers by the two branches of Methodism, was a joint project of the ME and ME, South Churches. A stated purpose of this hymnal was "to provide a worthy manual of song for use in the public and private worship of Almighty God, and to testify to the world the essential unity of the two great branches of Episcopal Methodism." The Order of Public Worship printed in the front of this volume helped make Methodist worship more uniform and structured.

"Lighting the candles."
This photograph shows two acolytes assisting in the worship service in Haymount United Methodist Church, Fayetteville, North Carolina.

As Methodist worship became more formal, robes and vestments came into use as a way to add to the sense of dignity and reverence. The use of candles symbolizes Jesus Christ as the light of the world. Candles, possessing both light and warmth, also represent the prayers of those at worship.

from the center to the side. This symbolic shift emphasized the centrality of the communion table and the priestly ministry of the clergy. Some congregations began using formal liturgies for Advent, Christmas, Epiphany, Lent, Easter, and Pentecost. Churches instituted choirs (sometimes paying singers), and adopted liturgical worship. It is not accurate to say that Methodism became a liturgical church. It is fair, though, to say that it became *more* liturgical, while retaining a blend of formal and informal worship.

The Book of Worship

In 1944 the Methodist Church adopted its first book of worship. In doing so, the church restricted the materials in the *Discipline* to matters of church law and government and placed worship materials in the new *Book of Worship*. The Preface to the *Book of Worship* stated:

Methodism has never been considered a liturgical church, but it always has had fixed forms to guide it in its recurrent acts of public worship.... Methodism has thus a twofold tradition of worship—both liturgical and free. It is liturgical in conducting its recurrent stated services with reverence...it is free in its ability to use extempore prayer, to bend each service to the glorifying of God and to the bringing of his saving grace unto [all].

The intent of this book of worship was to make available in one volume the historic offices and rituals of Methodism, along with a substantial collection of devotional material in the form of prayers, scripture readings, and orders of worship. The Book of Worship was prepared for public, family, and private use—and it enjoyed wide acceptance.

In 1964 the General Conference of the Methodist Church adopted a revision of the church's 1944 Book of Worship. The new book of worship anticipated the impending merger of the Methodist and Evangelical United Brethren Churches. Its introduction stated, "[The volume is] not intended in any way to fetter the spontaneity or reject the reliance upon the Holy Spirit which have characterized United Methodist worship throughout its history. Rather the Book of Worship seeks to claim for the church and its people the total United Methodist heritage in worship." This volume contained

The Church of the Saviour.

An example of Gothic revival and Methodism's move to formal worship is this picture of the chancel area of the Church of the Saviour in Cleveland Heights, Ohio. This large church, completed in 1928, was constructed in the style of thirteenth-century French Gothic architecture. The congregation obtained the cornerstone from Jerusalem, with the understanding that it may have been handled by Solomon's quarrymen some three millennia ago. Although the church can seat 1,100 people, it can be made to look well filled if only four hundred worshippers attend. The sanctuary is cruciform in plan, and for special occasions its wide aisles can accommodate 210 additional seats. The seven-sided pulpit features carvings of 18 Old Testament prophets, and the stained glass windows convey various aspects of the Christian message. The original congregation began in 1875 in a small house, where the people held what they termed "fiddled-singing meetings."

McKendree Methodist Church, Nashville, 1879.

During the 1840s numerous Methodist congregations built new churches in more favorable locations, with better accommodations, and in more elaborate architectural styles. Methodism came to believe that its permanent influence upon congregations, especially in the cities, depended on the convenience and beauty of its churches. In 1865 Methodist historian Abel Stevens declared, "True taste and true art ... are founded in original laws, that is to say, divine laws of human nature, and therefore meet a natural want of man.... True art should be recognized as one of the noblest handmaids of religion; elevating impressions and associations, through the senses in our temples, may ennoble even divine worship." He also said that the denomination that builds churches of beauty and quality "almost invariably finds its expense the best reimbursed, by its command of the people, their attendance, their intelligence, and their money."

The church pictured here illustrates that approach to church architecture. The first Methodist church built in Nashville was constructed in 1789 or 1790. It was a simple building, measuring 20 square feet. In 1812, the congregation erected a much larger building on a lot costing $160. This auditorium was the largest in Nashville, and the Tennessee Legislature used it between 1813 and 1817. The congregation built still another church in 1818.

Then, in 1833 the congregation built another church and named it after Bishop William McKendree. At the time, the 1,500-seat auditorium was the largest ME Church in America. The building measured 65 by 90 feet, and it cost $15,000. After the Civil War, the congregation voted to tear down the structure and construct a "high steeple" church. That church is pictured here. The building cost $36,000, including $2,800 for the main steeple, which soared 230 feet. The twin towers on either side rose 130 feet. As Methodists erected more stately buildings, their worship services became increasingly liturgical and formal.

worship aids arranged according to the Christian Year, and it included an expanded selection of scripture readings. As did its predecessor volume, this book of worship generated widespread interest.

In 1992 the United Methodist Church adopted still another *Book of Worship*, being a successor to the 1944 and 1964 editions of the *Book of Worship*. This new volume was based on the Anglican liturgical legacy as well as the Methodist and Evangelical United Brethren worship traditions. This current *Book of Worship* contains liturgies for such occasions as the Birth or Adoption of a Child, Farewell to Church Members, Commissioning to Short-term Service, Farewell to a Pastor, Dedication or Consecration of an Organ or Other Musical Instruments, Blessings of Animals, and Blessing of a Home. As well, it contains liturgies pertaining to Hope After Loss of Pregnancy, Persons Going Through Divorce, Persons Suffering Addiction or Substance Abuse, Persons with AIDS, Persons with Life-threatening Illness, and Persons in Coma or Unable to Communicate. This worship resource draws from many sources, deals with a wide scope of themes, and speaks to a broad spectrum of concerns.

The preface to United Methodism's 1992 *Book of Worship* states:

This book acknowledges our Anglican liturgical heritage and celebrates worship out of our cultural and ethnic diversity. It witnesses to our Evangelical United Brethren and Methodist heritage. Women, men, youth, and children have all contributed to the rich variety of ways of speaking with God in corporate worship. Underlying this diversity and variety, however, is the one God who calls us to be disciples of Christ Jesus."

This volume, the church's current official book of worship, contains a rich collection of materials for public and private worship.

The Book of Worship.

From left to right: the original 1944 Book of Worship and the 1964 and 1992 revisions.

Open and Closed Worship

At one level, early Methodist worship was open to everyone. The only condition for attending Methodist public meetings was to refrain from interrupting the services with inappropriate words or actions. Everyone was encouraged to attend these public services, especially the unconverted. Commonly, these early Methodist gatherings attracted crowds several times larger than the membership of the host congregation. If a society reported 100 members, it was not unusual for over 400 people to assemble for the public services. These open gatherings saw many people commit themselves to Christ as Lord.

At another level, certain Methodist services were closed to the public. Meetings of the members of the societies were often held on Sunday evenings; they were intended for members only. Tickets, to be renewed quarterly, were required for admission to the class meetings and love feasts. Asbury himself occasionally "kept the door" so as to admit only those who had the right to attend.

As one might expect, some people were offended because the Methodist classes and love feasts denied them admission. However, the early Methodists believed that their closed meetings needed to be continued, even if critics complained. In 1798 Bishops Coke and Asbury contended, "It is manifestly our duty to fence in our society, and to preserve it from intruders; otherwise we should soon become a desolate waste. God would write *Ichabod* upon us, and the glory would be departed from Israel." On one occasion, Francis Asbury criticized his fellow missionary Richard Wright for concluding a revival in New York with a general love feast for all. Asbury complained that this open meeting undermined "all he has done."

The closed worship services had positive effects: They helped create an environment in which God could work freely among those of like heart and mind. In this atmosphere of kindred spirits, the participants felt free to engage in the close personal examination and the intimate sharing that were significant parts of these services. The spiritual tone in Methodism's closed meetings was often glorious, and worshipers reported remarkable instances of divine blessing. Accounts of these services described the longing for heaven felt by many who attended. There, they would no longer need to part from their brothers and sisters in Christ, and they would forever dwell in the Lord's presence. William Watters wrote, "The holy fire, the heavenly flame, spread wider and wider, and rose higher and higher.... May we after having done the work alotted [sic] us, meet in our father's Kingdom to tell the wonders of redeeming love, and part no more." The closed meetings of early Methodism also helped fortify the participants for overcoming temptation and dealing with persecution. Class members left their meetings with a determination to bear witness to the grace and power of God. They sang:

> *Ye servants of God, your Master proclaim,*
> *And publish abroad his wonderful name;*
> *The name all victorious of Jesus extol,*
> *His kingdom is glorious and rules over all.*

In addition, closed worship services also caused non-Christians to ponder their lack of a personal relationship with Jesus Christ. Jabez Bunting, an outstanding leader in nineteenth century British Methodism, said, "Many attribute their conversion to their having attended a love-feast; I owe mine to having been shut out of one." As a child, he had attended closed meetings, sharing his mother's class ticket. When Bunting grew toward young adulthood, his pastor excluded him from the love feast because he made no personal profession of faith in Christ. Bunting began to search his heart and "once for all renounced sin."

Methodism's public services were aimed at those who were not yet believers. These open gatherings were designed to communicate the gospel in ways easily understood by non-Christians. The leaders used language that was familiar to unchurched people. The hymns contained straightforward texts, sung to familiar tunes or tunes easily learned by the visitors. The public meetings were, in today's terminology, seeker-sensitive services that aimed to reach those not familiar with the gospel or religious terminology. These open gatherings clarified the gospel and provided opportunities for people to accept Jesus Christ as their Savior.

Methodism's closed services were designed to nurture the saints and lead them on the path of sanctification. These non-public meetings of believers made use of the mystical symbols of bread, wine, and water. Deeper theological content and greater expectations characterized these closed gatherings designed for believers and those "desiring to flee the wrath to come." The open and closed meetings were instrumental both in the church's evangelistic outreach and in the church's ministry to those who had chosen to join in fellowship with the people called Methodists.

Today's United Methodist worship is perhaps as diverse as that of any church. The influences of worship traditions from various ethnic and national backgrounds add richness to United Methodist worship, demonstrating that United Methodism is an inclusive church. In the midst of this diversity, however, all United Methodists make the common confession that there is "one Lord, one faith, one baptism, one God and Father of us all, who is above all and through all and in all."

Gathering for worship.

This photograph shows the sanctuary of the Carmel, Indiana United Methodist Church. The church began in 1838 as the "Carmel Class." In 1848 the class moved from a house to a log cabin and took the name Carmel Methodist Episcopal Church. Today, the church has an imposing physical plant and a membership approaching 3,000.

Sunday morning solo.

The soloist in an African-American United Methodist congregation is accompanied by a pianist as well as a gospel choir, which is seated behind the pulpit.

One factor remains constant in authentic worship—the believer's complete devotion to God the Father, Son, and Holy Spirit—the holy Trinity that creates, redeems, and sustains life. All who worship God in spirit and truth know the joy of claiming God's promise: "Then shall you call upon me, and you shall go and pray unto me, and I will hearken unto you. And you shall seek me, and find me, when you shall search for me with all your heart." In the end, participating in that reality constitutes the fundamental intent of worship in the Wesleyan way.

Sunday morning Worship.

Pastor Dennis L. Blackwell is preaching to a Sunday morning congregation at Asbury United Methodist Church in Merchantville, New Jersey.

Grave marker for United Methodist ministers.

Frequently, funeral services for faithful Christian servants—laity and clergy—are times of worship. Far from being services of defeat and sorrow, Christian funerals are services of victory and joy. For Christians, burial ceremonies are occasions for celebrating God's grace and the sure hope of eternal life.

This grave marker, adopted in 1968, was designed to mark the gravesites of United Methodist ministers, and it can be used with various types of monuments. The five-inch medallion depicts a circuit rider facing west, as did many early Methodist ministers. The world globe suggests John Wesley's statement, "The world is my parish."

Seminary students at a chapel service.

The seminary preparation of the ordained ministry includes both knowledge and vital piety. Study in the classroom and worship in the chapel are equally important for the intellectual and spiritual formation of ministers in the making.

Traditionally, the language of Wesleyan worship consists of verbal communication through prayer, hymns, scripture, and testimony. These media can be supplemented by non-verbal modes of worship such as instrumental music, drama, dance, architecture, sculpture, and painting. Ideally, worship involves the mind, the emotions and the will.

10 *The Heritage of Hymns*

John and Charles Wesley each made distinctive contributions to the Christian church. John's theological balance, organizational genius, and inspired leadership made him the most significant religious figure of the eighteenth century. Charles Wesley's main legacy consists of his many hymns of enduring quality. He gained the distinction of being the greatest hymn writer in the history of Christianity. *The Cambridge Modern History* states, "His hymns, besides being something new in eighteenth century literature, are the purest revelation of its religious feeling, and embody...the truest and tenderest aspects of Methodism. [His hymns] are worth all the histories that have ever been written, as a revelation of the true power of Methodism, and teach us the secret, which brought men—degraded and brutalised beyond expression—to listen to [the gospel]."

Charles Wesley statue.
This bronze sculpture is located in Bristol, England. It appears here by the courtesy of the Charles Wesley Heritage Centre in Bristol.

As an undergraduate at Oxford, Charles Wesley translated Greek and Latin classics into English verse. Following his conversion and the rise of Methodism, he became one of the greatest hymn writers of all time.

Henry Moore, a friend of the Wesleys, recorded the following story about Charles Wesley: "When he was nearly eighty he rode a little horse, grey with age.... As he jogged leisurely along he jotted down any thoughts that struck him. He kept a card in his pocket for this purpose, on which he wrote his hymn in shorthand. Not infrequently he has come to ... City Road [Chapel, in London], and, having left the pony in the garden in front, he would enter, crying out, 'Pen and ink!' These being supplied he wrote the hymn he had been composing."

John and Charles alike understood the importance of hymns and hymn singing. Because the early Methodist hymnbooks carry the names of both John and Charles Wesley, the authorship of some of the hymns is not certain. In general, we credit Charles Wesley with having composed most of the original hymns and John Wesley with having translated the hymns written in other languages.

Most hymn writers prior to Charles Wesley wrote verses that carefully avoided personal sentiment or spiritual passion. By contrast, the Wesleyan hymns spoke freely about the deepest of religious emotions, while boldly using personal pronouns. The Wesleyan hymns expressed heartfelt repentance over sin, certainty about knowing Christ, gratitude for divine providence, and sublime joy at the prospect of heaven to come. This hymnody touched the souls of multitudes and helped to generate and sustain the Wesleyan revival. For more than two-and-a-half centuries, the depth and power of the Wesleyan hymns have helped millions of people to know Jesus Christ and to worship him in spirit and in truth.

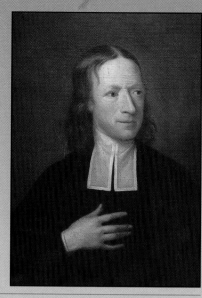

John Wesley.
Robert Hunter painted this portrait in 1765 when Wesley was 63 years old.

John Wesley's contributions to Methodist hymnody were important in several ways: (1) He personally wrote a number of excellent hymn texts. (2) He translated into English the best of German hymns. (3) He edited and improved the hymns of others. (4) He served as a collector, compiler, and publisher of important collections of hymns.

The following entry in Wesley's journal, written when he was about 65 years old, illustrates his concern for reaching all people with the gospel: "I rode to Bolton. So hot a day as this, I do not remember to have felt in England. The congregation seemed to forget the heat, though the Room was like an oven. For it was a comfortable hour: God refreshing many souls with the multitude of peace. The House was fuller this evening than the last, while I enforced that gracious invitation, 'Come unto me, all ye that are weary and heavy-laden.'"

John Wesley's first hymnal.

John Wesley's first hymnal was printed in 1737 in Charles-Town, South Carolina (later, Charleston). It was succeeded by numerous collections of Wesleyan hymns, published in England and in America.

Bicentennial edition of Wesley's works.

This 848-page volume containing the Wesleyan hymns is part of the Bicentennial Edition of Wesley's works. This book (as do the other volumes in this series) contains an introduction and editorial notes. A highly useful feature of this work is the inclusion of biblical references reflected in the Wesleyan hymns.

Charles Wesley (1707-1788).
Frank O. Salisbury painted this portrait, located in the World Methodist Building at Lake Junaluska, North Carolina. Permission to reproduce this picture is given by the World Methodist Museum.

Charles Wesley was the most gifted and prolific hymn writer Great Britain ever produced. He understood, as did his brother John, the value of hymns as a means of worship, instruction, and inspiration. His first collection of hymns appeared in 1739, and throughout his lifetime numerous other Wesleyan hymn collections appeared. In all, he wrote at least 7,300 hymns.

The Wesleyan hymns, particularly those for the major festivals of the Christian year, are sung far beyond the borders of Methodism. Charles Wesley's sacred verses have appeared more frequently in church hymnals than the verses of any other hymnwriter. The profound value of these hymns lies in their expression of the deep spiritual hungers, aspirations, and hopes that reside in all human hearts in every century. It has been said that Isaac Watts unlocked the door to evangelical singing, and the Wesleys threw that door wide open.

The Genius of the Wesleyan Hymns

With the advent of Methodism, hymn singing moved from a dispassionate observance to a fervent experience of joy and wonder. It is fair to say that the Wesleys transformed British hymn singing from an appendage to an essential component of Christian worship. Joseph Williams, an eighteenth-century contemporary of the Wesleys, wrote about Methodist hymn singing: "Never did I hear such praying and singing.... [It was] the most harmonious and delightful I ever heard. If there be such a thing as heavenly music upon earth, I heard it there."

John Wesley wrote in the preface to the 1780 *Collection of Hymns for Use of the People Called Methodists* that the hymnal contained "all the important truths of our most holy religion." The Wesleyan hymns possess theological integrity and intellectual substance. John and Charles did not write sentimental songs based merely on intuition, feelings, or private hunches. The Wesleyan hymns celebrate such pivotal biblical teachings as Christ's pre-existence, divinity, incarnation, atoning death, resurrection, ascension, and return. Charles Wesley's Advent hymn stirs us with its theological depth:

> *Hail, the heav'n-born Prince of Peace!*
> *Hail, the Sun of Righteousness!*
> *Light and life to all He brings,*
> *Ris'n with healing in His wings.*
> *Mild He lays His glory by,*
> *Born that men no more may die,*
> *Born to raise the sons of earth,*

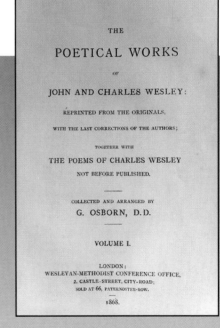

Title page of The Poetical Works of John and Charles Wesley.

In 1868 Dr. George Osborn began the task of publishing the hymns of John and Charles Wesley. This series contained 13 volumes, and was published during the years 1868-72 as *The Poetical works of John and Charles Wesley.*

Born to give them second birth.
Hark! The herald angels sing,
"Glory to the new-born King."

John and Charles Wesley's preparation for their ministries began in childhood. As soon as they learned to speak, their mother taught them to talk directly to God in simple prayers. As children, they acquired from Susanna Wesley a disposition to trust in God's providence in all situations—even disagreeable ones. In their youthful development, their father and older brother tutored them in the art of expressing themselves through poetic verse. This childhood training influenced their adult lives. There is scarcely a life experience for which there is not an appropriate Methodist hymn. Charles Wesley wrote verses for almost every situation, including weddings, embarking on a journey, persecution by a spouse, families in need, being unjustly accused, tending a sick child, and working in the mines. The early Methodists even sang themselves to sleep in the evening. With thoughts of God on their lips, they softly caroled:

How do thy mercies close me round!
For ever be Thy name adored.
Safe in Thy arms I lay me down,
Thy everlasting arms of love.

Wherefore in confidence I close
My eyes, for Thine are open still,
My spirit, lull'd in calm repose,
Waits for the counsels of Thy will.

Christian experience, of course, constitutes the main theme of the Wesleyan hymns. They lyrically express what one of John Wesley's favorite authors, Henry Scougal, called "the life of God in the soul of man."

These hymns have sustained the faith and hope of millions by keeping alive the eternal realities of the Christian faith. Charles Wesley captured an important truth in his hymns:

Through Thee, who all our sins hast borne,
Freely and graciously forgiven,
With songs to Zion we return,
Contending for our native heaven;
That palace of our glorious King,
We find it nearer when we sing!

Indeed, the gospel entered persons' hearts as much through singing hymns as through listening to sermons.

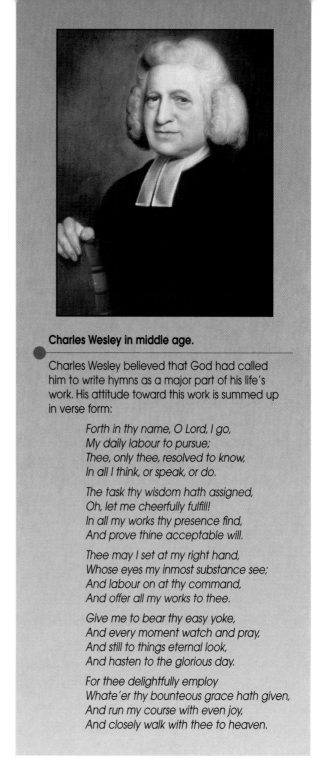

Charles Wesley in middle age.

Charles Wesley believed that God had called him to write hymns as a major part of his life's work. His attitude toward this work is summed up in verse form:

Forth in thy name, O Lord, I go,
My daily labour to pursue;
Thee, only thee, resolved to know,
In all I think, or speak, or do.

The task thy wisdom hath assigned,
Oh, let me cheerfully fulfill!
In all my works thy presence find,
And prove thine acceptable will.

Thee may I set at my right hand,
Whose eyes my inmost substance see;
And labour on at thy command,
And offer all my works to thee.

Give me to bear thy easy yoke,
And every moment watch and pray,
And still to things eternal look,
And hasten to the glorious day.

For thee delightfully employ
Whate'er thy bounteous grace hath given,
And run my course with even joy,
And closely walk with thee to heaven.

Charles and John held the conviction that scripture carries a message from heaven to earth and that God blesses the biblical texts in unique ways. Only those very familiar with the Bible can fully appreciate the extent of biblical citations or allusions found in the Wesleyan hymns. Hymnologist J. Ernest Rattenbury has stated, "A skillful man, if the Bible were lost, might extract much of it from [Charles] Wesley's hymns." The power of scripture in the Wesleyan hymns gives them self-authenticating authority and strength. As well, these hymns have ecumenical appeal because all Christian denominations accept the Bible as the authoritative revelation from God.

These hymns both extol God's exalted majesty and declare God's parental concern for the details of our individual lives. In a single verse, Charles Wesley shows that God is both transcendent and near at hand:

> *High throned on heaven's eternal hill*
> *In number, weight, and measure still*
> *Thou sweetly orderest all that is:*
> *And yet thou deign'st to come to me,*
> *And guide my steps, that I, with thee*
> *Enthroned, may reign in endless bliss.*

The Wesleyan hymns affirm that God the Sovereign One enters into the human realm with the offer of full redemption to all who turn to him in repentance and faith.

In a day when sermons and hymns said little or nothing about the Holy Spirit, the Wesleyan hymns were remarkable eighteenth-century testimonies to the importance of the third member of the holy Trinity:

> *Come, divine and peaceful Guest,*
> *Enter our devoted breast;*
> *Holy Ghost, our hearts inspire,*
> *Kindle there the Gospel fire.*
>
> *Now descend, and shake the earth;*
> *Wake us into second birth;*
> *Life divine in us renew,*
> *Thou the gift and giver too!*

The Methodists prayed that the Holy Spirit would enlighten their minds to understand the full meaning of scripture:

> *Come, divine Interpreter,*
> *Bring me eyes thy book to read,*
> *Ears thy mystic words to hear,*
> *Words which did from thee proceed,*
> *Words that endless bliss impart,*
> *Kept in an obedient heart.*

The Wesleyan hymns underscore the conviction that our first thoughts of God come because the Holy Spirit prompts them:

> *Thou dost the first good thought inspire,*
> *The first faint spark of pure desire*
> *Is kindled by Thy gracious breath;*
> *By Thee made conscious of his fall,*
> *The sinner hears Thy sudden call,*
> *And starts out of the sleep of death.*

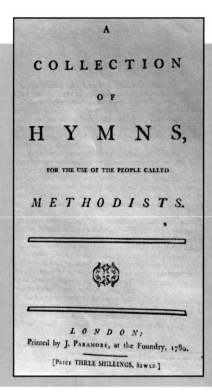

The 1780 Wesleyan hymnal.

Most people agree that John Wesley's 1780 hymnal ranks among the grandest hymn collections in existence. Hymnologist Bernard Manning said, "You may think my language about the hymns extravagant: therefore I repeat it in stronger terms. This little book ranks in Christian literature with the Psalms, the Book of Common Prayer, the Canon of the Mass. In its own way it is perfect, unapproachable, elemental in its perfection. You cannot alter it except to mar it; it is a work of supreme devotional art by a religious genius."

The Wesleys trusted that the Holy Spirit would work through scripture to bring God's truth into the hearts of saints and sinners alike. Prayerfully, the Methodists sang, "Spirit of Faith, Come down, Reveal the things of God."

The Wesleys lived in a day when the philosophy of Deism had crept into the church. Deism regards God as a remote being who remains indifferent to the details of human experience. Deism emphasizes what we must do to live honorable lives; the theism of the Wesleys leads to the evangelical doctrine that our salvation does not depend on our efforts or merit. Rather, redemption rests entirely on the work of Jesus Christ. The Wesleyan hymns lift praises to God, who came to earth not in wrath but in mercy. Charles Wesley captured this important Christian belief in one of the church's foremost Christmas hymns:

> *Hark! The herald angels sing,*
> *"Glory to the newborn King;*
> *Peace on earth, and mercy mild,*
> *God and sinners reconciled!"*
> *Joyful, all ye nations, rise,*
> *Join the triumph of the skies;*
> *With th'angelic host proclaim,*
> *"Christ is born in Bethlehem!"*
>
> *Christ, by highest heaven adored;*
> *Christ, the everlasting Lord!*

Late in time behold Him come,
Offspring of a virgin's womb.
Veiled in flesh the Godhead see;
Hail th' incarnate Deity,
Pleased as man with men to dwell,
Jesus, our Emmanuel.

In eighteenth-century England and America few of the Methodists had money, position, or status. Persons of social distinction tended to look down on those of a lower standing. The Duchess of Buckingham's oft-quoted letter to the Countess of Huntingdon typifies the opinion some held toward those less favored. She spoke about the Methodists:

Their doctrines are most repulsive and strongly tinctured with impertinence and disrespect towards their superiors, in perpetually endeavouring to level all ranks and do away with all distinctions. It is monstrous to be told that you have a heart as sinful as the common wretches that crawl the earth.

The Methodists cared little for the opinions of the lords and ladies who shared the views of the haughty duchess. The Methodists sang, "On all the kings of earth/ With pity we look down/ And claim, in virtue of our birth/ A never-fading crown." Charles Wesley wrote:

Thy sovereign grace to all extends,
Immense and unconfined;
From age to age it never ends;
It reaches all mankind.

The "unwashed masses" outside the pale of the church learned from Methodist preaching and singing that God loved them. Coal miners, whose tears washed white streaks down their blackened faces, sang of God's grace that had touched them with transforming power: "Its streams the whole creation reach/ So plenteous is the store/ Enough for all, enough for each/ Enough for evermore." Although the early Methodists had little money in their pockets, they sang about the fullness of grace in their hearts:

Riches unsearchable
In Jesu's love we know,
And pleasure from the well
Of life, our souls o'erflow.

Another mark of the Wesleyan hymnody is its affirmation that God's sustaining power is adequate to give us victory over sin. The Methodist hymns declare that we do not need constantly to transgress God's laws in thought, word, and deed. With serious intent, the Methodists sang:

Jesus, thine all-victorious love shed
in my heart abroad;
Then shall my feet no longer rove,
rooted and fixed in God.

Refining fire, go through my heart,
illuminate my soul;
Scatter thy life through every part,
and sanctify the whole.

My steadfast soul, from falling free,
shall then no longer move,
But Christ be all the world to me,
and all my heart be love.

This hope for victory over sin was not rooted in human effort. Rather, the belief that God expects and enables holiness was based on the work of Christ who came to save his people from their sins. Although the Wesleys never taught absolute perfection, they did take seriously the implications of the prayer, "Lead us not into temptation, but deliver us from evil." Their hymns accented the grace of God revealed in Jesus Christ, who came to conquer the powers of evil:

The length and breadth of love reveal,
The height and depth of Deity,
And all the sons of glory seal
And change, and make us all like Thee.

The theme of sanctification appears throughout the Wesleyan hymn texts, and it is usually expressed in the very words of scripture.

The hymns of John and Charles Wesley lift up the view that life's highest prize is becoming a son or daughter of God through faith in Jesus Christ. Shortly after his conversion to Christ, Charles Wesley wrote a hymn titled, "Where Shall My Wondering Soul Begin?" One of the stanzas celebrates his new standing as a child of God:

O how shall I the goodness tell,
Father, which thou to me hast showed?

That I, a child of wrath and hell,
I should be called a child of God!
Should know, should feel my sins forgiven,
Blest with this antepast of heaven!

The Wesleyan hymns remind us that our lives are not grounded in material things. Rather, a grace-filled life constitutes life's greatest treasure. Christians of many denominations value the Wesleyan hymns because they help us focus on the issues that are of ultimate significance.

The Hymns of American Methodism

Hymn singing has played a highly significant role in American Methodism. The preachers at the Christmas Conference of 1784 considered the question, "How shall we reform our singing?" They formulated the answer: "Let all our preachers who have any knowledge in the notes improve by learning to sing true themselves, and keeping close to Mr. Wesley's tunes and hymns." Bishop Asbury stated in the preface of Methodism's 1808 hymnal that it contained "a body of excellent divinity, explanatory of and enforcing the fundamental doctrines of the gospel." Bishops Thomas Coke and Francis Asbury advised the church on hymn singing: "We exhort you to sing with the Spirit, and with the understanding also: and thus may the high praises of GOD be set up from East to West, from North to South; and we shall be happily instrumental in leading the Devotions of Thousands, and shall rejoice to join you in Time and Eternity."

The American Methodist *Discipline* of 1805 advised: "In every large society let them learn to sing, and let them always learn our tunes first." Throughout the history of American Methodism, the *Discipline* repeats this counsel: "In every Society let due attention be given to the cultivation of sacred music.... As singing is a part of divine worship in which all ought to unite, therefore exhort every person in the congregation to sing." The Methodists sang hymns in their homes, about their work, around their family altars, and at their public assemblies. People referred to the followers of John Wesley as "singing Methodists."

American Methodism's first hymnal, adopted in 1784, was John Wesley's *Collection of Psalms and Hymns for the Lord's Day*. Six years later, in 1790, the church adopted a new hymnal titled *A Pocket Hymn Book: Designed as a Constant Companion for the Pious*. During the next 88 years the Methodist Episcopal Church produced a succession of five more official hymnals. Then, in 1878, the church approved a new *Hymnal of*

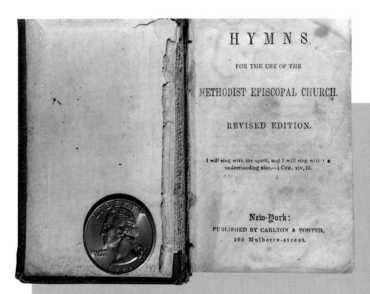

Methodist pocket hymnal.

The early Methodist hymnals were printed without musical notes and often in tiny editions for pocket or purse. The size of this 1849 hymnal can be gauged by comparing the title page with a modern twenty-five cent piece.

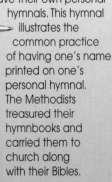

Personalized hymnal.

In early American Methodism, the preacher or worship leader "lined out" the verses for the congregation, two lines at a time. In time, the people were eager to have their own personal hymnals. This hymnal illustrates the common practice of having one's name printed on one's personal hymnal. The Methodists treasured their hymnbooks and carried them to church along with their Bibles.

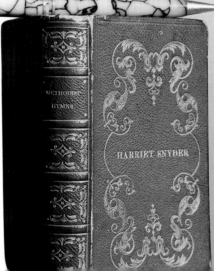

145

the Methodist Episcopal Church with Tunes, the first to contain musical notes. Those who served on this hymnal committee chose tunes of a "solid, enduring kind" to enhance "the spirituality of divine worship through the power of sacred song upon the heart."

In 1905 the Methodist Episcopal and Methodist Episcopal, South, Churches published a joint hymnal. This hymn collection featured "sound doctrine and healthful Christian experience" to "greatly enrich our worship." It introduced new hymns such as "Now Thank We All Our God," "He Leadeth Me," and "Lead on, O King Eternal." The social aspects of the gospel appeared in hymns such as "O Master, Let Me Walk with Thee" and "Where Cross the Crowded Ways of Life." Some of the older Methodists objected to the rituals in the hymnal and the addition of the Amen at the end of each hymn. They regarded these innovations as being too formal. Nevertheless, this hymnal gained acceptance in the church.

The 1878 hymnal of the Methodist Episcopal Church.

This 1878 hymn collection was Methodism's first hymnal printed with music. Recommending this hymnal to the church, the church's eleven bishops wrote, "We most cordially commend it to you as one of the choicest selections of evangelical hymns ever published; and we trust that it will increase the interest of public worship, give a higher inspiration to social and family services, and aid in private meditation and devotion. As it is published by the authority of the Church, and to meet the wants of the Church ... we do the more earnestly commend it to your liberal patronage. We exhort you, dear brethren, to 'sing with the spirit' and 'with the understanding also,' 'making melody in your heart to the Lord.'"

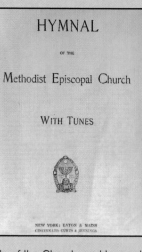

1862 United Brethren Hymnal.

The earliest United Brethren hymnals were printed in German. To encourage congregational singing, the church's General Conference of 1861 passed a resolution stating, "We ... kindly forbid the introductions of choirs into any of our churches." Four years later the denomination forbade the use of musical instruments in church. Later, these rules were relaxed, when the church came to believe that congregations could honor God with instruments of music and with choirs.

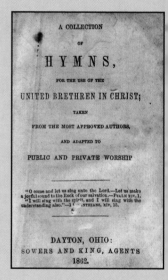

Joint Hymnal, 1905.

Anticipating a merger, the Methodist Episcopal Church and the Methodist Episcopal Church, South printed a joint hymnal in 1905. The hymnal's Preface concluded, "And now, praying that this Hymnal, prepared by a joint Commission whose brotherly harmony was never once broken and whose final meeting was a Pentecost, may be abundantly blessed of God to the edification of believing souls and to the glory of his name, we commend it to our churches, and we earnestly hope that it may everywhere supplant those unauthorized publications which often teach what organized Methodism does not hold, and which, by excluding the nobler music of the earlier and later days, prevent the growth of a true musical taste."

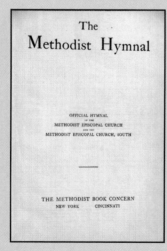

Evangelical Church hymnal.

This hymnal of the Evangelical Church, titled *Evangelical Hymn-book* or *A Collection of Spiritual Songs* (translation) appeared in 1850. The Evangelical Church continued to publish it until 1894.

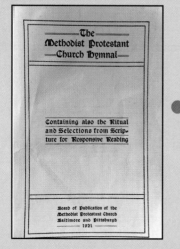

The Methodist Protestant Church Hymnal.

In 1838 Thomas H. Stockton edited the first official Methodist Protestant hymnal. In 1882 the Methodist Protestant Church adopted *The Tribute of Praise,* the first Methodist Protestant hymnal to contain both hymn texts and tunes. The hymnal pictured here was first adopted in 1901 and reprinted in many editions. The hymns are conveniently grouped under various topics. This hymnal was the last definitive collection published by the Methodist Protestant Church, which became a part of the Methodist Church in 1939.

The next Methodist hymnal was published in 1935. The hymnal committee consisted of representatives of the Methodist Episcopal, Methodist Episcopal, South, and Methodist Protestant Churches, in anticipation of the merger of these churches (in 1939) to form the Methodist Church. Committee membership consisted of persons of different backgrounds and theological perspectives. Influences as diverse as modern science and the camp meetings were apparent in this Methodist hymnal.

The theologically liberal members of the hymnal committee influenced the elimination of sections in the hymnal on The Need for Salvation, Warning and Invitations, the Ascension and Reign of Christ, Judgment, Retribution, and Heaven. In a quest for "new words for a new day," the editors changed the words in some of Charles Wesley's hymns. For instance, "Hark, the Herald Angels Sing" originally contained the words,

> *Late in time behold him come,*
> *Offspring of the Virgin's womb....*

The committee changed these words to:

> *Long desired, behold him come,*
> *Finding here his humble home....*

The theologically conservative committee members called for balance in the hymnal. The popular use of gospel songs, especially in the southern churches, led the committee to add a subsection titled "Songs of Salvation" (popularly called "gospel songs"). These songs focused on God's call to salvation, personal Christian experience, walking closely with Christ, victory over temptation, and heaven as the blessed hope of the redeemed. The Songs of Salvation in the 1935 hymnal included hymns such as "Saviour, More Than Life to Me," "Softly and Tenderly Jesus is Calling," "Pass Me Not, O Gentle Saviour," "What a Friend We Have in Jesus," "Blessed Assurance, Jesus Is Mine," "He Leadeth Me: O blessed Thought!" and "My Hope Is Built on Nothing Less."

Methodist union in 1939.

On May 10, 1939 in Kansas City, Missouri the Methodist Episcopal Church, Methodist Episcopal Church, South, and Methodist Protestant Churches united to form the Methodist Church. This photograph shows the senior bishops of these three churches. From left to right are Bishop James H. Straughn of the Methodist Protestant Church, Bishop Edwin Holt Hughes of the Methodist Episcopal Church, and Bishop John M. Moore of the Methodist Episcopal Church, South. The hymn chosen for this historic occasion was "O for a thousand tongues to sing my great Redeemer's praise."

Frances Jane "Fanny" Crosby (1820-1915).
Picture courtesy of the Billy Graham Center Museum.

Fanny Crosby, who wrote approximately 9,000 hymns, is sometimes called a Methodist saint. Due to a physician's mistreatment, she was blinded at the age of six weeks. She was reared in a religious environment, and memorized scripture and poetry. By the age of ten she could recite the first four books of both the Old and New Testaments from memory. Crosby possessed an ability to hear a tune and almost immediately write words to fit it. She said, "True hymns make themselves. I never undertake a hymn without first asking the good Lord to be my inspiration."

Out of modesty, Fanny Crosby used as many as 200 pseudonyms. She lived a frugal life and asked for only two dollars for each hymn she wrote. Crosby's hymns and gospel songs, which are still widely sung, earned her the admiration of her generation. Today's United Methodist hymnal contains seven of her hymns, including "To God Be the Glory," "Pass Me Not, O Gentle Savior", "Blessed Assurance", and "I Am Thine O Lord."

In 1960 the church's General Conference commissioned a new *Methodist Hymnal* and a new *Book of Worship*. Both publications appeared in 1964. The hymnal committee, chaired by Bishop Edwin E. Voigt, included EUB members, in anticipation of the coming (1968) merger. Bishop Nolan B. Harmon chaired the Committee on Texts. This hymnal reinstated many of Charles Wesley's texts that had been changed in the 1935 hymnal. For instance, the 1964 hymnal restored Charles's original words, *"Late in time behold him come, Offspring of the Virgin's womb."* The 1964 hymnal added melodies from the German Chorale and Plain Song traditions. For the first time, folk music and black spirituals appeared in the *Methodist Hymnal*.

Today's *United Methodist Hymnal* was published in 1989. This hymnal contains hymns from the Methodist and EUB traditions, and it is the most extensive revision of hymnal

Bishop Nolan B. Harmon (1892-1993).
This photograph of the original painting appears here by permission of the Southeastern Jurisdiction Heritage Center. Photograph by Dave Henderson.

Bishop Harmon was a member of both the 1935 and 1964 hymnal committees. As a member of the 1964 committee, he served as chairman of the sub-committee on texts. The stated intent of the 1964 hymnal committee was: (1) to draw upon the rich heritage of ecumenical hymnody, including our own Wesleyan traditions, (2) to bring to our people for use in worship a hymnal of sufficient diversity to allow for the variety of religious experiences, and (3) to reach into the future with a hymnal that will serve the religious needs of the next generation.

Charles Albert Tindley (1851-1933)

In 1801 Richard Allen published the first hymnal of predominantly black hymns, *A Collection of Hymns and Spiritual Songs from Various Authors,* the earliest hymnbook to contain refrains or choruses. Black Methodists pioneered the use of gospel songs and introduced them to white congregations. Although these songs did not find their way into the nineteenth and early twentieth century hymnals of the Methodist Episcopal Church, they have greatly influenced the gospel music widely used in Methodism. Moreover, the poignant power of the black spirituals gained worldwide recognition. They have been sung in many places, from slave cabins to formal concert halls. In the twentieth century, the gospel songs of Charles Albert Tindley and Thomas A. Dorsey have been especially popular.

Charles Albert Tindley, the son of slaves, was born in Maryland prior to the Civil War. As a slave, he was not permitted to attend public school. He learned to read at the age of 17 and developed a life-long thirst for knowledge.

He worked his way through college by working as a hod carrier and later as sexton of a Methodist church. Then, after earning his divinity degree through a correspondence course, he became a minister in an all-Black conference of the Methodist Episcopal Church. He served as pastor of the Calvary Methodist Episcopal Church in Philadelphia, the church where he had once worked as a janitor. This church became famous for its music; Tindley himself composed many of the gospel songs used by the church. During Tindley's thirty-one-year pastorate, the church moved to a new location and changed its name to Tindley Temple Methodist Episcopal Church. At his death, the church had 12,500 members and was the largest Methodist church in the world. In 1916 he published *New Songs of Paradise,* a collection that included "We'll Understand It Better By and By" and "I'll Overcome Someday." Today's United Methodist hymnal contains five of his gospel hymns, including "Stand By Me" and "Nothing Between My Soul and My Savior." In all, he wrote over 40 gospel hymns.

Charles Albert Tindley's songs incorporate black folk imagery that interprets the oppression African Americans met in urban areas. In contrast to the black spirituals, Tindley's songs are not merely other-worldly, although they do depict heaven as the final triumph over earthly oppression. His music speaks to oppressed people who are attempting to survive in the present world.

Tindley's gospel songs paved the way for the immensely popular gospel music of Thomas A. Dorsey (1899-1965), a talented African-American composer. His gospel song "Precious Lord, Take My Hand" appears in the present *United Methodist Hymnal*. Dorsey's gospel music became popular around 1930 and began the age of gospel hymns, earning him the title "The Father of Gospel." In 1931 he organized the first gospel choir, now an established institution in most African-American congregations. In the 1940s Dorsey's "Peace in the Valley" became the first gospel song to be added to America's "Hit Parade" of popular songs. Although Dorsey was not a Methodist, his songs influenced American Methodism's gospel music.

Bishop William Ragsdale Cannon (1916-1997).

Bishop Cannon, a member of the 1964 hymnal committee, represented those in the church who wanted to restore the number and accuracy of Wesleyan hymns that had been removed or altered in the 1935 hymnal.

Songs of Zion.

Songs of Zion was first published in 1973 as a collection of songs frequently used in African-American worship services. This hymnal reflects the pain of slavery, the struggle for freedom, and the belief in ultimate justice. In many ways, this hymnal is for all Christians who are "strangers and pilgrims" in any land. These songs help God's people sing the songs of Zion in an oppressive environment.

Voices: Native American Hymns and Worship Resources.

This hymn supplement, printed in 1992 by Discipleship Resources, contains hymns and worship resources for Native American Christians. The logo on the cover of this hymn collection puts the cross of Christ at the center and surrounds it with a number of Native American symbols.
The intersection of the two roads represents the centered life of harmony and balance, a Native American concept of beauty. The logo portrays the essential unity of many tribes as members of the one church of Jesus Christ.

content and format since the 1870s. It contains a broader base of musical styles than any of its predecessor hymnals. This hymnal includes new hymns reflecting concerns for peace, ecology, hunger, and justice. A concern for gender-inclusive language is reflected in text alterations of several traditional hymns. The current hymnal also includes hymns from ethnic traditions, especially hymns from the African-American, Hispanic, Asian-American, and Native-American communities.

During the past few decades the church has published supplements to its hymnals. Methodism's 1964 hymnal had included only six hymns representing the African-American tradition. In 1973 United Methodism's Board of Discipleship addressed this deficiency by publishing a hymnal supplement titled *Songs of Zion*. The intent of this publication was to bring to the church a resource "reflective of the musical heritage of black Christians." This supplement established a standard for future hymnals for African-American congregations. Also, the church needed a hymnbook to meet the needs of persons of Asian

The Upper Room hymn and worship supplement.

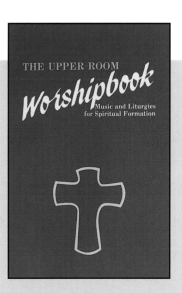

This hymnal, published by the Upper Room in 1985, contains a supplemental collection of music and liturgy for contemporary services of worship, praise, and prayer. *The Upper Room Worshipbook* is especially popular with the Emmaus Movement and the Academy for Spiritual Formation.

background. So, in 1983 the church published *Hymns for the Four Winds: A Collection of Asian American Hymns.* In 1985 the Upper Room published a hymn and worship book to supplement the official United Methodist hymnal. Then, in 1996, the church published a Spanish language hymnal, *Mil Vosec Para Celebrar.*

John and Charles Wesley believed that words put to music become potent influences in people's lives. They knew that people's religious songs tellingly express who they are and significantly shape what they become. Millions of people (including those who never learned to read) committed the Methodist hymns to memory, as the preachers lined them out for the congregation to sing. The hymns brought sinners to repentance and inspired saints in their daily Christian walk.

From the start, the Methodists sang during class meetings, prayer meetings, love feasts, watch night services, and at preaching services. Every gathering began and ended with a hymn. The impact of hymns on Methodism has been enormous. Hymns in the Methodist tradition continue to help worshipers understand and experience the gospel. They define what is truly Christian, and they point people to Jesus Christ. Through the singing of hymns, congregations worship the God whose Spirit imparts grace to their own spirits:

How happy every child of grace,
Who knows his sins forgiven!
"This earth," he cries, "is not my place;
I seek my place in heaven;
A country far from mortal sight,
Yet O by faith I see
The land of rest, the saints' delight,
The heaven prepared for me

O what a blessed hope is ours!
While here on earth we stay.
We more than taste the heavenly powers,
And antedate that day;
We feel the resurrection near,
Our life in Christ concealed,
And with his glorious presence here
His life in us revealed.

The Wesleyan hymns endure because of their self-authenticating excellence. The energy released by congregational hymn singing elevates our worship of God and enhances the communion of the saints.

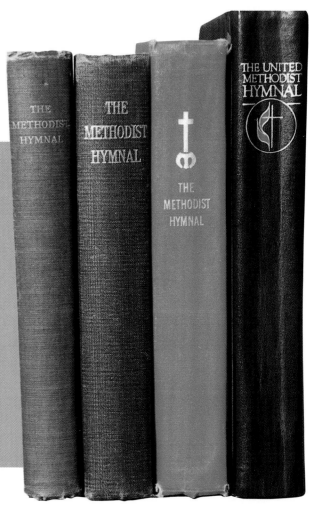

Twentieth Century Methodist hymnals.

Next to the Bible, the most loved book in the church is the hymnal. An eighteenth-century Methodist woman, Mary Benson, referred to "the dear Methodist hymn-book." Her love for the hymnal has been shared by millions of Methodists to the present day. The hymnal continues to echo the grand heritage of American Methodism.

From left to right in this picture are the Methodist hymnals published in 1905, 1935, 1964, and 1989. The 1905 hymnal was a joint work of the northern and southern branches of Methodism, and it featured their shared Wesleyan heritage. The 1935 hymnal echoed the social and scientific mood of the day and also introduced gospel songs into the hymnal. The 1964 hymnal represented a cultural diversity that spoke to a variety of religious experiences. The 1989 hymnal features inclusiveness of language and sensitivity to a variety of social and environmental concerns. Although these hymn collections are products of their particular times, the common thread of Wesleyan worship runs through them all.

11

Offering Them Christ

John and Charles Wesley rank among history's most effective Christian evangelists. They viewed those without Christ as sheep without a shepherd, lost people who were "fast bound in sin and nature's night." The Wesleys devoted their lives to taking Christ to those who did not know him. Some church leaders objected to the scope of the Wesleys' ministries and some of the methods they used to reach those who were not Christians. However, the Wesleys let nothing stand in the way of offering Christ to the unconverted. In a now famous declaration, John Wesley answered those who criticized his zeal for reaching lost people: "I look upon all the world as my parish...in whatever part of it I am, I judge it meet, right, and my bounden duty, to declare unto all that are willing

John Wesley preaching in the open air.
This picture of John Wesley preaching in Ireland is from a painting by Maria Spillsbury. It is on display in the Museum of Methodism in Great Britain.

In 1742 John Wesley wrote the following account in his journal: "I rode to Horsley. The house being too small, I was obliged again to preach in the open air; but so furious a storm have I seldom known. The wind drove upon us like a torrent; coming by turns from east, west, north, and south; the straw and thatch flew round our heads; so that one would have imagined it could not be long before the house must follow; but scarce any one stirred, much less went away, till I dismissed them with the peace of God."

Early Methodist preachers did not invite people to accept the gospel without first proclaiming it, and they did not proclaim the gospel without afterward exhorting people to accept it. On hearing a sermon in Scotland, Wesley commented, "I heard many excellent truths ... but, as there was no application, it was likely to do as much good as the singing of a lark.... No sinners are convinced of sin, none converted to God, by this way of preaching."

to hear, the glad tidings of salvation. This is the work which I know God has called me to; and sure I am, that his blessing attends it." Wesley told his preachers, "You have nothing to do but to save Souls. Therefore spend and be spent in this Work...save as many Souls as you can...bring as many Sinners as you possibly can to Repentance...build them up in that Holiness without which they cannot see the Lord."

Methodism's Main Mission

From the 1730s when Wesley was in Georgia, he took a keen interest in the American colonies. After he returned to England, he became concerned that most of the Anglican priests in America had ineffective ministries. Wesley told the bishop of London that these priests "knew something of Greek and Latin; but knew no more of saving souls, than of catching whales." Taking matters into his own hands, Wesley assumed the authority to send missionaries of his own to America. He chose preachers who had a passion for winning the lost. One of those early preachers, Joseph Pilmore, wrote in his journal, "O that the great Master of the vineyard would raise up and thrust out laborers into his field...that the knowledge of God may be increased, and poor wandering sinners brought into the fold of Christ!" Another of these missionaries, Richard Boardman, wrote John Wesley a letter that revealed Boardman's love for evangelism:

> Our [preaching] House contains about seventeen hundred [the typesetter who transcribed the letter may have misread seven hundred] hearers. About a third part of those who attend get in; the rest are glad to hear without. There appears such a willingness in the Americas to hear the word as I never saw before. They have no preaching in some parts of the Back Settlements. I doubt not but an effectual door will be opened among them. O may the Most High now give His Son the heathen for His inheritance.

This scene depicts John Wesley's farewell to the team of three ministers he sent to America to help establish the Methodist Episcopal Church. Here, the men are boarding a small boat to row out to the ship that will take them to New York. In the boat with Thomas Coke are Thomas Vasey and Richard Whatcoat, newly ordained by John Wesley for ministry in America.

As American Methodism grew, it produced an army of circuit riders and lay preachers. These Christian workers labored sacrificially in their efforts to take the gospel to every soul in the land. Nineteenth-century Methodist Bishop Holland McTyeire observed, "It was not new doctrine but new life the first Methodists sought for themselves and for others.... The Methodists came forth as evangelists. They persuaded men.... Their controversy was not with Church or State authorities, but with sin and Satan; and their one object was to save souls."

American Methodism's first *Discipline* (1784) gave a clear charge to Christian workers: "Go into every House in course, and teach every one therein, young and old...to be Christians inwardly and outwardly." In 1798 Bishops Coke and Asbury instructed the preachers with plain words:

> The preacher must...Convince the sinner of his dangerous condition. He must

"break up the fallow ground." "Cry aloud, spare not," says the Lord to his prophet, "Lift up thy voice like a trumpet, and shew my people their transgression, and the house of Jacob their sins.... He must set forth the depth of original sin, and shew the sinner how far he is gone from original righteousness; he must describe the vices of the world in their just and most striking colours, and enter into all the sinner's pleas and excuses for sin, and drive him from all his subterfuges and strongholds. He must labour to convince the formalist of the impossibility of being justified before God by his ceremonial or moral righteousness. Myriads are continually perishing.... He must set forth the virtue of the atoning blood. He must bring the mourner to a present Saviour; he must shew the willingness of Christ this moment to bless him, and bring a present salvation home to his soul.

Bishops Francis Asbury and Thomas Coke personally exemplified the ministry of evangelism. For example, Asbury wrote in his journal, "Little sleep last night. Let me suffer, and let me labour; time is short, and souls are daily lost." Taking Christ to the people was so important to him that he had little patience with disputes over trifles. He noted a controversy that disturbed a Methodist society in Charleston, South Carolina: "There is a holy strife between its members and the Episcopalians, who shall have the highest steeple; but I believe there is no contention about who shall have the most souls converted." Asbury often declared, "Heaven is my object, not earth."

Bishop Coke's strong interest in evangelism led him to give his considerable fortune to the cause of foreign missions. He even solicited from door to door, raising money to send Christian workers to unevangelized lands. Throughout his adult life, Coke personally took numerous missionary voyages. He died at sea on his way to begin a Methodist mission in India and Ceylon. His missionary zeal won him the title "Foreign Minister of Methodism."

The Methodist Episcopal Church demonstrated that its main mission was saving souls. Even unchurched people recognized that Methodism existed for one primary reason—to bring people to Jesus Christ. The Methodists believed that spiritually transformed people would make America a great nation. They purposed to reform the continent and to spread scriptural holiness over the land. That was their main mission.

Religious Revivals in Early Methodism

During American Methodism's early decades, evangelism was a conspicuous part of almost every kind of gathering. The bishops stressed soul winning at Annual and General Conferences. Preaching services, love feasts, watch nights, and communion services saw people converted to Christ. Also, the local and district conferences were times of revival and spiritual refreshing. When a preacher delivered an especially effective evangelistic message, people commonly said, "He preaches like a bishop."

The early journals and histories of Methodist people recorded hundreds of fruitful revivals. For instance, Jesse Lee wrote the following account:

Many sinners were powerfully convinced, and cried for mercy. The news of convictions and conversions were common; and the people of God were inspired with new life and vigour, by the happiness of others.... Numbers of old and gray-headed, of middle-aged persons, of youth, yea, of little children, were the subjects of this work.... This out-pouring of the spirit extended itself, more or less, through most of the circuits.

Summarizing Methodist work during 1791, Lee wrote, "We had a pleasing revival of religion in many places during this year; and a door was opened for the spreading of Methodism in the New-England states; where many people were inviting us, and sending for us to come and preach among them. Some of them also cast in their lots with us, and joined our society."

Entire territories felt the positive effects of Methodist evangelistic efforts. A striking example was the remarkable transformation of the Kentucky frontier. At one time Kentucky had been called "that dark and bloody ground," a

A frontier home.

The early Methodists considered heads of households to be spiritual leaders who were responsible for conducting daily devotional exercises for the family. Numerous Methodist households set up "family altars" for daily Bible reading and prayers. A nineteenth-century Methodist author wrote, "The heads of families owe a duty ... to those whom God has committed to their care and guidance.... Who can properly estimate the magnitude of that responsibility?"

Many lay people also evangelized in their personal contacts and daily work. Some lay people talked to their neighbors about Christ; others ministered as lay speakers and class leaders. As exhorters and lay preachers, numerous church members carried on significant ministries while the traveling elders made the rounds of their circuits.

reference to the fighting and lawlessness that blanketed the territory. Religious revivals, however, changed the area. The 1803 *Methodist Magazine* printed a report of an 1801 visit of the president of Washington (Virginia) College to the frontier:

> I found Kentucky...the most moral place I had ever been. A profane expression was hardly ever heard. A religious awe seemed to pervade the country. Upon the whole, I think the revival in Kentucky the most extraordinary that has ever visited the Church of Christ; and all things considered, it was peculiarly adapted to circumstances of that country.... Something of an extraordinary nature seemed necessary to arrest the attention of a giddy people who were ready to conclude that Christianity was a fable.... This revival had done it. It has confounded infidelity, awed vice into silence, and brought numbers beyond calculation under serious impressions.

If the Methodist revivals attracted supportive crowds, they also stirred up resistance. In 1789 Francis Asbury described a conflict produced by a revival in rural West Virginia:

> Our quarterly meeting began in the woods near Shepherdstown: we had about seven hundred people: I felt energy and life in preaching, and power attended the word. Brother Willis spoke, and the Lord wrought powerfully. [Sunday] was a high day—one thousand or fifteen hundred people attended; sinners began

to mock, and many cried aloud; and so it went. I was wonderfully led out...and spoke, first and last, nearly three hours. O, how the wicked contradicted and opposed!

Such opposition was often followed by the conversion of the demonstrators; God sometimes came upon them and brought them to their knees in prayer. A preacher reported the following account to Bishop Asbury: "One man who was intoxicated, and came into the assembly to make disturbance, was struck to the ground by an invisible power, and is since soundly converted, and joined society."

> Methodism's revivals led to the establishing of many new churches. During a trip through Ohio in 1812, Bishop Asbury wrote, "We had a solemn meeting. I preached to about three thousand people.... We came away thirty miles to Barnesville, where I delivered my testimony.... The Methodists seem to have almost entire influence in this town. Our chapel is forty by fifty feet."

In 1805 Bishop Asbury edited and published reports of revivals that had taken place throughout the church. He titled that book, *Extracts of Letters, Containing Some Account of the Work of God Since the Year 1800.* This collection of revival reports includes William Thacher's account of a revival in New Haven, Connecticut:

> On Sunday morning the people flocked from every direction; the computation of numbers that day was from seven to eight thousand. Prayer-meeting at 8, preaching

half past 9, by brother [Nicholas] Snethen, with mighty energy; two or three more sermons and a number of prayers and exhortations were delivered from the stand, and then a short intermission, after which the worship continued in different groups till Monday 9 o'clock, when the sacrament was administered to numbers, who were overwhelmed with love divine. Then preaching with great clearness, freedom and power by brother [Freeborn] Garrettson; a lively pathetic exhortation by brother Moriarty, and a crowning discourse by brother Snethen, while tears of joy flowed down the animated faces of the saints, shouts of rapture filled the place, and convictions seemed to fasten on every auditor. After a very fervent prayer, and the accustomed benediction, the parting scene was truly affecting.

Another preacher's account concluded, "About one hundred and thirteen white and black were joined in society yesterday; and from what I hear, I doubt not, but as many, if not twice the number...will be joined in different parts of the country—all the fruits of this blessed meeting."

The Camp Meeting

A major Methodist means of taking Christ to the people was the camp meeting, a distinctively American religious phenomenon which had no exact precedent. Camp meetings originated in 1799 on the Kentucky frontier, and then spread across America. These "brush arbor" meetings constituted one of the church's most effective means of evangelism, and they mark the start of what historians call the Second Great Awakening in America.

Camp meeting sites required little preparation for making them ready for religious services. It was relatively easy to assemble a simple wooden speaker's stand, plank seating, and straw for stuffing mattresses. People slept in tents, covered wagons, makeshift shelters of tree boughs, and sapling-pole sheds. As the camp meetings became established, the people built tabernacles for the preaching services. In time, they constructed large dormitories, with dining halls on the ground level and sleeping rooms above. Later, individuals and congregations built cottages for these summer "encampments."

Methodist camp meeting.
This picture is taken from Barlow Weed Gorham's 1854 book, Camp Meeting Manual. *The scene is of a frontier camp meeting circa 1848.*

Camp meeting crowds of from five to ten thousand were common, and some meetings were much larger. The famous Cane Ridge camp meeting in Kentucky peaked at from 20,000 to 25,000 people, in a time when nearby Lexington, the largest settlement in the state, registered less than 1,800 citizens. Generous farmers allowed people's horses to graze in their pastures.

In the days before electric amplification, it required a strong voice to speak to large camp meeting crowds. In Virginia, a camp meeting preacher thundered out a sermon on the second coming of Christ. His voice carried so far that a presiding elder remarked, "That sermon can almost be heard in hell."

A citizen who lived near a United Brethren campground in Sandusky County, Ohio reported the following account: "A stranger called at my home one day about eleven o'clock to inquire the way to the campmeeting, which was then in progress. I told him to listen, and, on being silent for a moment, the voice of Michael Long, in the full exercise of its powers, came wafted upon the breezes. I told the stranger to follow the sound through the wood, and he would find the campmeeting about three miles distant in that direction."

Methodist people looked forward to the camp meeting as the highlight of their year. One observer said, "Age snatched his crutch, youth forgot his pastime, the laborer quitted his task [to go to the camp meeting]." In 1803 Fanny Lewis wrote Bishop Asbury:

Camp meeting! Why the very name thrills every nerve!.... Every foot of ground seemed to me sacred. I saw nothing, heard nothing to molest my peace. Not one jarring string. Every thing seemed to combine together to promote the glory of God, and his gospel. Such indeed, my dear father [Bishop Asbury], was our meeting; and I can but lament my inability to give you an account of it; but it was better felt than expressed. Sometimes you would see more than one hundred hands raised in triumphant praise with united voices, giving glory to God, for more than one hour together, with every mark of unfeigned humility and reverence.... The preachers all seemed as men filled with new wine. Some standing crying, others prostrate on the ground, as insensible to every earthly object; while the Master of assemblies was speaking to the hearts of poor sinners, who stood trembling under a sense of power and presence of a sin-avenging God.

The early camp meetings attracted people of different ages and religious backgrounds. Crowds came from great distances, prepared with bedding and food to stay for several days

John Berry (J. B.) McFerrin (1807-1887).

McFerrin, a frontier preacher in Tennessee and Alabama, described the daily schedule at a camp meeting: "At daybreak a trumpet roused the camp. A second blast was the signal for private prayer. At the third peal all who could leave their tents collected at the preaching stand for public prayer. Then came breakfast. At 8 and 11 A.M., at 3 P.M., and early candlelighting there was preaching with exhortation, followed by a prayer meeting with the penitents. The preaching was expected to be animated, and after the sermon the second man, or exhorter, was to apply the subject and move the congregation to action. Choristers led the singing, but the whole multitude would join in some chorus hymn."

or longer. Jesse Lee described an 1803 camp meeting held in South Carolina:

In July, there was a camp-meeting held in Sandy River circuit, which was said to be the greatest time among sinners that some of them ever saw. On Saturday the Lord began to shake Satan's kingdom in a powerful manner. On Sunday, and Sunday night, the power of darkness gave back. Many sinners were on the ground crying for mercy, and many believers crying for perfect love. About twenty persons found redemption in the blood of Jesus at that time.

Family at camp meeting.

Frontier camp meetings helped spread a national revival called the Second Great Awakening. Camp meetings began at the end of the eighteenth century, and by 1820 the Methodists in America supported over 500 camp meetings. Many of these "encampments" became significant centers of evangelism and spiritual renewal.

Nineteenth-century Methodists took their entire families to camp meetings. In this picture note the mother and her small children near the tent. Women cared for the infants, prepared meals, nursed the sick, and tended to additional domestic chores. These responsibilities often prevented women from hearing the messages. Many women, however, willingly made these sacrifices in the hope that their children would have a personal experience with Jesus Christ.

Writing about camp meetings, James B. Finley concluded: "For practical exhibition of religion, for unbounded hospitality to strangers, for unfeigned and fervent spirituality, give me a country camp meeting against the world."

Bishop Francis Asbury was enthusiastic about camp meetings; he referred to them as "harvest seasons." In 1802 he wrote to the Presiding Elder of the Pittsburgh District, "I wish you would also hold campmeetings; they have never been tried without success. To collect such a number of God's people together to pray, and the ministers to preach...this is field fighting, this is fishing with a large net." Numerous entries in his journal tell about the conversions of hundreds to Christ, many of whom became Methodists. In a letter dated in 1801, Asbury reported, "The work of God is running like fire in Kentucky. It is reported that near fifteen if not twenty thousand were present at [a camp meeting]...and one thousand if not fifteen hundred fell and felt the power of grace." He declared, "All earth and hell is roused against field meetings, but we will endure fines, imprisonment, and death sooner than we will give them up."

In 1801 Bishop Asbury appointed William McKendree to serve as the Presiding Elder of the Kentucky District. This district was part of the Western Conference, which covered Kentucky, Ohio, Tennessee, Western Virginia, and a part of Illinois. McKendree started camp meetings wherever he labored. When he became a bishop in 1808, he continued to promote camp meetings throughout the vast territories of the Western conference. These gatherings significantly contributed to the growth of Methodism on the frontier.

Asbury was so convinced of the worth of camp meetings that he held Annual Conferences in the summer during camp meetings so that preachers and lay people could benefit from the spiritual inspiration they provided. He wrote in the (1811) *Arminian Magazine*:

> *Our camp meetings, I think, amount to between four and five hundred annually, some of which continue for the space of six or eight days. It is supposed that it is not uncommon for ten thousand persons...to be present at one of those meetings. On such occasions many become subjects of a*

Valentine Cook (1765-1820).

Cook was a student at Cokesbury College and later he became its most renowned alumnus. After leaving Cokesbury College, he served as an itinerant Methodist preacher, gaining a reputation for his compelling sermons. In time, Bishop Asbury appointed him a presiding elder in Pennsylvania and Kentucky. In 1799 Cook became the principal of the newly founded Bethel Academy in Jessamine County, Kentucky. After the school closed, he preached, taught, conducted revivals, and spoke at camp meetings. Cook was fluent in English and German, and was considered one of Methodism's most powerful orators. At this time it was customary for "seekers" to kneel for prayer at their pews or benches, where designated persons came to pray with them. Cook seems to have been responsible for introducing the "altar call" during which seekers came forward to kneel at a railing for counsel and prayer.

A listener who heard Cook preach in a camp meeting in 1820 wrote the following account: "Every eye was fixed and every ear was opened to catch the words of eternal truth as they rolled in thrilling torrents from his almost-inspired lips. No human tongue, untouched by flames fresh from the altar of God, could have spoken as he did. No language can adequately describe the scene that followed. The whole assemblage was in tears. Sinners were crying to God for mercy, while the saints of the Most High were shouting aloud for joy. Many souls were converted before the meeting closed. A great revival succeeded in all that section."

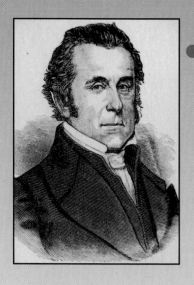

Nicholas Snethen (1769-1845).

In 1803 Snethen organized the first camp meeting in Maryland. The meeting proved successful despite the lack of support from a number of his colleagues. His inspiration for this venture came from his having attended a southern camp meeting the previous year. He described that event: "The scene by night was solemn and novel. The lofty trees, and the light from the different fires, with the stand for preaching, were awfully pleasing. Fifteen of our (Methodist) preachers were present, besides Baptist and Presbyterian ministers. All were engaged at once on religious subjects, and many happy conversions took place."

Snethen was one of the most effective pulpit orators of his day. On one occasion he preached for 40 minutes and was overcome by "the surging waves of his own emotion." Another preacher finished the sermon and by the end of the service 500 converts had been added to the church. Snethen spent part of his ministry as a traveling companion of Bishop Asbury, who knew him well. The bishop called him a "silver trumpet" in reference to his "far-reaching, melodious, and silver-toned voice."

work of grace, and many experience much of the sanctifying influences of the Holy Spirit. Backsliders are restored, and the union of both preachers and people is greatly increased.

Asbury died in 1816, and for another fifteen years after his death, the presiding elders continued to schedule fourth Quarterly Conferences in conjunction with camp meetings.

The main theological themes of the Methodist camp meetings were God's love for all, repentance, justification by faith, regeneration by the power of the Holy Spirit, the witness of the Spirit, and God's provision for holiness. Underlying this preaching was the urgent message that "Today is the day of salvation." Sometimes camp meetings reported over 1,000 conversions during a week of services. The yearly conference journals reported the statistics of the camp meetings held in their areas.

During the nineteenth century, the Methodists institutionalized the camp meetings by establishing

Camp meeting scene.

This picture captures some of the many concurrent activities at a typical nineteenth-century camp meeting. Penitents are kneeling in prayer; well-dressed folk are engaged in social conversation; one woman is swooning; another is dancing with joy. The camp meetings were interracial events, and sometimes there were more black worshipers present than white. At night, numerous campfires burned, making it appear that the whole woods were aflame. Sometimes black and white worshipers sat together on the rows of seats; at other times they sat on separate sides of a center aisle. The black preacher Daniel Coker once preached at a gathering of 5,000 in a camp meeting in Maryland, where many white people assembled to hear his inspired speaking.

many permanent camp meeting sites. Before the end of the century supporters of some camps built large and impressive buildings. Especially notable were the camps that developed at Chautauqua, New York; Ocean Grove, New Jersey; Lake Junaluska, North Carolina; Oak Bluffs, Massachusetts; and Bayview, Michigan.

Methodist Emotion

Perhaps the most interesting phenomena connected with the eighteenth and nineteenth centuries were the displays of religious emotion that sometimes occurred in Methodist services. Excitement was especially evident in Methodism's revivals and camp meetings. These emotional displays were not unique to Methodism. Earlier in the eighteenth century Jonathan Edwards reported on the physical demonstrations he observed during the Colonial revivals in New England. "Boiling hot" religion, however, was a Methodist trademark.

Joseph Pilmore, one of Wesley's first missionaries to America, wrote, "Our meetings, in general, were lively, and the souls of the people were so refreshed, that they greatly rejoiced to run the heavenly race."

Faultfinders objected to excitement and emotion as violating "dignity and order." In 1805 the General Assembly of another denomination summarily denounced camp meetings: "God is a God of order and not of confusion, and whatever tends to destroy the comely order of his worship is not from him." These critics charged Methodism with promoting "intemperate zeal."

Without question, the Methodists *were* enthusiastic. The preachers shouted, waved their Bibles, banged on pulpits, and walked about as they delivered their extemporaneous sermons. In public meetings, some preachers at times shook so powerfully that they needed to stop speaking and recover their composure before continuing their messages. One circuit rider expressed gratitude for a good woman who regularly sewed up the armhole seams of his coat. He explained that while preaching he regularly burst the seams, and no doubt he would burst them again.

Ocean Grove Auditorium.

Ocean Grove Camp was founded in 1869 at Ocean Grove, New Jersey as a facility of the Methodist Episcopal Church. The camp operates throughout the summer from June until after Labor Day. The summer season reaches a climax with the famous Ocean Grove camp meeting, a 10-day program of preaching and evangelism. The Great Auditorium shown in this picture was built in 1894 in the span of 92 days. Across the front of the auditorium are the words, "Holiness unto the Lord, be ye holy."

The most common physical phenomena consisted of moaning, crying, laughing, swooning, and shouting. Even more dramatic physical displays consisted of dancing with joy, jerking, and "the singing exercise." Barton Stone (one of the founders of the Christian Church, or Disciples of Christ) wrote a treatise on the unusual religious demonstrations he observed in camp meetings. Discussing the singing exercise, he wrote, "The singing exercise is more unaccountable than anything else I ever saw. The subject in a very happy state of mind would sing most melodiously, not from the mouth or nose, but entirely in the breast, the sounds issuing thence. Such music silenced everything, and attracted the attention of all. It was most heavenly. None could ever be tired of hearing it."

Describing an emotional camp meeting, Methodist preacher John McGee reported:

Many thousands of people attended. The mighty power and mercy of God was manifested. The people fell before the Word, like corn before a storm of wind, and many rose from the dust with divine glory shining in their countenances, and gave glory to God in such strains as made the hearts of stubborn sinners to tremble; and after the first gust of praise they would break forth into whole volleys of exhortation.

As a circuit rider discreetly put it, "The camp meetings were marked by some peculiarities."

The early Methodist leaders were not entirely comfortable with the physical demonstrations that sometimes accompanied religious revivals. Yet they were reluctant to restrain emotional displays, for fear of quenching the work of God. Thomas Rankin, Wesley's assistant in America, did not encourage emotional displays in religious services, but he refrained from suppressing them because he saw the good that often followed. Rankin said, "Numbers were calling aloud for mercy, and many were mightily praising God.... Husbands were inviting their wives to go to heaven with them and parents calling upon their children to come to the Lord Jesus.... All was wonder and amazement." A participant in a Methodist meeting wrote:

On the one hand you would have seen a poor sinner leaning with his head against a tree, with tears running from his eyes, and somebody going and pointing him to the Lamb of God upon the cross. On the other hand you would have seen a whole group of people, and from the midst of them you would have heard the piercing outcries of the broken-hearted penitent; and to turn your eyes in another direction you would see a gray-headed father and his children crying to God to have mercy on their souls.... I could have led you to a place where the divine blessing was manifested, similar to the glory which appeared in the tabernacle of the congregation when the wandering Israelites fell upon their faces and shouted.

Expressing his tolerance for physical demonstrations, a preacher said, "When I see a different sort of apple on a branch I am not prepared to sever it from the tree."

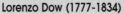
Lorenzo Dow (1777-1834)   Peggy Holcomb Dow (1780-1820).

Lorenzo Dow began preaching at the age of 18, and he became noted for his zealous and successful evangelistic ministry. He did not receive ordination because he did not want to accept the constraints of conference membership. Dow traveled widely, often preaching six or seven time a day. Some of his travels took him into the South, where he preached after dark to the slaves on plantations. He won many of them to Christ. His eccentric dress and unconventional ways gained him the nickname "Crazy Dow." He kept a journal that detailed his adventures, refuted unbiblical teachings, and defended the camp meetings against those who criticized them.

Lorenzo Dow's wife, Peggy, was a devoted companion who supported her husband's work, despite the sacrifices brought about by his exhausting schedule. Prior to meeting Lorenzo, Peggy often said, "I had rather marry a preacher than any other man, provided I was worthy; and I would wish him to travel and be useful to souls." On meeting Peggy, Lorenzo Dow asked her sister questions about her: "Does she profess religion? For how long? Does she keep wicked company?" Satisfied with the answers, Lorenzo talked with Peggy, and within 24 hours he asked her to marry him. Almost immediately after Lorenzo's proposal, he left for a preaching tour and did not return for almost two years. They were then married in a late evening wedding service. Early the next morning Lorenzo left for a seven-month preaching tour in the Mississippi Territory. On his return, he stayed with Peggy for two weeks before starting out on another round of preaching. Later, Lorenzo told Peggy that he was preparing to sail to England for a long evangelistic tour. She decided to sail with him, and thereafter she accompanied him whenever she could. Her autobiography, *Vicissitudes: Or the Journey of Life*, was printed in the same volume that contained Lorenzo's journal and his other writings. The book saw a wide circulation among nineteenth-century Methodists.

Those who were "struck down" by the power of God were sometimes converted to Christ, and their lives were profoundly transformed. In 1798 Valentine Cook preached on God's coming judgment. A listener in the congregation arose and exclaimed, "Stop! Stop till I can get out of this place!" Cook declared to the congregation, "Let us pray for that man." The agitated person began his exit, but on reaching the edge of the assembly, he dropped to his knees and began to cry aloud for mercy. He soon became a new person in Christ.

Lorenzo Dow, a Methodist evangelist, vigorously defended these emotional displays in an essay, "Defense of Camp Meetings." Dow responded to a critic who had written, "[The] exercises and engagements of the people at [camp meetings] are absurd. Their opinions are enthusiastic, and their practices disgusting. In a word, the whole business is intolerable." Forthrightly, Dow replied, "I am at liberty to suppose it to be your opinion in opposition to the manner of the Methodists, that men may have all necessary religion in secret. That it is improper to make any proclamation of its attainment, and that all external show of it is hypocrisy. Under the influence of this opinion you had rather be considered irreligious than be classed with any people who make a noise about religion."

Concerning displays of religious emotion, Bishop Thomas Coke wrote to Freeborn Garrettson, "All the shouting seasons, in spite of my proud reluctance to yield to them at first, were a matter of great praise and rejoicing to me very soon: and I shall defend them, both from the pulpit and the press." Coke also recorded in his journal, "Souls are awakened and converted by multitudes; and the work is surely a genuine work.... Whether there be wild-fire in it or not, I do most ardently wish, that there was such a work at this present time in England."

Methodist Evangelism and Evangelists

Bishop Asbury set the tone for Methodist evangelism and evangelists. He crossed the Appalachian Mountains at least 60 times, using various routes in order to reach as many people as possible. Following his example, numerous Methodist evangelists have continued the ministry of offering Christ to the people. It will be remembered that all the early Methodist circuit riders were evangelists. They understood that their primary mission was to proclaim the message of salvation and to invite their listeners to become genuine Christians. Out of the ranks of the preachers came a number of outstanding evangelists, both lay and clergy.

One such early evangelist was Benjamin Abbott (1732-1796), who wrote *The Experience and Gospel Labours of the Rev. Benjamin Abbott*, an account of his ministerial work. A typical passage reads,

> *I met brother [Freeborn] Garrettson at brother B's on Fish-kill-mountain, and held a love-feast: brother G. opened it; and after handing about the bread and water, the people spoke feelingly of God's dealing with their souls, and we had a melting time with them—after love-feast, brother G. preached and I exhorted. When I came to this circuit, there were but few that knew the Lord, and when I left it, I think there were about one hundred that had found peace in Him, of whom Moses and the prophets wrote.*

Following Abbott's death, the Conference Minutes of 1796 stated, "He was an innocent, holy man. He was seldom heard by any one to speak about anything but God and religion; and his whole soul was often overwhelmed by the power of God." For many decades after Abbott's death, conference notices of deceased Methodist preachers mentioned their work in evangelism.

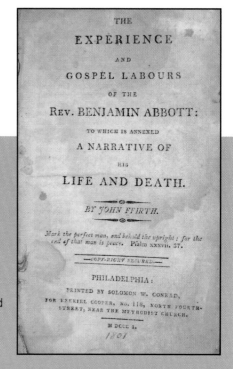

Title page of Benjamin Abbott's memoirs.

Benjamin Abbott (1732-1796) was one of the earliest American-born Methodist evangelists. He lacked formal education, but his earnest preaching was remarkably eloquent and effective. His ministry brought thousands into the Methodist Episcopal Church. During America's War of Independence, Abbott was a major figure in preserving the spiritual life of the Methodist societies throughout New Jersey.

In Abbott's account of his work he wrote the following passage: "Sunday 14th, I was very unwell; but I besought God, that if it was his will that I should go to my appointment, that he would strengthen me for this one, as he did Sampson (sic) among the Philistines; and he did so: for I was enabled to attend my morning appointment, and preach; and blessed by God he laid to his helping hand and we had a shout in the camp, and four joined society. I attended my other appointment and preached, and the Lord poured out his Spirit in power.... This was a happy day to my soul."

The roster of effective Methodist evangelists is a long one. Any listing would include such notables as Harry Hosier, Freeborn Garrettson, George Shadford, Jacob Albright, William Otterbein, John Seybert, William McKendree, John Stewart, Elijah Hedding, Phebe Palmer, Margaret Van Cott, Sam Jones, Ira Sankey, E. Stanley Jones, Lawrence Lacour, and Harry Denman. A number of historians believe that the single most important factor in the development of American Methodism has been its evangelistic outreach.

Bishop William McKendree (1757-1835).

As a youth, McKendree lived a morally upright life. He said that prior to his conversion he remembered having sworn only one profane oath in his life. Yet he sensed that he did not know God. Reading the Bible confirmed his deep spiritual need. McKendree said that he was convinced that his heart was "deceitful and desperately wicked." He experienced a profound conversion: "I ventured my all upon Christ. In a moment my soul was relieved of a burden too heavy to be borne, and joy instantly succeeded sorrow. For a short space of time I was fixed in silent adoration, giving glory to God for his unspeakable goodness to such an unworthy creature."

McKendree became a Methodist preacher, but at the start of his ministry he lacked confidence. At a time when the despondent McKendree considered leaving the ministry, an elderly minister encouraged him: "Brother, my mind is powerfully impressed that God has a great work for you to do, and I believe the impression is from the Lord. Don't start from the cross—take it up—go to the work, and be faithful!" These tearful delivered words of support greatly encouraged the young preacher, and he entered his work with fresh enthusiasm. McKendree eventually became the first native-born American to be elected a Methodist bishop. He gained the reputation of being one of the most effective preachers and leaders in Methodism. Always, McKendree helped establish camp meetings in the areas he served. During his episcopacy, his area increased dramatically in numbers and geographical expansion. Many have referred to him as "the Apostle of Western Methodism."

John Stewart (?-1823).

John Stewart, a freeborn person of mixed race, was converted around 1815 in a Methodist camp meeting near Marietta, Ohio. At the time of his conversion he was a poverty-stricken alcoholic, intent on suicide. His conversion transformed his life, and he soon became a powerful Methodist evangelist. In 1816 Stewart sensed that God had called him to preach to the American Indians. His ministry among them was highly successful. This pioneering work among Native Americans in Ohio was the first sustained Methodist ministry among the American Indians.

Bishop Elijah Hedding (1780-1852).

In 1789 the evangelist Benjamin Abbott conducted evangelistic meetings near the home of Elijah Hedding, who at the time was nine years old. The meetings resulted in the conversion of many members of his family. Later, Elijah was converted and became a Methodist minister. He preached with great power, and was a particularly effective evangelist. The General Conference of 1824 elected Hedding bishop, and he became famous in Methodist circles as a gentleman of integrity, piety, and wisdom. Throughout his long tenure as bishop, he continued his evangelistic work.

On his deathbed Hedding said, "I was reflecting upon the wonder of God's mercy—how a just and infinite and holy God could take such vile creature to dwell with him in so holy a place.... I thought of his great mercy to me—how much he had done for me—and I had such glorious view of the atonement of Christ ... that my soul was filled in a wonderful manner. I have served God more than fifty years. I have generally had peace, but I never saw such glory before, such light, and such clearness, such beauty! Oh, I want to tell it to all the world.... But I cannot. I never shall preach again; never shall go over the mountains, the valleys, the woods, and the swamps, to tell of Jesus any more. But oh, what glory I feel! It shines and burns all through me, and it came upon me like the rushing of the mighty wind upon the day of Pentecost."

Phebe Worrall Palmer (1807-1874).

Mrs. Palmer, a Methodist lay woman, was an evangelist, author, editor, and social reformer. She evangelized in over 300 camp meetings and revival campaigns in America, Canada, and England. Bishop Matthew Simpson wrote that Mrs. Palmer "was a clear, fluent, forcible speaker, (who) persuaded many to bow at the foot of the cross."

Margaret Van Cott (1830-1914).

"Maggie" Van Cott was unusually successful in personally winning individuals to Jesus Christ. And so she decided to give herself to the work of evangelism. In 1869 the Methodist Episcopal Church granted her a preacher's license, making her the first American woman to receive this authorization.

For more than 30 years she preached evangelistic meetings throughout the United States. At the conclusion of her revivals she organized prayer bands for the purpose of conserving the converts. It is estimated that she won 75,000 people to Christ, about half of whom joined the Methodist Episcopal Church.

Ira David Sankey (1840-1908).

Ira Sankey joined the Methodist Episcopal Church at the age of fifteen, and soon developed an effective music ministry. Accompanying himself on a reed organ, he sang in a rich baritone voice that could fill concert halls. The dramatic quality of his clear and pleasant tones deeply affected congregations. Sankey helped establish the singing of gospel hymns as an important part of revival meetings.

In 1870, Dwight L. Moody heard Sankey sing at a YMCA convention in Indianapolis. Moody was so impressed with Sankey's ministry that he invited the singer to come to Chicago to join the Moody team as a singing evangelist. Sankey accepted the invitation and for the next twenty-five years he was an indispensable member of Moody's team. Sankey's music deeply moved congregations across America and abroad. In addition to promoting gospel songs, Sankey developed "story hymns" that presented the gospel with emotional power. Two of his most popular songs were "The Ninety and Nine" and "Jesus of Nazareth Passeth By." Sankey's collections of gospel hymns became enormously popular. He accepted none of the royalties from the thousands of copies sold; these earnings he gave to Christian education. Ira Sankey's singing ministry made him one of the most effective evangelists of his time.

Samuel Porter ("Sam") Jones (1847-1906).

Sam Jones was converted to Christ as a result of the death of his father. In his father's final hours he reproved Sam for his lack of concern for the Christian faith, and for his profligate life. This exchange deeply moved the young man. Soon afterward he was converted under the preaching of his grandfather. Jones served briefly as a pastor of small churches in Georgia, and then he began to receive invitations to conduct revivals. Jones's clear and strong voice enabled him to speak to large crowds. Leading successful revivals, Jones won many converts who joined the church. As his popularity spread throughout the country, he held evangelistic meetings in nearly every state in the nation.

Jones vigorously opposed drunkenness, and his outspoken sermons led him to a place of prominence in the national prohibition movement. His humor and clever adages enhanced his fame. To one who accused him of rubbing the cat's fur the wrong way, Jones said, "Then let the cat turn around." It is estimated that he won over 700,000 people to Christ, sometimes as many as 2,700 in a single meeting. After his death, over 30,000 people filed past his casket, which was displayed in the Georgia State Capitol Building. Across the nation there were over forty memorial services held to commemorate the life and ministry of Sam Jones.

E. Stanley Jones (1884-1973).

This original oil painting by Letty McComb Lykens hangs in the E. Stanley Jones School of World Mission and Evangelism at Asbury Theological Seminary.

Many consider Jones the most eminent Methodist evangelist in the twentieth century. Beginning evangelistic preaching while a student at Asbury College, Jones devoted most of his life's work to India, where he had an especially effective ministry among educated Hindus. In 1928, the church elected him a bishop, but he declined the office so that he could devote himself to missionary evangelism.

Jones articulated for the twentieth century the Wesleyan balance of personal conversion and social responsibility. He was the author of about 30 books, many of which became best sellers. His first popular book, *The Christ of the Indian Road*, encouraged missionaries and evangelists to present the gospel in culturally relevant forms. *The Way, Abundant Living, Christian Maturity* and other books demonstrated that following the way of Christ leads to abundant life and personal fulfillment. His teaching helped the church understand the necessary bond between faith and works, and between personal and social holiness.

Lawrence ("Larry") Lacour (1914-1999).

Dr. Lacour was one of Methodism's most popular and effective evangelists during the middle years of the twentieth century. He served as a pastor, chaplain with the U. S. Navy, denominational executive, radio speaker, author, seminary professor, and vocational evangelist.

Reflecting on his childhood call to preach, Lacour wrote, "I can recall the overflow crowds that sang the great hymns with the same enthusiasm one finds today at sports events. As a small boy, I heard many a sermon that lasted for more than an hour—and most of them seemed to end entirely too soon! Those preachers made me feel that living for Christ was the greatest thing a boy could do. Their preaching produced living illustrations of how Christ changes lives. To speak for God in this way made a lasting impression on me. I got the idea that this was more important than being the president, a corporation executive, a movie star, or a sports hero."

Harry Denman (1893-1976).
This original oil painting hangs in the Lambuth Inn in Lake Junaluska, North Carolina. Photograph by Dave Henderson.

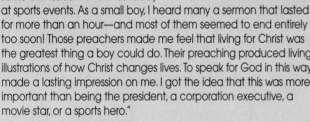

Denman was a layman who traveled extensively throughout America and abroad, holding evangelistic rallies and revivals. In 1939, following the union of the Methodist Episcopal, Methodist Episcopal, South, and Methodist Protestant Churches, Denman became the General Secretary of the Commission on Evangelism of the Methodist Church. He was particularly effective as a preacher and personal worker, bringing many people to Jesus Christ.

The story of Methodist evangelism reminds us that God calls the church perpetually to demonstrate and declare the gospel. A hymn of Charles Wesley captures this expectation:

A charge to keep I have, a God to glorify,
A never dying soul to save, and fit it for the sky.

To serve the present age, my calling to fulfill;
O may it all my powers engage to do my
*   Master's will!*

Arm me with jealous care, as in thy sight to live,
And O, thy servant, Lord, prepare, a strict
*   account to give!*

Help me to watch and pray, and on thyself rely,
Assured, if I my trust betray, I shall forever die.

In a sermon titled "The General Spread of the Gospel," John Wesley spoke optimistically about the future:

I cannot induce myself to think that God has wrought so glorious a work [as Methodism], to let it sink and die away in a few years. No: I trust, this is only the beginning of a far greater work; the dawn of 'the latter day glory.' And is it not probable, I say, that he will carry it on in the same manner as he has begun? At the first breaking out of this work in this or that place, there may be a shower, a torrent of grace; and so at some other particular seasons, which 'the Father has reserved in his own power:' But in general, it seems, the kingdom of God...will silently increase, wherever it is set up, and spread from heart to heart, from house to house, from town to town, from one kingdom to another.

National Association of United Methodist Evangelists.

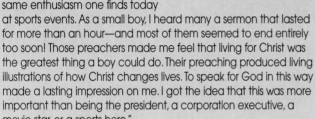
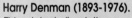

NAUME (The National Association of United Methodist Evangelists) is an affiliate of the church's General Board of Discipleship. The association brings together United Methodist evangelists for fellowship and inspiration at the annual meetings of the Council on Evangelism. NAUME provides a network of support for United Methodist evangelists and interprets their work to the church so that their services may be effectively utilized.

The Foundation for Evangelism.
This logo for the foundation was prepared by Kenneth Wyatt.

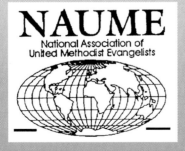

In 1949 Harry Denman organized the Foundation for Evangelism. The foundation, based at Lake Junaluska, North Carolina, is an affiliate of the General Board of Discipleship. This organization seeks to preserve Methodism's heritage of evangelism by emphasizing that Christ's command, "Go, make disciples," is a continuing mandate for the church. A major component of the work of the foundation is to fund chairs of evangelism in United Methodist seminaries. The foundation also sponsors a denominational program, Discover God's Call, founded by Gus Gustafson. This program of the church is designed to help Christians understand their spiritual gifts and use them in some form of ministry.

12 The Whole Gospel for the Whole World

Methodism's missionary spirit began with its founder, John Wesley, who declared, "The world is my parish." Wesley's interest in taking the gospel to new areas motivated him to spend his life as an itinerant preacher, even though he would have preferred to live a life of settled contemplation. His continuous travels throughout Great Britain led Canon J. H. Overton to observe, "He seems to fly about like a meteor." The famous Dr. Samuel Johnson enjoyed conversing with John Wesley, but Johnson was baffled by Wesley's drive to travel almost without ceasing. Johnson said, "John Wesley's conversation is good, but he is never at leisure. He is always obliged to go at a certain hour. This is very disagreeable to a man who loves to fold his legs and have his talk out, as I do." Having chosen a different focus, Wesley liked to quote the maxim, "Man was not born in the shades to lie." Wesley commented on his "vagabond life": "It is not pleasing to flesh and blood; and I would not do it, if I did not believe there was another world."

The story of American Methodism is one of small beginnings that developed into a mighty movement intent on taking the whole gospel to the whole world. Persons like Robert Strawbridge, Barbara Heck, and Philip Embury faithfully shared the gospel with their families, friends, and neighbors. Their converts, with excitement, spread the message of Methodism in ever-enlarging circles. After Methodism in America became a denomination, its missionary spirit continued, expanding its borders. Bishop Joshua Soule explained how the church went about its work:

> When it is ascertained that there is a tract of country lying beyond the limits of our regular itinerant work, with a population sufficient to justify the employment of a missionary, one is selected, the field of his labour is prescribed, his instructions furnished him, and he is sent forth to preach the gospel, raise societies, and form a circuit.

The Missionary Spirit of American Methodism

Francis Asbury echoed John Wesley's missionary passion. Concerning his coming to America, he wrote in his journal, "In 1771 I came as a missionary." After he became a bishop, he often referred to those who went out on circuits as "missionaries." Concerning those that Wesley sent to America, Bishop Asbury stated, "[They] came as missionaries [and] now behold the consequences of this mission." When founded in 1784, the Methodist Episcopal Church did not establish a distinct missionary society because the people regarded the entire church as a missionary movement. Once, an unfriendly cleric asked Thomas Ware, "Are you a missionary?" Ware replied, "I am a Methodist, and we are all missionaries."

Because preachers were so important to Methodism's mission, the church gave careful attention to their selection. The bishops asked probing questions about would-be Methodist preachers: (1) Have they the knowledge and love of God? (2) Have they gifts for ministry? (3) Have they fruit in their ministry? In 1798 Bishops Coke and Asbury declared:

> *[The preacher] must set forth the virtue of the* atoning blood. *He must bring the mourner to a* perfect *Saviour; he must shew the willingness of Christ* this moment *to bless him, and bring a perfect salvation home to his soul.... He must, like a true shepherd, feed the lambs and sheep of Christ. He must point out to the newly justified the wiles of Satan, and strengthen them if they stagger through unbelief. He must set before them the glorious privileges offered to them in the gospel. He must nourish them with the pure milk of the word. Those who are more adult in grace, he must feed with strong meat. He must shew them the necessity of being crucified to the world, and of dying daily: that "if they mortify not the deeds of the flesh, they shall die".... He must hold forth our adorable Redeemer as a prophet to teach, a priest to atone, and a king to reign in us and over us. He must break the* stony *heart, as well as bind up the* broken. *But still* holiness inward and outward must be his end: *holiness must be his aim.... Who is fit for these things? O Lord God, help us all! Let us do our utmost, and leave the blessing to the Lord.*

Each of the Annual Conferences certified yearly the character of its preachers. The 1796 General Conference adopted a rule requiring the removal of any minister guilty of improper behavior or of spreading "false doctrines." Bishops were subject to the same conference standards; the members of the conference could expel any of them for doctrinal deviation or improper conduct.

To the ministry of preaching, the American Methodists added the ministry of publishing. At first a few individuals imported Wesley's publications and sold them. Others privately published Wesley's writings, but without denominational permission or supervision. To bring order to this state of affairs, the 1773 conference

The emblem of the Methodist Publishing House.

This logo depicts a circuit rider, with a book in hand, making his rounds. The phrase "Since 1789" refers to the year that the church founded the Methodist Book Concern. It was decided at the time than any profits would be designated "for the use and benefit of the Methodist Church in America."

John Dickins (1747-1798).

There are many "firsts" connected with Dickins and his ministry. He was the first to welcome Thomas Coke to America, the first at the Christmas Conference to suggest the name "Methodist Episcopal Church," the first book editor of the denomination, and his wife was the first woman in America to live in a Methodist parsonage. When named the steward of the Methodist Book Concern in 1789, Dickins donated £125 ($600) of his own money to begin the church's publishing work in Philadelphia. Bishop Matthew Simpson said, "His skill and fidelity as editor, inspector, and corrector of the press were exceeding great, conducting the whole of his business with punctuality and integrity."

In 1798 the City of Philadelphia suffered a severe plague of yellow fever. Friends urged him to leave the city (more than 40,000 people had already left). Dickins, however, remained in Philadelphia to minister to those afflicted with the disease. He contracted the fever which was to lead to his death. From his bed, he said to his wife, "My dear, I am very ill; but I entreat you in the most earnest manner not to be the least discomposed or uneasy.... Glory be to God, I can rejoice in his will whether for life or death! I know all is well, glory be to Jesus!"

of preachers voted to bring all publishing under the authority of the "connection." Then in 1789 the young church founded the Methodist Book Concern.

The ministers selected one of their colleagues as the church's first book agent. His name was John Dickins. Bishop Asbury sent him to Philadelphia to establish the new ministry. Because the church had no money to support the new publishing venture, Dickins and his successor voluntarily sustained it with contributions of their own money. By 1793, the publishing house had 27 publications in print, and in 1795 Dickins issued a catalog. Dickins's service to the church was notable. Bishop Asbury referred to him as "the generous, the just, the faithful, skillful Dickins."

Ezekiel Cooper (1763-1847).

In 1798 Cooper succeeded John Dickins as the second editor of the Methodist Book Concern. Under his leadership the Book Concern became the largest publishing establishment in America. Cooper's associates regarded him as a "living encyclopedia" of theology and good judgment. A contemporary wrote, "He became one of the most able pulpit orators of his day. At times an irresistible pathos accompanied his preaching, and, in the forest worship (outdoor services) audiences of ten thousand would be so enchanted by his discourses that the most profound attention, interest, and solemnity prevailed. In public debate he possessed powers almost unequaled, and he seldom advocated a measure that did not prevail. He always treated his opponents with great respect."

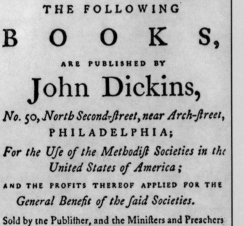

First catalog of the Methodist Book Concern, 1795.

In 1795, John Dickins released the first catalog of Methodist books. The list included John Wesley's *Notes Upon the New Testament*, volumes I and II of the *Arminian Magazine*, Thomas à Kempis's *Imitation of Christ* (printed under the title *An Extract of the Christian's Pattern*), the *Discipline*, *The Experience and Travels of Mr. Freeborn Garrettson*, *A Pocket Hymn-Book*, *An Extract on Infant Baptism*, *Children's Instructions*, *An Abridgment of Mrs. Rowe's Devout Exercises of the Heart*, *The Works of John Fletcher*, and Richard Baxter's *The Saints' Everlasting Rest*.

Ezekiel Cooper became John Dickins's successor as Methodism's book agent. Cooper had started his ministry as a traveling preacher in 1784, when Bishop Asbury assigned him to his first appointment with the charge, "[Go] on the Caroline Circuit and make a trial [at preaching]." Cooper rode circuits and served as a presiding elder until 1798, when the church elected him book steward. He remained a bachelor (as did many Methodist preachers), giving himself to preaching, managing the church's publishing house, and writing poetry. During Cooper's tenure as "Editor and General Book-steward," the Book Concern moved to New York, where Cooper, a competent manager, greatly expanded the church's publishing ministry. Under Cooper's leadership, the Book Concern set forth its publishing policy: "We confine ourselves to the publication of books and pamphlets, upon subjects of morality and divinity; more especially such as treat on experimental [experiential] and practical religion."

First New York headquarters of the Methodist Book Concern, 1824.

Cokesbury Press.

The Publishing House of the Methodist Episcopal Church, South adopted the name Cokesbury Press. When church union took place in 1939, Cokesbury Press merged with Abingdon Press. The mounted circuit rider on the logo for Cokesbury Press inspired the present trademark of the Methodist Publishing House. The name Cokesbury is now used to designate the bookstores of the publishing house.

Devoted circuit riders served as book and tract distributors. With leather saddlebags stuffed full of printed materials, these preachers ventured forth onto their circuits, always carrying reading matter to the people. The following order for tracts was typical of those received by the publishing house:

> You will please send us tracts suitable for the people in the wilderness. If you send us narratives, give us plain truth: if you send us instruction, give us good evidence and argument—no fiction—no romance; but plain, old fashioned, gospel work. O give us what will do our hearts good—our children and our neighbors good. Give us what will stir us up for usefulness on earth and holiness, and happiness in heaven.

A contemporary of Cooper stated that Methodism's tracts "covered the land like the leaves of autumn."

The Book Concern printed the sermons of John Wesley, the hymns of Charles Wesley, and the apologetic writings of John Fletcher with the purpose of nourishing the intellectual life of the church. The publishing house also produced materials explaining practical Christianity. At one point, the Methodist Book Concern was the largest publishing house in America.

The Missionary Society

American Methodism, in its early stages, devoted most of its attention to the English-speaking people who streamed westward to settle America's vast territories. This missionary work strained available resources, thereby limiting additional ministries. A larger missionary vision, however, was never out of mind. Soon after the founding of the Methodist Episcopal Church, Bishop Thomas Coke had expressed hope that the church would eventually develop an outreach to the American Indians: "We have in [North Carolina] got up to the Cherokee Indians, who are in general a peaceable people. I trust the grace of God will in time get into some of their hearts." In 1789 Asbury recorded in his journal, "I wrote a letter to Cornplanter, chief of the Seneca nation of Indians. I hope God will shortly visit [them], and send messengers to publish the glad tidings of salvation amongst them."

Despite Methodist interest in the Indian population (as well as the unreached slaves throughout the South), the church did not become strong enough to develop formal missions among them until after Coke and Asbury had died. The first local missionary society developed in 1819, when ministers in New York City drafted plans to reach "new and remote settlements." The vision of the New York Missionary and Bible Society was a large one:

> [We] are not restricted to our own nation or colour; we hope the aborigines of our country, the Spaniards of South America, the French of Louisiana and Canada, and every other people who are destitute of the invaluable blessings of the Gospel, as far as our means may admit, will be comprehended in the field of the labours of our zealous missionaries.

The chief founders of this new society were Nathan Bangs, Freeborn Garrettson, and Laban Clark. At the time that the New York Missionary

Society organized, ministers in Philadelphia were also taking steps to establish missionary work. However, neither the New York society nor the one in Philadelphia was an official agency of the denomination. These two societies raised funds to enable the bishops to send missionaries to new areas (in America).

Then in 1820 the General Conference took over the New York Missionary and Bible Society. That date marks the official founding of the Missionary Society of the Methodist Episcopal Church. At that 1820 General Conference, Bishop William McKendree gave the episcopal address in which he declared:

> *Perhaps we have not paid sufficient attention to the voice of Providence, calling to...[a] spread of the Gospel among the Indians, and among the destitute of our cities, and of many remote and scattered settlements...at this moment your attention is emphatically called to this subject by an address from the Wyandotte Indians, requesting us to send missionaries among them, by the wants of thousands of uninstructed souls in the cities, towns, and cottages of our widely extended country, and by societies already formed with a design to raise money for such purposes.*

McKendree believed that evangelized Indians could and should play a significant part in the development of the United States. Moreover, his experiences with Indian tribes encouraged him to believe that the prospects were favorable for winning them to Christ. McKendree asked a converted Indian Chief on one occasion, "Have you any temptations to go back to your former course of life?" The chief replied, "Yes, both from within and without. Often the devil throws them in my way; but I resist them by praying to God." McKendree's urging prompted the church to begin a mission to the Native Americans.

Christian work among the Indians encountered severe obstacles: (1) There were mass murders of Christian Indians by their former comrades. (2) Tragic consequences resulted from federal government policies promising the Indians that, in exchange for their land, the Great Father in Washington would take care of them.

Nathan Bangs (1778-1862).

In 1819 Bangs became one of the principle organizers of Methodism's Missionary Society. His contributions to the church were significant. Following his ordination in 1804, Bangs served six years as a missionary in Canada. Later, he helped found the church's Missionary Society. In 1820, Bangs began a twenty-year period of service as the book agent of the Methodist Book Concern. In this position he edited *The Christian Advocate, The Methodist Magazine,* and *The Quarterly Review.* Bangs wrote a four-volume *History of the Methodist Episcopal Church* (published 1838-1841).

As a missionary to Canada, Bangs had the opportunity to preach to an Indian gathering. Bangs reported, "Having ended my discourse, the chief threw his arms around my neck, hugged and kissed me, called me father, and asked me to come and live with them and be their instructor. The simplicity with which they received my words, and their affection greatly affected me: and this interesting interview with these sons of the forest more than compensated for the inconveniences I had suffered. I hoped the time was not far distant when these Heathens should be given to Christ for His inheritance."

Laban Clark (1778-1868).

Clark began preaching in 1800 and in 1801 he went to his first Annual Conference in New York City. It was a moving experience for the young man. He wrote, "The conference was composed mostly of young men in the prime of life and none past the meridian and vigour of manhood ... looking at them I said to myself, with such men we can take the world." In 1803 Clark went as a missionary to lower Canada. In all, he served over fifty years in the ministry. His interest in education led him to become one of the founders of a number of Methodist academies, as well as Wesleyan University.

(3) Whiskey traders supported (and even encouraged) the abuse of alcohol, and lied to the Indians that the missionaries were their enemies. (4) Many Indians were in the grip of a pagan worldview that regarded the natural world as the source of life and the answer to ultimate questions.

Despite these problems, the Methodists saw some successes among the Native Americans. One Indian convert said, "Religion wears better than my coat, and is made of more lasting stuff. My coat wears out and gets into holes, but the longer I wear religion the better it is. It gets thicker and warmer and stronger, and I think will last me through this world of sin and trouble." Accounts of Indian conversions appeared in the *Methodist Magazine*. Encouraged by the possibilities, some of the Annual Conferences began their own Indian missions.

Preachers also began to minister to the plantation slaves. In some cases the slaves' owners did not permit them to leave the plantations to attend churches. Therefore, some circuit riders included preaching stations among the slaves on cotton, rice, sugar, and indigo plantations. Some of these plantations were located in remote malaria-ridden river deltas.

In 1829 the South Carolina Annual Conference organized the first conference-sponsored mission devoted entirely to slaves. William Capers, the presiding elder of the Charleston District, became the superintendent of this enterprise. The first two missionaries were John Honour and John Massey. Although the plantation owners were not always eager to support this mission, Capers and the two missionaries persisted in their work. In time, some of the slaveholders began to welcome missionary efforts to reach the slaves because the gospel "took well with them" and "made them better workers."

The favorable response of the slaves to the preaching of the gospel inspired other conferences to follow the example set by South Carolina Methodism. In 1837, the Annual Conferences supported at least ten missions to slaves. By 1840, this mission work had three superintendents and seven full-time missionaries working on 234 plantations. In 1844 there were more than 150,000 black converts who had joined South Carolina Methodism. Other conferences reported significant numbers of slaves becoming Christians due to plantation ministries. By 1860, the membership of the M. E. Church, South, included 207,000 slaves. Many more slaves attended Methodist meetings.

The missions to Indians and African Americans raised up Indian and black converts who preached among their own people. John Stewart, who was partly Indian, excelled as a preacher and evangelist among the Wyandotte tribes of Ohio. One of the outstanding black preachers was the popular Henry Evans. A Methodist bishop reported that Evans was "so remarkable as to have become the greatest curiosity of the town, insomuch that distinguished visitors hardly felt that they might pass a Sunday in Fayetteville [North Carolina] without hearing him preach." Regrettably, the Annual Conferences ordained only a small number of Indian and black preachers.

German–American Methodism

In addition to ministering among Indians and slaves, the Methodist Episcopal Church developed other missions in America, including work among German immigrants. In certain sections of the United States growing communities of German Americans were becoming prominent. For example, in 1840, twenty-three percent of Cincinnati's population was German. St. Louis and other cities also had sizable German populations. Religion among these people, however, was not strong.

Many Germans had come to America without having found Christ in their churches in Germany. Consequently, in their new environment they tended to neglect religion altogether. Rationalism and religious doubt, moreover, were persistent influences in nineteenth-century Germany. Many immigrants to the United States brought these secular philosophies with them. The Methodist Episcopal Church decided that it must combat the "spiritual night" that had fallen on German Americans.

Furthermore, those Germans who wished to attend Methodist services usually did not know enough English to follow the sermons. To meet the spiritual needs of these immigrants, the church recruited preachers fluent in German, and encouraged other preachers to learn the language. In 1835, the Ohio Conference designated the small sum of $100 for work among German Americans. The bishop appointed a "missionary among the German immigrants in and near Cincinnati." The missionary's name was Wilhelm Nast.

Nast was exceptionally well educated, energetic, and fearless. His work at first showed little fruit. He observed, "[The Germans] are not like those who hear the word and, anon, with joy receive it.... They will not lay their hands to the Gospel plough until they have fully made up their minds." Because it was not easy to persuade the Germans to attend a church, Nast preached in homes, schools, and wherever he could gather a congregation.

This cultured man encountered severe difficulties, including crude and ill-mannered opposition. Sometimes people in Nast's audiences threw rotten eggs and plugs of half-chewed tobacco at him. On several occasions drunken detractors drove a pig or a cow under the meetinghouse during his sermons. Once, a mischief-maker loosed a flying rooster during a service. Another time someone slipped behind him while he was preaching and cut his coattails with scissors. People often rudely left the meeting in the midst of his sermon. The Cincinnati press ridiculed him unmercifully.

At the end of his first year, Nast had gathered a class of 12, with a total of three converts. He continued tenaciously ringing doorbells, handing out tracts, and standing outside beer gardens to engage people in religious conversation. One of Nast's early converts, Eduard Hoch, became his bodyguard, giving him needed protection from intoxicated and violent people. Another of Nast's converts, John Zwehlen, led in the construction of the world's first German Methodist Episcopal church (in Wheeling, West Virginia). Nast made friends with James Gamble, an Irish soapmaker, who was to become a financial benefactor of American Methodism. Many of Nast's converts became pillars of Methodism. The work he started expanded into Kentucky, Illinois, Wisconsin, Iowa, Missouri, and Pennsylvania.

Wilhelm Nast (1807-1889).

Born in Germany, Nast came to America at the age of 21. As a young man, he began seeking certainty that he was a Christian. Meanwhile, he took a position as librarian and professor of German at West Point, the U. S. Military Academy. Later he served as a professor of Greek and Hebrew in a college in Ohio. In 1835 he found a satisfying Christian experience and entered the Methodist ministry. His life's calling was to minister to German immigrants, and because of his work he became known as the "Apostle of German Methodism."

In 1838 Nast urged the Ohio Conference to establish a German language press. Nast said, "We might exercise a saving influence upon the Germans through the press, by publishing in the German language some of our doctrinal tracts, the Wesleyan Catechism, Fletcher's Appeal, and some of Wesley's sermons, and, as soon as possible, a German Methodist periodical." Although some members of the conference argued that little could be accomplished among "the infidel foreigners," the conference approved Nast's appointment as Editor of the *Christian Apologist*. One of Nast's most important ministries was his service as the editor (1839-1889) of the official paper of German Methodism in America, *Der Christliche Apologete*.

Another significant home mission outreach was to Texas. The 1836 General Conference, while in session in Cincinnati, received word of General Sam Houston's defeat of General Santa Anna's Mexican forces at San Jacinto. This news prompted the conference to send missionaries to the republic of Texas. At the time, Texas was an independent, sovereign nation (1836-1845). Therefore, Texas was considered a "foreign mission field." Martin Ruter, who played such an important part in the development of higher education in American Methodism, pioneered Methodist expansion into Texas. Accompanying Ruter to Texas were Robert Alexander of the Mississippi Conference and Littleton Fowler of the Tennessee Conference. Within a decade of Methodist beginnings in Texas, the work had grown so large that it established two Annual Conferences.

Foreign Missions

The first overseas work of Methodism's missionary society began in 1833. That year, the bishops sent to the African continent a young minister named Melville Cox. Because Cox suffered from acute tuberculosis, he knew that his life would be short. An acquaintance advised him to take his coffin to Africa with him, and a friend warned that he was "flying directly in the face of Providence." Cox wrote, "The Episcopacy has concluded to send me to Liberia.... I thirst to be on my way. I pray that God may fit my soul and body for the duties before me; that God may go with me; then I have no lingering fear. A grave in Africa shall be sweet to me, if he sustain me." During Cox's short time in Liberia, his manner of life and faithful gospel witness won the hearts of many. Cox organized and preached at probably the first camp meeting in Africa. He organized a Sunday school, engaged in personal evangelism, and planned a missionary strategy for those who followed him.

One of Cox's successors was Ann Wilkins. She had married at the age of 17, and her husband soon abandoned her. Following this experience, she decided to devote the rest of her life to Christian service. In 1836 while attending a camp meeting near Sing Sing, New York, she sent a note to one of the platform speakers, Nathan Bangs, Secretary of the Mission Society. Writing in the third person, she said, "A sister who has a little money at command gives that little cheerfully, and is willing to give her life as a female teacher if she is wanted. [Signed] Mrs. Ann Wilkins." The society commissioned Wilkins as a missionary, and she sailed for Liberia in 1837. She was American Methodism's first female missionary to a foreign field (other than spouses of

Melville Beveridge Cox (1799-1833).

Cox was the first foreign missionary commissioned by the Methodist Episcopal Church Missionary Society. Prior to sailing for Liberia, Cox knew that he was terminally ill. He wrote his own epitaph, "Let a thousand fall before Africa be given up." Cox sailed for Liberia in 1832, and soon established the headquarters for Methodist work in that country. Because of his poor health, he died at the age of thirty-three.

One of Methodism's historians of missions wrote, "His holding aloft of the missionary standard, his utter fearlessness, his giving of himself to the last ounce of his strength, have been an inspiration to thousands who have come after him."

Ann Green Wilkins (1806-1857).

Mrs. Wilkins was the first female missionary assigned to a foreign field by the Methodist Missionary Society. She served in Liberia, Africa 1836-57. In an era when missionaries succumbed alarmingly to illness and death, her relatively long tenure in Africa was remarkable.

missionaries). Mrs. Wilkins had remarkable gifts and graces for this work, and she became a highly successful missionary. Among her numerous contributions was the founding of Millsburg Female Academy, Methodism's first overseas school for girls.

Meanwhile, in 1834 the Missionary Society decided to send a missionary to South America. To pioneer this work, the board selected Fountain E. Pitts, pastor of McKendree M. E. Church in Nashville. Pitts arrived in Brazil in 1835, and within two weeks of reaching Rio de Janeiro, he formed a Methodist class. Then he rode to Montevideo, Uruguay, where he quickly formed another Methodist society. Pitts went next to Buenos Aires, where he found that Protestants needed government permission to preach. He had brought with him to South America complimentary letters of recommendation from President Andrew Jackson and Senator Henry Clay. These references promptly gained him permission to preach, and his sermons attracted large crowds of people who were eager to hear the gospel.

Pitts appealed to the missionary board to send a permanent missionary to the area. The board responded promptly. In 1836 Bishop Elijah Hedding appointed Justin Spaulding. Soon after Spaulding's arrival, he was joined by John Dempster, who later became a leader in theological education in America. Dempster reported that he was much impressed with the work in South America, having had "conversations with several influential persons in [Buenos Aires], native citizens and others." Within a short time Methodism in Brazil had a thriving church and a well-attended school.

The promising work in Brazil, however, suffered a serious reversal. In 1842, during a period of temporary recession in the United States, the Missionary Society abandoned its support for South American Methodist missions. This severe action came at a time when continued financial assistance for missions in Brazil was crucial. Brazil, at that time in its history, particularly needed the strong proclamation of the gospel that Methodism could have provided. Ironically, the finances of the Missionary Society soon improved, and the drastic decision of the board would not have been necessary.

Dwight Judson Collins (1823-1852).

Collins was the first Methodist missionary to China. He was reared in a deeply religious household; four of the eight sons in the family became Christian ministers. In 1841 Collins became a member of the first freshman class at the University of Michigan. Following graduation, he became Professor of Natural and Moral Science at the recently established Albion College, at the time a female college. He felt a strong calling to go as a missionary to China. His bishop, however, informed him that the church had no mission in China nor money to begin one. Collins replied to the bishop, "Secure me a position before the mast (of a ship)—my strong arms can pull me to China and support me after I get there. God is calling and I must go."

Methodism's other foreign missionary endeavors steadily grew and soon spread to five continents. One of the new mission fields was the Orient. In 1847 the Missionary Society chose a young preacher named Judson Dwight Collins to take Methodism to China. Accompanied by his wife and a colleague, Moses White, Collins founded three schools there and helped prepare a Bible in the Chinese language. Within a year of arriving in China, Mrs. Collins died. Because of Collins's poor health, his doctors advised him to return to America. Although he died at the age of 29, he left the lasting legacy of having taken Methodism to Asia.

Ludwig Sigismund Jacoby (1813-1874).

Jacoby, an immigrant from Germany, was converted in Cincinnati under the preaching of Wilhelm Nast. Following Jacoby's conversion, he became active in ministry among the German-speaking Methodists, serving eventually as the superintendent of the Methodist work among Germans in St. Louis. In 1849 he responded to a call to take Methodism to Germany. There, he organized a publishing house and a theological seminary. Also, Jacoby served as the superintendent of German Methodism and oversaw the expansion of Methodism throughout that country.

In 1849 Ludwig S. Jacoby, who was converted under the ministry of Wilhelm Nast, opened Methodist work in Germany. Robert S. Maclay took Methodism to Japan in 1873, and in 1885 Henry G. Appenzeller helped plant Methodism in Korea. Methodism entered India and Mexico through the pioneer work of William Butler. In 1879 James M. Thoburn took Methodism into Burma, and in 1899 he supervised Methodist beginnings in the Philippine Islands.

Henry Gerhard Appenzeller (1858-1902).

In 1886 Appenzeller went to Korea, where he opened a school. Eventually, he founded the first Methodist Church in that country. As superintendent of the Methodist Mission, he traveled extensively throughout Korea, and the people came to love him. Appenzeller served as a member of the Board of Translators, which produced a Korean Bible. He also authored and translated many tracts, and helped establish a Methodist publishing house. He served the missionary community by editing and publishing the weekly *Korean Christian Advocate* and the monthly *Korean Repository*.

Three of Appenzeller's children became missionaries in Korea, serving there for a combined total of 68 years. One of his daughters (the first American child ever born in Korea) became the long time president of Ewha College, Korea's first university for women, and the largest female university in the world.

William Butler (1818-1899).

While Butler was a pastor in Lynn, Massachusetts, Bishop Matthew Simpson commissioned him to take Methodism to India. Butler and his family arrived there in 1857, and within three years he had established mission stations in nine strategic locations.

After Butler returned to America to resume a pastorate, Bishop Simpson asked him to pioneer another Methodist mission, this time in Mexico. Butler arrived in that country in 1873 and established mission stations in key places. His leadership in Mexico was crucial. He helped change the Protestant missionary practice of denouncing Roman Catholicism, instructing the Methodist missionaries to teach the positive truths of the gospel. *Zion's Herald* said of Butler, "So completely had he mastered the subject of universal missions that he was at home in every phase of it.... In his public prayers he seemed a Moses talking face to face with God; as a preacher an platform speaker he had few superiors. His piety was apostolic."

Conflicts with the New York Board of Missions over administrative matters caused Butler to return to America where he resumed a pastorate and became active in the Freedman's Aid Society. Bishop J. Wascom Pickett said of Butler, "Contemporaries agreed, and historians confirm, that notwithstanding Butler's lack of administrative finesse, he was a wise and devoted missionary who rendered great service. His foresight and grasp of the opportunitie and the needs in both India and Mexico were remarkable.... (His work) registered an achievement rarely, if ever, equaled in so short a time in Methodist missionary history."

James Mills Thoburn (1836-1922).

In 1859 Thoburn went to India as a missionary and became a highly effective Methodist leader in that country. He was the first editor of *The Indian Witness*, and through its pages he encouraged support for missions in India. William Taylor joined Thoburn, and the two established Methodist evangelism and church growth in India. When Thoburn attended Methodism's General Conference in 1864, his missionary zeal helped gained him wide recognition as a missionary leader. It was said that Thoburn "put India on America's heart." The church eventually elected him the first bishop of India and Malaysia. Thoburn's sister, Isabella, was the first missionary appointed by the Woman's Missionary Society of the Methodist Episcopal Church.

The southern branch of Methodism began its first venture into foreign missions in 1848, sending Charles Taylor to China. Soon thereafter, the Church of the United Brethren began foreign missions (to Africa). The moving story of Methodist missions is a drama of exceptional vision, courage, and sacrifice. The list of the church's distinguished missionaries is a very long one, and in many instances their work grew into strong national Methodist churches.

During the nineteenth century and well into the twentieth century, Methodist missions loomed large in the church. In America, many congregations had yearly missionary conferences with guest missionary speakers who informed and inspired. Some congregations "adopted" missionaries and supported them. Families often kept pictures of missionaries on the breakfast table and prayed daily for their work. Women's groups collected clothing and food to send to overseas missionaries. Children saved pennies for missions and presented them at the altar of the church on "missionary Sunday." Missionary Prayer Bands dotted the Methodist landscape.

Overseas, the missionaries met with both agony and ecstasy. Many of them contracted tropical diseases, lived with unfamiliar and inadequate food, and coped with strange customs. Some suffered martyrdom. Often, missionaries needed to send their children to distant boarding schools, depriving parents and children of a normal family life. Ann Wilkins wrote about the

Charles Taylor (1819-1897).

Taylor was one of the first foreign missionaries of the Methodist Episcopal Church, South. He graduated from the University of New York with his class's highest academic honors.

Taylor's ministries were diverse. After college he taught ancient languages. Then he joined the South Carolina Conference. In 1848 Taylor graduated from the Philadelphia College of Medicine with the MD degree. That year he went to Shanghai, China as a medical missionary. In addition to practicing medicine and preaching, while in China he published a work on *Harmony of the Gospels* and a number of religious tracts in the Chinese language. After returning to America, he served as president of Spartanburg Female College and later as Sunday School Secretary for the M.E. Church, South. Taylor later joined the Kentucky Conference and became president of Kentucky Wesleyan College. His missionary concern continued to the end of his life.

Daniel Kumler Flickinger (1824-1911).

In 1855, Flickinger, a United Brethren minister, pioneered United Brethren missions in Ghana, where he served for 40 years. He founded the magazine *Missionary Visitor* and edited this journal for twenty years. He also wrote books about missionary topics, including *Ethiopia, or Twenty-six Years of Missionary Life in Western Africa, Our Missionary Work,* and *Fifty-five Years in the Gospel Ministry.* The Africans called him "a little man with a big heart." For his work, he gained the title "Father of United Brethren Missions."

Bishop Arthur James Moore (1888-1974).

Bishop Moore was an effective evangelist and long-time president of Methodism's Board of Missions. In 1937 he led a "Bishop's Crusade" aimed at reviving interest in Christ's mandate to make disciples of all nations. This campaign cleared the Mission Board of a debt of seven million dollars. He continued to promote a missionary spirit in the church until his death in 1974.

Bishop Moore wrote, "Christianity was intended to be, and of necessity is, a missionary religion. To take away its world view, to steal away its missionary passion, is to rob it of its character and leave it something other than its true self. Christianity.... lives and expands only when this world vision is constantly before its eyes and when its ministers and people are heroic adventurers and brave pioneers, ready to follow their Leader in the dangerous way of the cross."

obstacles she faced in recruiting girls for her school in Liberia: "The great difficulty...lies in the fact of their being contracted for, for wives at a very early age...often in infancy, and sometimes even before they are born." Due to limited financial support, the missionaries often lived with only the bare necessities. Melville Cox wrote his mother:

> I have bought a table, a candlestick, a few cups and saucers, a pound of tea, a kroo of rice, a few mackerel, borrowed one tea-spoon, a cot to sleep on, and am living on rice morning, noon, and night. But I assure you it eats sweetly. We have [meats] here, but they are so exorbitantly high I don't choose to indulge myself with them.

Despite their difficulties, the missionaries saw wonderful successes. From Africa, missionary George S. Brown wrote his superintendent, "Come up and see the bush burn. Come up and see the desert blossom. Come up and see God convert the heathen.... do not stop to change your clothes." The missionaries echoed the attitude of John Wesley: "It is not pleasing to flesh and blood; and I would not do it, if I did not believe there was another world."

In his sermon "The General Spread of the Gospel," John Wesley appraised the growth of Methodism, and in doing so he captured the essence of its missionary spirit:

> From Oxford, where it first appeared, the little leaven spread wider and wider. More and more saw the truth as it is in Jesus, and received it in the love thereof. More and more found "redemption through the blood of Jesus, even the forgiveness of sins." They were born again of his Spirit, and filled with righteousness, and peace, and joy in the Holy Ghost. It afterwards spread to every part of the land, and a little one became a thousand. It then spread into North Britain and Ireland; and a few years after into New York, Pennsylvania, and many other provinces in America.... So that, although at first this "grain of mustard-seed" was "the least of all the seeds;" yet, in a few years, it grew into a "large tree, and put forth great branches.".... There are very many heathen nations in the world that have no intercourse, either by trade or any other means, with Christians of

The Do-without Band.

During the nineteenth century, Methodist women throughout America supported missions by joining the "Do-without Band." This organization had no membership fee. Methodist women agreed to "look about for opportunities to do without for Jesus' sake." For instance, to save money some chose to do without sugar for their tea or do without starch for their ironing. These women placed these small "do-without" savings into a handy envelope and gave the money to Methodist missions.

"IF ANY MAN WILL FOLLOW ME, LET HIM DENY HIMSELF."

HANDY ENVELOPE FOR
(SLIT FOR MONEY.)
"Do Without" Money

TO BE USED FOR THE DEACONESS WORK IN CHICAGO.
Office, 114 Dearborn Avenue, Chicago.

I will look about—
In my purchases,
In my home affairs,
In my amusements,
In my luxuries—
For opportunities to "Do Without

For Jesus' Sake.

I WOULD RATHER MY MONEY SHOULD GO TO WIN A SOUL FOR CHRIST, THAN TO PURCHASE A PASSING PLEASURE FOR MYSELF.

Do—without Band Collection Envelope

any kind.... Now, what shall be done for [them]? 'How shall they believe,' saith the Apostle, 'in Him of whom they have not heard? And how shall they hear without a preacher?'

American Methodism gratefully acknowledges its debt to earlier generations of faithful missionaries who were obedient to Christ's Great Commission. Their lives and labors endure.

Charles Wesley wrote a short hymn about the eternal rewards of those who live selfless lives of faithful service:

> Servant of God, well done! Thy glorious warfare's past;
> The battle's fought, the race is won,
> And thou art crowned at last.
> With saints enthroned on high,
> Thou dost thy Lord proclaim,
> And still to God salvation cry, Salvation to the Lamb!
>
> O happy, happy soul! In ecstasies of praise,
> Long as eternal ages roll, Thou seest thy Savior's face.
> Redeemed from earth and pain,
> Ah! When shall we ascend,
> And all in Jesus' presence reign
> Through ages without end?

The drama of Methodist missions is the story of those who heard and obeyed Christ's mandate to go into all the world and make disciples. Most of those who prayed, gave, went, sacrificed, and suffered did not see the full fruit of their labors during their lifetimes. We are today surrounded by this cloud of witnesses who esteemed the treasures of heaven greater than the treasures of earth. They looked to Jesus, the pioneer and perfecter of our faith, who for the sake of the joy that was set before him endured the cross, disregarding its shame, and has taken his seat at the right hand of the throne of God.